RELATIONAL INTEGRATION OF PSYCHOLOGY AND CHRISTIAN THEOLOGY

Relational Integration of Psychology and Christian Theology offers an in-depth, interdisciplinary relational framework that integrates theology, psychology, and clinical and other applications. Building on existing models and debates about the relationship between psychology and theology, the authors provide a much-needed examination of the actual interpersonal dynamics of integration and its implications for training and clinical practice. Case studies from a variety of clinical and educational contexts illustrate and support the authors' model of relational integration. Using an approach that is sensitive to theological diversity and to social context, this book puts forward a theological and therapeutic framework that values diversity, the repairing of ruptures, and collaboration.

Steven J. Sandage, PhD, is Albert and Jessie Danielsen Professor of Psychology of Religion and Theology at Boston University School of Theology, with a joint appointment in the Department of Psychological and Brain Sciences. He also serves as research director and senior staff psychologist at the Danielsen Institute at Boston University.

Jeannine K. Brown, PhD, is professor of New Testament at Bethel Seminary in St. Paul, Minnesota, and San Diego, California.

RELATIONAL INTEGRATION OF PSYCHOLOGY AND CHRISTIAN THEOLOGY

Theory, Research, and Practice

Steven J. Sandage and Jeannine K. Brown

Routledge
Taylor & Francis Group

NEW YORK AND LONDON

First published 2018
by Routledge
711 Third Avenue, New York, NY 10017

and by Routledge
2 Park Square, Milton Park, Abingdon, Oxon, OX14 4RN

Routledge is an imprint of the Taylor & Francis Group, an informa business

Library of Congress Cataloging-in-Publication Data
Names: Sandage, Steven J., author. | Brown, Jeannine K., 1961- author.
Title: Relational integration of psychology and Christian theology :
    theory, research, and practice/Steven J. Sandage, Jeannine K. Brown.
Description: New York, NY : Routledge, 2018. | Includes bibliographical
    references.
Identifiers: LCCN 2017044441 (print) | LCCN 2017045057 (ebook) |
    ISBN 9781315671505 (eBook) | ISBN 9781138935921 (hardback) |
    ISBN 9781138935938 (pbk.) | ISBN 9781315671505 (ebk)
Subjects: | MESH: Psychotherapy | Religion and Psychology |
    Christianity | Cultural Diversity
Classification: LCC RC480.5 (ebook) | LCC RC480.5 (print) |
    NLM WM 460.5.R3 |
DDC 616.89/14—dc23
LC record available at https://lccn.loc.gov/2017044441

ISBN: 978-1-138-93592-1 (hbk)
ISBN: 978-1-138-93593-8 (pbk)
ISBN: 978-1-315-67150-5 (ebk)

Typeset in Bembo
by Apex CoVantage, LLC

To Carla Dahl, who embodies the interdisciplinary virtues of curiosity, humility, and hospitality

CONTENTS

ACKNOWLEDGMENTS

We are dedicating this book to Carla Dahl, who has been a key mentor and friend to both of us, but also an exemplar of relational integration. We were each formed by team teaching integrative courses with Carla at Bethel Seminary, along with many informal conversations and moments. It's cliché but true to say that relational integration is "more caught than taught." Carla's profound integrative wisdom is closely matched by her huge heart and Olympic-level sense of humor. Carla's leadership, which moved her over many years from faculty secretary to a dean position at Bethel Seminary, put in place the integrative ecology that led to our collaboration on this project.

Leland Eliason was Provost at Bethel Seminary during some of our shared time there, and Leland fostered an integrative vision of theological education which also shaped the ethos that contributed to our development as integrative scholars and educators. Leland's personal commitment to integration was catalyzing and inspiring to our efforts.

We both also enjoyed integrative collaborations with many faculty, staff, and student colleagues at Bethel, including interdisciplinary scholarly projects, team teaching integration seminars, and working on administrative or committee efforts aimed at different aspects of integration. Special shared gratitude goes to Kyle Roberts, Mary Jensen, Peter Vogt, Mark Harden, Mark McCloskey, and Thorsten Moritz for so many highly textured relationally integrative influences. Too many students to name have engaged in integrative dialogues, assignments, and projects that have stimulated our learning about relational integration. We appreciate all these collective influences.

In this book, we describe some parts of our personal journeys of integration. But we each want to briefly acknowledge some key influences here, especially since this is a book about relational influences on integration.

Jeannine's Acknowledgments

I am grateful for the great number of colleagues and friends who have shaped my integrative journey. An early influence was Dr. Al Wolters, who gave a lecture at a conference on "Scripture and the Disciplines" in 2004, for which I was a respondent. His gracious hospitality toward my questions and insights before and during that conference set a wonderful tone for other integrative interactions to come. A more recent influence is my daughter Katherine Agre, a genetic counselor at the Mayo Clinic. It is my greatest joy to "do integration" with such an amazing clinician whose expertise in areas far different from mine has such interesting implications for theological reflection.

Carla Dahl, whom we have already mentioned, has provided for me the most formative influence for integration. As a colleague and friend, she was the person I trusted to look at my first attempts at integration from the Gospel of Matthew. Our team teaching on the topic of the Gospels and formation remains a highlight over a decade later. I am grateful for the grant that Carla and I received, along with Wyndy Corbin Reuschling, from the Lilly Theological Research Grants program of the Association of Theological Schools in 2009–10, that helped the three of us write *Becoming Whole and Holy: An Integrative Conversation about Christian Formation*. It was a delight to have Wyndy join our work, as an expert in ethics and a true exemplar of relational integration.

Two other influential colleagues and conversation partners across disciplines have been Peter Vogt (Old Testament) and Kyle Roberts (Theology). Both have demonstrated the humility and curiosity that have made for fruitful and fascinating dialogue. Kyle has been a co-author on a forthcoming theological commentary on Matthew (Two Horizons series), and I am grateful for his partnership and friendship in that process. So many other colleagues have graciously joined my classes to offer their cross-disciplinary perspectives and/or invited me into theirs, including Denise Muir Kjesbo (Ministry Leadership), Mark McCloskey (Ministry Leadership), Mary Jensen (Formation), Ben Lim (Marital and Family Therapy), and Norah Caudill (Old Testament). I have recently enjoyed team-teaching Bethel's Senior Integration Seminar (first taught with Steve) with Jim Smith, who has enriched the conversations in that course with his wide-ranging interests from church history to baseball history to pastoral leadership. I would also thank all the students who were a part of integrative courses I have taught; they have contributed profoundly to my growth as an integrator.

I want to express my particular thanks to Ken Reynhout for giving feedback on ideas for and drafts of Chapter 2 (on the history of theology's interaction with psychology). His willingness to engage in long conversations, his insights into interdisciplinarity, as well as his own work on the dialogue between theology and science have been important for my learning (and any shortcomings of that particular section remain my own). Finally, I am grateful to my teaching assistant, Chao Ma, for his tireless and cheerful work on this project, from providing valuable input to formatting bibliographies.

Steve's Acknowledgments

I benefitted in life-changing ways from working with Gary Collins and Everett L. Worthington, Jr., two of the most important figures in shaping the integration of psychology and theology. Their scholarship was deeply impactful, but close exposure to their personal lives of integration was even more helpful. Randy Sorenson was perhaps the most important influence for me on the specific conceptual understanding of relational integration advanced in this book, and I dedicated my lectureship on relational integration at the 2017 Fuller Integration Symposium to Randy. I also owe a great deal to some other key intellectual mentors in the integration of psychology and theology who have been gracious and encouraging to me personally—Alvin Dueck, Peter Hill, Eric Johnson, Micah McCreary, Ken Pargament, Scott Richards, Mark McMinn, Charles Ridley, and Jack and Judith Balswick.

My first substantive collaboration and exploration of relational integration was with LeRon Shults. Our two books and other projects, including team teaching and joint speaking opportunities, had a huge impact on my understanding of real interdisciplinary engagement, both the joys and the formative challenges. I am also grateful to my current theological research collaborators at Boston University School of Theology (BUSTH)—Claire Wolfteich, Hee An Choi, Shelly Rambo, and Wesley Wildman—who each guide me into new vistas of integration. BUSTH Area colleagues Nancy Ammerman, Chris Schlauch, Barbod Salimi, and Jonathan Calvillo contribute fresh integrative questions and contours to my work. Dean Mary Elizabeth Moore has also empowered my integrative thinking at BUSTH and modeled her own interdisciplinary work and commitment.

Several other former Bethel colleagues continue to have a significant impact on my understanding to integration. Peter Jankowski is one of the most talented "relational integrators" I know and certainly one of the most generative influences on my scholarship. I want to also thank Jason Li, Judy Tiesel, Catherine Lally, Andy Johnson, Tina Watson Wiens, Ruben Rivera, Becky Eller, Jane McCampbell, Bernard Walker, Judy Johnson, Ken Reynhout, Andrea Hollingsworth, and Cher Moua for their integrative influences and, more importantly, their support during my own periods of dis-integration. They are joined by other key colleagues in the wider field of integration who have influenced and motivated my work, including Brad Strawn, Todd Hall, Liz Hall, Keith Edwards, Kaye Cook, Nathaniel Wade, Julie Exline, Mike McCullough, Doug Hardy, Charlotte Witvliet, Nils Friberg, Donnie Davis, Josh Hook, and Jennifer Ripley. Funding from the John Templeton Foundation, the Lilly Endowment, and the Fetzer Institute has supported many of these efforts mentioned above.

Jim Maddock and Noel Larson have been my most significant mentors in the existential, systemic, and clinical dimensions of integration. Quite simply, they transformed my approach to integration in clinical practice. They also introduced me to a network of differentiation-based "integrative" therapists, and I am particularly grateful to my long-time consultation group colleagues—Sheryl Cohen, Michael Radkowsky, and Winifred Reilly—the people who keep me clinically honest and model soulful therapeutic work. My current clinical and training setting at the Danielsen Institute includes a surplus of relationally integrative influences, but special thanks to our management team of George Stavros, Miriam Bronstein, Lauren Kehoe, David Rupert, and Michael Tschiderer. Much of my clinical integration work also evolved during years at Arden Woods Psychological Services, where Tom Hainlen and Carol Morgan carefully stewarded a clinical setting and Friday Forum tradition where I could learn about practical dimensions of relational integration.

Given the developmental orientation of this book, I want to also acknowledge my undergraduate influences at Iowa State University of Norm Scott, Doug Epperson, and Judith Bunyi, whose integrative generosity was tremendously influential. I have also profited from so many hours of dialogue with students and clients who have trusted me with their integrative and dis-integrative questions and discoveries. All of the cases described in this book are either constructed or masked composites with identifying information altered. I also appreciate grant funding (#60622) from the John Templeton foundation for humility research which has contributed many ideas to this book.

FIGURES AND TABLE

Figures

Table

1

INTRODUCTION

Psychology and theology are constitutive parts of everyday life. Psychology involves observations and interpretations of human behavior, and theology involves understandings of God, the sacred, and ultimate concerns. Psychology and theology are certainly formal academic disciplines but also occur at "everyday" or "folk" levels. These folk forms can be intentional and reflective processes, for example, a person might try to interpret the reasons for a friend's uncharacteristic irritability on a given day (psychology). And that same person might try to explain the reasons they do or do not believe in God amidst the incredible tragedies in the world to a curious co-worker or their adolescent child who asks about the basis of their faith (theology). But psychology and theology are also more implicit dynamics that operate beneath our conscious awareness most of the time. As humans, we embody psychological processes which constantly influence our thoughts, feelings, and behaviors. Personality factors, such as attachment style, often influence our habitual ways of coping with stress or responding to unfamiliar persons and situations (Mikulincer & Shaver, 2007). We also live out certain theological beliefs or assumptions about what is good, valuable, and ultimate in our behaviors and as we try to make sense of experiences. In some cases, those implicit theologies and ultimate concerns might arguably be destructive to the individual or those around them, such as when vengeance, personal superiority, hedonism, or hateful bigotry become ultimate and supersede claimed theological views. For others, nihilism or the avoidance of caring about much of anything in life can operate as a kind of theological stance. Thus, psychology and theology are unavoidable dimensions of human experience.

In this book, we will suggest that a relational dialectic exists between psychology and theology consisting of descriptive and prescriptive orientations. Theology tends to emphasize the prescriptive—how things *should be*, while psychology and other social sciences emphasize the descriptive—or interpretations of how things *are* (Brown, Dahl, & Corbin Reuschling, 2011). It is not difficult to track interactions between descriptive and prescriptive orientations within everyday conversations. For example, these orientations are discernable in the following hypothetical conversation among co-workers at a construction site:

ANDRE: Where's Samuel today?

MARIA: He's out again. Must still be sick.

ANDRE: *Sick?* He's not sick . . . he's lazy!

JAMES: He's got *something* going on. Hasn't seemed like himself for months now. What do you think it is?

ANDRE: I will tell you what it is. He doesn't like to work.

MARIA: No, I think he's probably depressed. His mother is very ill and close to death, and his siblings don't help out . . . And I don't think he's gotten over the divorce. With Theresa [his former wife] now getting married again so quick, it's got to be tough for him.

ANDRE: Ah . . . you're just making excuses for him. People need to show up for work, regardless of what's going on.

JAMES: Andre, I wish *you* would take some days off.

(Laughter from Maria and James)

ANDRE: No, I am serious! Samuel talks about God and religion all the time but then mopes around and lays in bed to make more work for the rest of us. He's a hypocrite! The way I was raised, God wants you to show up and do your work and that's how you take care of yourself and your family.

JAMES: Wow . . . I guess compassion wasn't part of the way you were raised, huh, Andre? Give the guy a break. He works hard when he's here, and you don't know, he may very well be sick this week.

MARIA: Yeah, Andre, you need to get a little *heart*.

ANDRE: "Heart" doesn't get the work done and doesn't pay the bills. You all are too soft! What about holding people accountable?!

This vignette illustrates a number of quite fluid movements between interpretations of behavior (description) and expressions of values or ideals (prescription); the "is" and the "ought" weave together quite seamlessly in the processes of meaning-making in everyday conversation. As in most conversations, there is limited differentiation explicitly noted in this vignette between these descriptive and prescriptive orientations. Andre moves abruptly between making interpretations or talking about what he thinks *is* going on with Samuel (description) and expressing his own ideals—what he thinks *should be* going on with Samuel (prescription). The others characters in the story make different interpretations and articulate contrasting values and concerns; yet they also interweave description and prescription. This vignette illustrates that resonance as well as tension between psychology and theology can and do emerge at a folk level in everyday conversations among people who may have little awareness that they are wrestling with the "integration of psychology and theology."[1] Additionally, and central to the thesis of this book, we would suggest that these movements between psychology and theology unfold in the context of relational dynamics, such as we see in this story: confrontation, humor, compassion, and judgment.

The Interdisciplinary Turn

The recognition that psychology and theology, in their basic outworkings, are constituent parts of human reflection on life suggests that they cannot and should not be completely divorced from each other in the academy. Scholarly interdisciplinary exploration relating psychology and theology can be located within the wider context of a rising interest in interdisciplinary research and collaborative team science over the past two decades (Raasch, Lee, Spaeth, & Herstatt, 2013; Stokols, Hall, Taylor, & Moser, 2008). This integrative impulse can be seen across the academy. In the humanities (English, literature) diverse methodologies are employed to expand and to cross disciplinary boundaries (Moran, 2002). Religion and science is a broad endeavor at the intersection of various beliefs/practices and contemporary science. Within this wider integrative conversation, (Christian) theology and science has been a fertile area of engagement for over fifty years (Reynhout, 2013). Additionally, certain disciplines have emerged as (inherently) integrative endeavors, such as practical theology, with its desire to reflect deeply and theologically upon Christian tradition and practice.

This growing interest in interdisciplinarity is evident, for example, in the increasing number of funded research proposal requests calling for interdisciplinary collaboration. This suggests a developing recognition that interdisciplinary research endeavors can be particularly productive in their provision of knowledge validation from significantly different angles or differentiated perspectives. The distinct lenses, methodologies, and assumptions that distinct disciplines bring to interdisciplinary collaboration potentially offer greater levels of corroboration for knowledge gained. This might seem counter-intuitive to those who raise the question of how significant difference can yield anything other than a multiplication of contradictory, subjective perspectives. Yet interdisciplinary pursuits of knowledge that draw upon more than one discipline offer a unique set of constraints or boundaries as well as resources for the conversation—constraints and resources that can positively impact epistemological outcomes and generate novel solutions to problems (Raasch et al., 2013). As Moran (2002) notes, interdisciplinary endeavors can "be seen as a way of living with the disciplines more critically and self-consciously, recognizing that their most basic assumptions can always be challenged or reinvigorated by new ways of thinking from elsewhere" (p. 187). In fact, the rise of interdisciplinarity and increased interest in team science can, in part, be attributed to funding bodies seeking to solve real world problems that are too complex for any single disciplinary perspective (Aldrich, 2014).

The integrative impulse is also evident beyond the academy in various professional contexts. For instance, in healthcare settings, integration is increasingly a theme in collaborative care models as frameworks for integrating mental health and primary care. There is a growing body of evidence supporting the clinical and financial benefits of collaborative care that integrates professional healthcare disciplines in efficient coordination of treatment planning. Regulating bodies (e.g., Medicaid) have made calls for the integration of medical and psychological services (Unutzer, Harbin, Schoenbaum, & Druss, 2013). This emphasis, along with the near ubiquity of managed care, highlights the need for professionals to develop skills and competencies for working integratively with professionals from various healthcare disciplines. It seems clear that individual professionals differ in their levels of motivation and capacities to work collaboratively and integratively across disciplines. A willingness to acknowledge the strengths of other disciplines rather than defend one's disciplinary "turf" may require humility as a personal and professional virtue (Paine, Sandage, Rupert, Devor, & Bronstein, 2015).

Christian pastoral ministry is another professional context that highlights growing interest in integration. The Association for Theological Schools (ATS) includes in its standards for seminary faculty that they "foster integration for the diverse learning objectives of the curriculum" (ATS, 2010, p. 15). Although this has not always happened in an educational context that has participated in academic specialization and its resulting fragmentation, seminaries and theological schools are attempting to move toward integration in significant ways, including team-taught courses and integrative classes. Illustrative of the integrative nature of ministry is the related field of pastoral theology—"an independent branch of theology that studies the praxis of faith and faith communities" (Dingemans, 1996, p. 16). As Heitink (1999) notes, pastoral theology is inherently interdisciplinary.

Location for Language of Integration

In this book, we articulate an approach to the integration of psychology and theology we call "relational integration." Our focus is on a relational integration of psychology and theology, and, because of our own religious traditions, Christian theology provides our primary (though not exclusive) focus. Yet interdisciplinary engagements between psychology and theology can be found within various theological and religious traditions (e.g., Abu-Raiya & Pargament, 2015; Bland & Strawn, 2014; Jennings, 2010; Sharma & Tummala-Narra, 2014; Spero, 1992; Starr & Aron, 2008). Although the language of "theology" is often used to indicate theoretical formulation within the Christian tradition, Neville (2006) has broadened the definition of theology to expand beyond any particular religious tradition. His vision for a public theology is focused on symbolic engagement with ultimate concerns, regardless of any particular religious tradition. This coheres with our interest in relational and diversity dynamics for the process of integration, which leads us to consider what it means to pursue constructive relational integration between psychology and *various* theological and religious traditions (Strawn, Wright, & Jones, 2014). In fact, many of the concepts, competencies, and strategies we employ for a relational model of integration may be suggestive for interdisciplinary conversations between and among various academic and religious domains (Morgan & Sandage, 2016). It is our hope that readers from a wide range of disciplines and vantage points interested in "inter"-conversations of various kinds will find something of value in our contribution.

Introducing Relational Integration

We now turn to introduce some of the key features of our model of relational integration. We begin by providing the impetus and some of the essential contours of relational integration. Then we locate our view in reference to other ways of pursuing interdisciplinary work and integration. We continue describing our integration model by identifying it as collaborative (involving more than one scholar) and contextual (and so not the only way to do integration).

Contours of Relational Integration

Our relational view of integration builds on the prior work of integrative theorists in both psychology (e.g., Balswick, King, & Reimer, 2016; Collins, 2000; Dueck & Reimer, 2009; Jones, 2010; Sorenson, 1996; Worthington, 1994) and theology (e.g., Green, 2005; Murphy, 1990; Reynhout, 2007; Shults, 2003; Wolters, 2007). Yet we shift emphasis to a consistently "relational" approach to integration, arguing that *differentiated relationality is formative for shaping collaborative integration*. Our commitment to a Trinitarian and incarnational understanding of differentiation-based relationality provides the grounding for a theological anthropology that values community, difference, collaboration, contextualization, alterity, and social justice. At the center of our project, we define relational integration as embodied (Chapter 4), hermeneutical (Chapter 5), developmental (Chapter 6), and intercultural (Chapter 7). Relational integration "matters," because healthy interpersonal collaboration is not a given in interdisciplinary endeavors (Callard & Fitzgerald, 2015). Interpersonal processes can either facilitate or hinder interdisciplinary work depending upon the team or organizational dynamics, which has led to the formation of a "science of team science" field with researchers studying the conditions of interdisciplinary effectiveness (Stokols, 2008). More broadly, healthy collaboration is a vastly underrated challenge in human relationships for reasons that are both theological and psychosocial. Yet it is essential in our increasingly diverse world to develop capacities for healthy, just, and ethical collaboration across difference. We offer relational integration as a set of perspectives, approaches, and commitments that can serve to integrate conceptually and practically several positive trends in the contemporary discourse on the integration of psychology and theology, including emphases on relationality, spiritual formation, collaboration, diversity, ethics, and social justice.

The neglect of attention to relationality in integrative literature is curious since the research of Sorenson (2004) and his colleagues—the only systematic program of empirical research on integration among Christian graduate psychology trainees to date—identified relational dynamics between faculty and trainees as the most influential factor in doctoral trainee reports of learning integration across four different training programs. Sorenson found that students were often experiencing various implicit relational dynamics with faculty, for better and for worse, which shaped their process of understanding the possibilities for how psychology and Christian faith might come together (i.e., integrate) in a person. Students often reported desiring "open dialogue" and a kind of access to the personhood of the instructor and evidence of the instructor's "ongoing relationship with God" (Sorenson, 1997). The latter was not referencing student desire for instructors with an idealized relationship with God but rather authentic relational access to the personal dimension of instructors' ongoing ways of working out integration of relational spirituality. In trying to describe what she found helpful in "integrative instructors," one doctoral student explained these relational qualities in the following way.

> There is something that feels very solid about them. They know who they are and don't need to brag or build themselves up in any way. They are often very modest about what they do. You feel like you can critique them if necessary. They are the kind of people who actually open themselves up for evaluation. They ask for feedback in such a way that it feels safe to give it. There is a sense of collaboration with them. You sense that you're in "this" (whatever it may be) together. You're on the same team. On the one hand they feel very open and yet on the other, they feel somewhat immovable. Perhaps it's the sense of strength that comes from being firmly rooted in knowing themselves that makes them feel strong enough to take feedback from others. They feel strong. You get the sense that you can't hurt them or damage them, that you won't intrude on them—or perhaps that you will but you're invited to intrude to some extent. You get the sense of knowing them.
>
> *(pp. 543–544)*

Sorenson (1996) does not use the term "relational integration," but his work has framed integration as deeply personal and relational and in ways that fit the above description from the student:

> Integration is personal in the sense that it occurs through contact with persons-in-relation, including other creatures and God . . . Who we are to each other, how we treat each other has direct bearing on the quality of integrative models we can imagine and sustain.
>
> *(p. 206)*

Throughout this book, we want to outline the contours of a relational approach to the integration of psychology and theology by thematizing relationality at the levels of both content and process. Relationality provides a useful theme for the content of integration, particularly within the Trinitarian Christian tradition which emphasizes a God who is relational. As Trinity, God always exists and acts in relationship (LaCugna, 1991). Theological anthropology is also illuminated by understanding relationality as part of the *imago dei* and as a central dynamic of human nature (Shults, 2003; Grenz, 2006). Various theories within social science also highlight the relational dynamics of humans nested within social or ecological contexts. For example, emerging connections between research on attachment and the field of interpersonal neurobiology reveal how relational experiences form relational templates in the brain used to configure working models of self and other. These internal working models of relationship shape "alterity," that is, interpretative schemas and levels of openness to those who are deemed "other." This social science emphasis on the profound significance of human relationships in both development and transformation coheres in significant ways with the biblical emphasis on community and loving one's neighbor.

Plotting Relational Integration on the Methodological Landscape

In recent years, views on ways of relating psychology and Christianity have multiplied and grown more distinct, with ongoing dialogue between proponents of various views (Johnson, 2010). Christian practitioners and scholars have also articulated a variety of stances related to counseling and psychotherapy (Greggo & Sisemore, 2012). At times, contemporary "integration" of psychology and theology (e.g., Collins, 2000; Jones, 2010; McMinn, 2012) or science and religion (e.g., Barbour, 1990) is offered as an explicit, defined position. For example, Jones (2010) articulates and defends the integration view in Johnson's (2010) edited volume on five views of psychology and Christianity; and McMinn (2012; McMinn & Campbell, 2007) has proposed an approach to psychotherapy based on an integration position. Alternately, integration is sometimes suggested as a more ambiguous interdisciplinary goal. Typically, the goal of integration is expressed as bringing together understandings from different disciplines to synthesize a more constructive holistic perspective (Stevenson, Eck, & Hill, 2007).

In the 1990s, Eck identified and reviewed twenty-seven approaches for relating psychology and theology. Specific models for relating psychology and theology continue to be debated among Christian scholars and practitioners (and we will review various models in Chapter 2). Models typically take a particular stance (or at least imply a stance) on a few central issues, including (1) the prioritization of disciplines; and (2) the level(s) at which coherence can be attained (e.g., linguistic, conceptual, methodological, and/or assumptive). The prioritization of disciplines is a long-standing conversation and debate in interdisciplinary work across many disciplines (Callard & Fitzgerald, 2015), often including questions of whether to privilege epistemologically one discipline over the other and the practical implications of such privileging. This commonplace concern to establish a hierarchy of the disciplines arises from a history of disciplinary ordering that must be acknowledged and accounted for in delineating a comprehensive integrative process. For example, between theology and psychology, there has been robust discussion of which field should take priority, with a historical precedent for treating theology as "queen of the sciences" going back to the Middle Ages (Porter, 2010; Sandage & Brown, 2010). Conservative religious communities often continue to privilege theology over psychology and over other disciplines, whereas more progressive communities may reverse this privileging or seek to hold disciplines in an egalitarian tension.

Our own view—suitable to a relational model and building on our prior work (Sandage & Brown, 2010; Brown, Dahl, & Corbin Reuschling, 2011)—is an egalitarian approach to interdisciplinarity. As we will explore in Chapter 5, hermeneutical considerations in both theology and psychology, particularly the locatedness of all who engage in scholarship as they embody particular interpretive traditions and frameworks, lead us to argue for mutuality and shared power in interdisciplinary conversation. Additionally, we will suggest there is value in fostering relationships between psychologists and theologians, so that the relationship itself provides the context for and so is the precursor to the integrative work. A relational schema for integration encourages a differentiated model of interaction rather than allowing anxieties over maintaining an "upper hand" to set the agenda for interdisciplinary collaboration (see Chapter 3).

Another aspect of integrative method has to do with how or at what level resonance is pursued and recognized between disciplines (Brown, 2004). Although not all theorists attend to this aspect of their methodology explicitly, the level at which integration is sought can distinguish differing views of integration. A rather more simplistic way to seek integration is to look for common language between two disciplines. Yet pressing toward the level of disciplinary "judgments" assists in determining whether specific linguistic or even conceptual similarities between two disciplines indicate coherence in their determinations, i.e., their judgments about their object of study (Brown, Dahl, & Corbin Reuschling, 2011; Vanhoozer, 2005). For example, reference to New Testament *language* of "spirit, soul, and body" (1 Thess 5:23) to support a tripartite perspective on human persons without attending to corresponding *judgments* from the Bible that suggest a unitary view of the personhood (e.g., Green, 2008) can lead to meager or misconstrued integrative results. Looking for conceptual resonance and then testing judgments about these related concepts in different disciplines provide a stronger methodology for integration.

Finding coherence at the level of disciplinary methodology is a common approach to integration. For example, social scientific criticism has enjoyed a significant place at the table in biblical studies, in part because it coheres well with historical-critical method, which has been the predominant approach in the guild in the modern era. Though it has not been without its critics (e.g., Stanton, 1992), social science has entered the field with relative ease, given that it has overlapping goals with historical criticism and augments the latter by focusing on sociological dimensions of the biblical texts and their settings (Elliott & Via, 1993).

Probably the most elusive kind of integration sits at the level of core disciplinary assumptions. An important methodological question for integration is whether coherence at this level is required for integration at other levels. The biblical counseling movement would seem to provide an example of an affirmative answer to this question. In the view of its practitioners, unless psychology can conform to what are understood to be biblical assumptions, then very little if any fruitful conversation between psychology and theology is possible. In any event, attention to the ways any particular integration approach "does integration" involves assessing at what levels integration is sought.

Relational Integration: Multiple Persons in Conversation

To round out this introduction to our relational approach, we explore what we consider to be a significant misstep in the conceptualization of integration among various disciplines and how our model of relational integration may fill an important gap in this regard. This misstep consists in a tendency toward abstraction in discussion of integrative method or philosophy, not surprising as the modern academy has the same propensity (see Chapter 4). And since scholars have often been the primary contributors to published literature on integration, it is not particularly surprising that the focus is typically placed on *integrating disciplines or abstract bodies of knowledge*. While increasingly diverse approaches to interdisciplinary study have begun to emerge in the fields of both psychology and theology, much of the historical and even contemporary discourse continues to be characterized by an implicitly individualistic, Cartesian model of a single individual exploring a new area of study in order to enhance their primary disciplinary focus. Yet it is obvious that disciplines are not "doing integration." For that matter, books and journal articles are not the actors in the work of integration. Rather, it is real people who attempt (or avoid) collaborative integration as part of relational and cultural systems that shape the process of interdisciplinary discourse.

We do acknowledge that, within this model of a single scholar or practitioner doing integration, it seems to be increasingly the case that such interdisciplinary work attempts to bridge more thoroughly the two disciplines being engaged. For example, conversations about how biblical scholars might bridge psychology and biblical studies account for the inception of the Psychology and Biblical Studies section of the Society of Biblical Literature (1991) and a subsequent project of psychological analysis of the Bible in the four-volume *Psychology and the Bible* (Ellens & Rollins, 2004). We cite this volume to indicate that more sophisticated work is being done in this area. Yet it is also telling that the essays in this volume (other than the introduction) are written by single authors, the majority of whose home disciplines are biblical studies or theology. Two of the views in the *Psychology & Christianity: Five Views* (Johnson, 2010) book are represented by co-authors (a philosopher and psychologist in both cases), however it is noteworthy that none of the eight contributors to this key volume is a biblical scholar or theologian in terms of formal academic training.

The interdisciplinary terrain, however, is shifting, even if somewhat slowly. Examples of integrative volumes representing collaboration between theological and social science scholars can be enumerated and suggest an encouraging trend (Brown, Dahl, & Corbin Reuschling, 2011; Browning & Cooper, 2004; McMinn & Phillips, 2001; Shults, 2003; Shults & Sandage, 2006; Strawn, 2012; Whitehead & Whitehead, 1995). Yet, within the growing literature on interdisciplinary method, the actual interpersonal dynamics of integration have received scant attention. This limited consideration (see Coe & Hall, 2010; Entwistle, 2010) of actual relational dynamics among psychologists and theologians is striking, particularly among Christians who hold a relational view of God and a relational ontology of personhood.

In our relational integration model, we desire to move beyond a single-integrator construct toward two-person and systemic understandings of relational integration among psychologists and theologians. While providing a careful comparison of multiple views for relating psychology and Christianity, none of the authors in Johnson (2010) focuses specifically upon the challenges or potentialities of actual relational interaction and collaboration between theologians and psychologists, nor do any focus on the positive aspects of diversity and differentiation with respect to their particular view. We think attention to relational dynamics can assist in navigating potential challenges of integration that involves actual conversations between two or more scholars (or practitioners) of different disciplines. Such attention to relationality also highlights the strengths (and not just the challenges) that emerge from multiple disciplinarians in the conversation. This relational view is also promising for integrative applications to counseling and psychotherapy which involve processes of relational negotiation between two or more persons across differing values, worldviews, and treatment preferences. Counselors and therapists may have their preferred ways of approaching spiritual and theological concerns, but that cannot be effectively delivered in a "prepackaged" way that looks the same with each client or group of clients.

Sociocultural Contexts of Integration

Another downside of the tendency to view integration abstractly—that is, as occurring between psychology and theology rather than between psychologists and theologians—is the corresponding propensity to lose sight of the contextual nature of disciplinary and integrative work. A relational perspective helpfully attends to the reality that the processes of relational integration of psychology and theology unfold within diverse social contexts and personal experiences (e.g., Moriarty, 2010). Theology and psychology are formal scholarly disciplines, but at a more basic folk level everyone is both a theologian and psychologist, as we have suggested in our opening vignette, since everyone holds assumptions, however implicit, about ultimate concerns (theology), and everyone also engages in observations about people and the world around them (psychology). At times, individuals will need to make their best attempts at integration "on their own," that is, they will need to seek to integrate their own understandings of theology and psychology for a situation at hand. But there are also actual interpersonal and contextual dynamics at play between theologians and psychologists, pastors and therapists, which influence the relational and social processes of integration or disintegration. These dynamics can be avenues toward productive "real-time" interdisciplinary conversations, as well as possible barriers to dialogue (see Chapter 3).

Even as our relational model encourages collaboration among psychologists and theologians, the disciplines of psychology and theology are also significant resources for making sense of some of the challenges and barriers to the kinds of relational integration we envision. In fact, we want to avoid promoting an idealistic fantasy or some kind of "cheap integration" (cf. Bonhoeffer's notion of cheap grace) that promises integrative synthesis without anxiety, conflict, or sacrifice. Generating interaction between scholars or professionals of differing disciplines hardly guarantees that interdisciplinary understanding or collaboration will result. In some cases, paradigms and languages seem too dissonant, or understanding breaks down in the anxiety of concerns about power and control (i.e., regarding disciplinary hierarchies). There is also the risk of scholars in one discipline unilaterally assimilating the other by "cherry picking" selected pieces of data from it (what Reynhout, 2007, terms, "overreach") rather than engaging in more responsible and collaborative relational integration. Having more than one discipline represented in the room does not guarantee that each person will have equal presence and voice.

Relational integration also presses against abstraction by affirming the multiple contexts in which integration can and does occur. We resist a "one-size fits all" approach to integration and affirm the value of a plurality of integrative models. Early discussions of integration in the 1960s–1980s tended to invoke the idea that "all truth is God's truth" and often spoke of the quest to integrate psychology and theology in ways that might have implied these were singular, unified disciplines rather than diverse, poly-theoretical bodies of knowledge. We resonate with the recent articulation of a "tradition-based" approach to integration which calls for integrators to acknowledge the particularity of their theological and theoretical traditions and sociocultural embodiment rather than implying it is possible or desirable to integrate generic or monolithic versions of either discipline (Strawn, Wright, & Jones, 2014, p. 300; also see Dueck & Reimer, 2009). As examples, the methods and products of integration will be different when seeking to synthesize Kierkegaardian theology and Lacanian psychoanalytic theory (Pound, 2007),

Womanist theology and Kohutian self psychology (Sheppard, 2011), or Wesleyan theology and psychoanalysis (Armistead, Strawn, & Wright, 2009). Throughout this book, we try to be explicit about our particular theoretical and theological assumptions, recognizing that others who embrace differing traditions and assumptions will articulate different models. It is our hope that one unique contribution of our work is the articulation of a model that is not only theoretically consistent across both psychology and theology, but also accounts for the unique intrapersonal and interpersonal tensions of integration in lived experience.

Finally, an additional consequence of viewing integration in more abstract terms is that the turn to praxis can be sluggish. This concern shows up in the literature, with a complaint that the integration of psychology and theology has remained too conceptual and divorced from practical applications. As noted above, a major influence on the historical turn toward interdisciplinarity has been the interest in finding better solutions to "real world" problems, so it is crucial to orient interdisciplinary integration in relation toward praxis. A key feature of our relational integration approach is an emphasis on using (a) case study methodology and real life cases involving problems and human suffering to help catalyze the integrative process in (b) relational or group processes of conversation, consultation, and mutual learning. We also make the assumption that the ultimate goal of relational integration is to foster constructive changes and transformations in practical, embodied ways. There is evidence that interdisciplinary collaborations are more common in strategic or applied disciplines oriented toward understanding practical applications (van Rijnsoever & Hessels, 2011). We have found good integrative "traction" often comes when working inductively from cases and practical issues toward theological and psychological reflection.

Our Personal Histories of Integrative Engagement

In line with our relational integration model, we value naming and exploring the embodied nature of the integrative process. So, we offer here brief rehearsals of our own formative influences and journeys into interdisciplinary integration.

Steve

My (Steve) own journey toward relational integration includes many episodes and narratives but I will highlight a few formative periods that convey the contrasting relational themes of hospitality and absence. My interests in both psychology and theology first developed during my undergraduate studies in the 1980s at Iowa State University. I majored in psychology and was interested in pastoral ministry but I had been warned by my pastor that the religious studies courses in that context would be too "liberal" for my evangelical Christian faith. So I loaded up on psychology courses while longing for a greater theological understanding of the existential issues or "ultimate concerns" that seemed to lie behind or beneath many of the psychological concerns I was studying. Religion and spirituality were virtually never mentioned in any of my psychology courses. However, two psychology professors, Norm Scott and Douglas Epperson, invited me into their research groups and welcomed me to use independent study credits to read about religious values in psychotherapy and even Christian counseling. This felt like a welcoming act of hospitality by these psychologists in an environment my faith community considered dangerous.

After my undergraduate degree, I went to Trinity Evangelical Divinity School (TEDS) to satisfy my theological interests and to study with Gary Collins, a leader in the integration of psychology and theology. To my delight, conversations about integration with Gary were often around the dinner table at his house enjoying meals or dessert with other students and his family amidst lively banter and stimulating discussions. Gary pressed for international and intercultural awareness, both in theorizing but also in his own life and relationships. At this same time in seminary, I was growing to both love theology and also lament the reality that much of the theology I was learning was ethnocentric, excessively cognitive or abstract, and largely disengaged from issues of social justice and tragic realities of human suffering. During my last quarter of seminary, I naively signed up for a ministry practicum at a county-run geriatric center, and I was unprepared for the deplorable conditions, the rampant mental illness and severe dementia, and the overall level of trauma and despondency. I would often leave the facility with a headache and sit in my car wrestling with my own despair, groping to try to make sense out of residents' questions about the absence of God or how I should relate to seniors who were floridly psychotic or profoundly bitter. Theologian James Loder (1989) says transformation toward integration often starts with an existential crisis or a "rupture in the knowing context" (p. 32), and this was an important dis-integrative rupture that helped me see that I needed deeper psychological and spiritual formation to undergird my desire to bring together theology and psychology in my learning and vocation.

During my doctoral program in psychology at Virginia Commonwealth University, I was working with Everett Worthington (another leader in the integration of psychology and theology) and again enjoying the hospitality of integrative conversations at his family dinner table. This relational dynamic and "explicit integration" was grounding and allowed me to explore the diversity of perspectives on psychology and theology in that pluralistic, supposedly "secular" context. I became intrigued by the variety of ways different people I met held the tensions between theology and psychology or what we might call more implicit dynamics of integration. These included a psychologist who frequently referenced religion in passive-aggressive ways along with disclosures about hurtful church experiences from his past; a chaplain at the prison where I worked who liked to discuss the theories of various psychologists (with mixed accuracy) and how their insights paled in comparison to his theological tradition; a seemingly non-religious social worker who surprised me one afternoon with her "out of the blue" explanation of how her relationship with God motivated her work with prison inmates; an accomplished psychopathology researcher who declared that "any attempt at the scientific study of religion is absurd"; and a clinical supervisor who appeared to seamlessly integrate his faith identity, progressive theological perspective, and therapy work without the angst and hesitations I was experiencing. I could not articulate it at the time, but looking back I know I benefitted greatly from relationships with this diverse array of professionals and professors across various religious and cultural traditions and contexts, who modeled such differing approaches to relating psychology and theology, that it set the stage for me to eventually work on differentiating my own approach to "integration."

Jeannine

I (Jeannine) understand my own journey toward relational integration as woven together with and emerging from my gender coupled with my ecclesial location in conservative evangelical circles. I have early memories marked by traces of my calling and gifting for an eventual career in biblical studies, including a love of Bible study and a sense of Christian vocation in the few areas of service available to women in my tradition (these were missionary, Sunday School teacher, or choir director). Yet much of God's calling was muted by these restrictive options. So given my musical interest, I headed to college to study music therapy, with its focus on social service fulfilling some measure of ministry calling. Music therapy was and is a highly integrated degree program, so I took a good number of courses across a spectrum of biology, psychology, and sociology, in addition to music, before moving into music therapy courses that worked to bridge these disciplines. I appreciated this integrative impulse and thrived in the academic environment.

My college years were also a time of developing ministry and leadership gifts in a para-church college ministry, coupled with theological crisis around the question of ministry as a woman. After college, I went on staff with InterVarsity Christian Fellowship, and it was this experience of ministry that led me to seminary. Since I had (like Steve) been warned about taking religious studies courses at college, I lacked and now felt the need for formal theological training. It was at seminary that my calling to academic work and teaching became clear, through the mentorship of New Testament professor Robert Stein. This brings me to reflect upon a theme of my own movement toward vocation and integration—namely, that in my academic journey virtually all of my professional mentors have been men. In seminary and doctoral work, my advisors and closest mentors were men. Not until my PhD work did I encounter a female mentor. Given this reality (and while I am thankful for these male mentors), I had significant integrative work to do around gender, vocation, and identity. A consistent and pressing question during these years of study was, *What does a female biblical scholar look like?*

This question slowly morphed into the question of *How will I look as a biblical scholar?* I suspect that one reason I have been so drawn to integration and to what

I have come to understand as relational integration is my ever-present aware-ness that my gender (especially in my ecclesial location) has complicated any "traditional" or prescribed career path. For example, beginning a PhD program with two preschoolers in tow pressed me to new levels of integrative reflection. This social location also drew me toward questions of hermeneutics, which itself involves an exploration of interpretative locations.

My first teaching post was at Bethel Seminary, where I continue to teach today. I arrived on the faculty during the tenure of Provost Leland Eliason, whose vision for the seminary focused on integration of three "centers" of learning: Bible, theology, history; personal and spiritual formation; and trans-formational leadership. Given my earlier experiences with integration, I was drawn to this model of theological education and the work of interdisciplinary integration and conversation that were being promoted among our faculty to foster it. The relational development that occurred around and in these conver-sations became influential for my ongoing integrative pursuits. One particular emerging motif suggested a fruitful direction for integrative conversation: col-leagues offering from their areas of expertise provided opportunities for oth-ers to hear resonance in their own fields. This inverted a paradigm that I had previously intuited about interdisciplinary collaboration—that of an individual scholar attempting to draw on insights from a second discipline for their work in their primary discipline.

A key movement in my development toward integration was the opportu-nity and choice to team-teach with colleagues across disciplines. Teaching a class on "Gospels and Formation" with Carla Dahl (social scientist) was stimu-lating and often surprising; it also seemed to promote a deeper kind of learn-ing for students than single-discipline courses usually did. Another significant outcome was a co-writing project, *Becoming Whole and Holy: An Integrative Con-versation about Christian Formation* (Brown, Dahl, & Corbin-Reuschling, 2011)—patterned as a reflective conversation among a social scientist, a biblical scholar, and an ethicist.

More recently, with the introduction of a capstone integrative course into our seminary curriculum, I have had the opportunity to co-teach regularly and focus attention on interdisciplinary methodologies, providing opportunities to hone my hermeneutical thinking around interdisciplinarity. The chance to consistently teach with colleagues from other disciplines, such as psychology, systematic the-ology, and church history, has sharpened my understanding of integration and the kinds of conversations that are helpfully illuminated by it. Even more, these in-class conversations have been places of risk and reward, as the framework for conversation is sketched ahead of time but the direction and details freely con-form to the conversation as it happens. This kind of unanticipated, and some-times anxiety-producing, conversation comes with integrative teaching, and it has fostered various relational capacities for integration like humility, a non-anxious presence, clarity of thinking, and curiosity (Sandage & Brown, 2015).

A Concluding Case: The Complexity of Theological and Psychological Dynamics

Antoine (age 52) and Lenelle (age 48) were a Haitian couple who had immigrated to Boston to live with extended family members in the 1990s. They recently contacted a Christian counseling center for help regarding family conflicts that emerged after their son, Daniel (age 28), told them four months prior that he would be getting married to his male partner, Malcolm (age 26, African-American). This was when they learned Daniel was gay, which conflicted with the conservative theological views of the church where they had been faithfully involved since shortly after their arrival in Boston. They had been very proud of Daniel when he became the first person in their extended family to go to college, as he attended an evangelical Christian college on an athletic scholarship and studied youth ministry. They had expected he would eventually go to seminary but were surprised and concerned when he enrolled at a very "liberal" seminary in his mid-twenties. They had thought his theology seemed to be changing after he started attending an Episcopalian church, which was a significant departure from their own Bible-centered, congregational-ruled church where Daniel grew up. Lenelle made the call to the counseling center and explained to Robert (the assigned therapist, age 42, male, Italian- and Hungarian-American) that she and Antoine were shocked and dismayed at the news that Daniel was gay and that they had felt alienated by a series of arguments with him since that time before breaking off contact a month prior. She said she "felt they were losing their precious son" and "wanted help figuring out what to do" since "the Bible says marriage is to be a man and a woman." She wanted to come to counseling as a family to heal this rift and also wondered if the counseling center might offer "specialized ministries for people like Daniel," by which she meant counseling to change his sexual orientation to heterosexuality. Her closing comment was "I've dreamed of seeing him get married and starting a ministry for so long . . . and now my hopes are shattered."

Robert also received a call from Daniel who wanted to discuss some things before attending any sessions with his parents. He explained that he had known he was gay since adolescence but had mostly avoided dealing with it until around the time he started seminary. His theological studies and participation in an "open and affirming" congregation had, in fact, led to shifts toward "a more progressive Christian faith" and his own "his acceptance of his own sexuality." He also said he and Malcolm (fellow seminary student) had dated for two years and were "deeply in love and a great support to each other." Daniel said he also loved his parents and wanted them to be involved in his life but was feeling extremely hurt and angry. He said he knew they would struggle with his disclosure but was devastated when, in the heat of their last argument, Antoine said, "I thought you were a Christian, not a sodomite! You are an embarrassment to our family!" Daniel said, "I was trying to explain a broader Christian perspective and that the Bible doesn't even address committed gay relationships of today, but my dad's statement was so rejecting . . . something broke inside me. I'm not yet sure how I can handle being in the same room with him." Despite his feelings, Daniel said he was open to counseling sessions with his parents, but wanted to clarify the goals up front and find out whether Robert would sympathize with his parents' desire to "try to make me straight through some kind of 'conversion therapy' or something."

This complicated case depicts several contours that are relevant to our relational integration approach. First, explicit theological and hermeneutical understandings are intricately related to psychological or emotional experiences and relational processes. A counselor will be unlikely to help this family without explicitly engaging the ways their theologies are tied to their psychologies and vice versa. Second, the profound and conflictual differences in this family show the complexity of relational integration when counseling or therapy moves beyond individuals to work with couples, families, or groups. The counselor will need an integrative model that can effectively navigate or even make use of these differences in the family and help cultivate a strong therapeutic alliance with each family member. Third, we can see that differing sociocultural contexts and experiences intersect with differing theological perspectives to generate psychological pain and conflict *within part of a single family.* As Robert moved into working with this family, he was challenged to empathize with *both* (a) Daniel in his newly found integrity of identity as a progressive Christian gay man and the hopefulness he experienced in his relationships with Malcolm and a gay-affirming community, and (b) Lenelle and Antoine in their confusion about Daniel and his future, their nagging guilt over whether they had done something wrong as Christian parents, and their embarrassment within their own church community which would not affirm Daniel's sexuality. Like most counselors would in this kind of situation, Robert found it easier to empathize with one side of this conflict than the other given his own personal theological convictions. However, he needed to manage his countertransference and maintain a differentiated stance with each family member, while respectfully engaging the strengths and tensions within each person's particular set of theological and psychological concerns.

In the chapters that follow, we will describe how a relational integration approach might apply to the systemic challenges of these kinds of cases. However, in Chapter 2 we first want to trace some of the history of how the term "integration" arose in the psychology and theology dialogue and offer a summary of differing models for relating psychology and theology.

Note

1 Green (2003) speaks of the "erroneous assumption that science and religion have lives separate from one another" (p. 184).

Bibliography

Abu-Raiya, H., & Pargament, K. I. (2015). Religious coping among diverse religions: Commonalities and divergences. *Psychology of Religion and Spirituality*, 7(1), 24.

Aldrich, J. H. (2014). *Interdisciplinarity: Its role in a discipline-based academy.* Oxford: Oxford University Press.

Armistead, M. K., Strawn, B. D., & Wright, R. W. (Eds.). (2009). *Wesleyan theology and social science: The dance of practical divinity and discovery.* Newcastle: Cambridge Scholars Publishing.

The Association of Theological Schools (2010). *Standards of accreditation.* Pittsburgh, PA: The Association of Theological Schools. Online version available at: https://www.ats. edu/accrediting/standards-and-notations

Balswick, J. O., King, P. E., & Reimer, K. S. (2016). *The reciprocating self: Human development in theological perspective* (2nd ed.). Downers Grove, IL: InterVarsity Press.

Barbour, I. G. (1990). *Religion in an age of science.* San Francisco, CA: Harper & Row.

Beilby, J. K., & Eddy, P. R. (Eds.). (2009). *The Historical Jesus: Five views.* Downers Grove, IL: InterVarsity Press.

Bland, E. D., & Strawn, B. D. (Eds.). (2014). *Christianity & psychoanalysis: A new conversation.* Downers Grove, IL: InterVarsity Press.

Brown, W.S. (2004). Resonance: A model for relating science, psychology, and faith. *Journal of Psychology and Christianity, 23,* 110–120.

Brown, J. K., Dahl, C. M., & Corbin Reuschling, W. (2011). *Becoming whole and holy: An integrative conversation about Christian formation.* Grand Rapids, MI: Brazos.

Browning, D. S., & Cooper, T. D. (2004). *Religious thought and the modern psychologies.* Minneapolis, MN: Fortress Press.

Callard, F., & Fitzgerald, D. (2015). Social science and neuroscience beyond interdisciplinarity: Experimental entanglements. *Theory, Culture & Society, 32*(1), 3–32.

Coe, J. H., & Hall, T. W. (2010). A transformational psychology view. In E. L. Johnson (Ed.), *Psychology & Christianity: Five views* (pp. 199–226). Downers Grove, IL: InterVarsity Press.

Collins, G. R. (2000). An integration view. In E. L. Johnson & S. L. Jones (Eds.), *Psychology & Christianity: Four views* (pp. 102–129). Downers Grove, IL: InterVarsity Press.

Dingemans, G. D. (1996). Practical theology in the academy: A contemporary overview. *The Journal of Religion, 76*(1), 82–96.

Dueck, A., & Reimer, K. (2009). *A peaceable psychology: Christian therapy in a world of many cultures.* Grand Rapids, MI: Brazos Press.

Ellens, J. H., & Rollins, W. G. (Eds.). (2004). *Psychology and the Bible: From Christ to Jesus* (Vol. 4). Westport, CT: Praeger.

Elliott, J. H., & Via, D. O. (1993). *What is social-scientific criticism?* Minneapolis, MN: Fortress Press.

Entwistle, D. N. (2010). *Integrative approaches to psychology and Christianity: An introduction to worldview issues, philosophical foundations, and models of integration* (2nd ed.). Eugene, OR: Cascade Books.

Green, J. B. (2003). Science, religion and the mind-brain problem—the case of Thomas Willis (1621–1675). *Science & Christian Belief, 15*(2), 165–185.

Green, J. B. (2005). Body and soul, mind and brain: Critical issues. In J. B. Green & S. L. Palmer (Eds.), *In search of the soul: Four views of the mind-body problem* (pp. 7–32). Downers Grove, IL: InterVarsity Press.

Green, J. B. (2008). *Body, soul, and human life: The nature of humanity in the Bible* (studies in theological interpretation). Grand Rapids, MI: Baker Academic.

Greggo, S. P., & Sisemore, T. A. (2012). *Counseling and Christianity: Five approaches.* Downers Grove, IL: InterVarsity Press.

Grenz, S. (2006). The social God and the relational self: Toward a theology of the Imago Dei in the postmodern context. In R. Lints, M. S. Horton, & M. R. Talbot (Eds.), *Personal identity in theological perspective* (pp. 70–92). Grand Rapids, MI: Eerdmans.

Heitink, G. (1999). *Practical theology: History, theory, action domains*. Grand Rapids, MI: Wm. B. Eerdmans Publishing.

Hook, J. N., Worthington, E. L., Davis, D. E., Jennings, D. J., Gartner, A. L., & Hook, J. P. (2010). Empirically supported religious and spiritual therapies. *Journal of Clinical Psychology*, *66*(1), 46–72.

Jennings, P. (2010). *Mixing minds: The power of relationship in psychoanalysis and Buddhism*. Somerville, MA: Wisdom Publications.

Johnson, E. L. (Ed.). (2010). *Psychology & Christianity: Five views* (2nd ed.). Downers Grove, IL: InterVarsity Press.

Jones, S. L. (2010). An integration view. In E. L. Johnson (Ed.), *Psychology & Christianity: Five views* (pp. 101–128). Downers Grove, IL: InterVarsity Press.

LaCugna, C. M. (1991). *God for us: The trinity and Christian life*. New York, NY: HarperSanFrancisco.

Loder, J. E. (1989). *The transforming moment*. Colorado Springs: Helmers & Howard.

McMinn, M. R. (2011). *Psychology, theology, and spirituality in Christian counseling* (rev. & updated ed.). Carol Stream, IL: Tyndale House Publishers, Inc.

McMinn, M. R. (2012). An integration approach. In S. P. Greggo, T. A. Sisemore, S. P. Greggo, T. A. Sisemore (Eds.), *Counseling and Christianity: Five approaches* (pp. 84–109). Downers Grove, IL, US: InterVarsity Press.

McMinn, M. R., & Campbell, C. D. (2007). *Integrative psychotherapy: Toward a comprehensive Christian approach*. Downers Grove, IL: InterVarsity Press.

McMinn, M. R., & Phillips, T. R. (Eds.). (2001). *Care for the soul: Exploring the intersection of psychology & theology*. Downers Grove, IL: InterVarsity Press.

Mikulincer, M., & Shaver, P. R. (2007). *Attachment in adulthood: Structure, dynamics, and change*. New York, NY: Guilford Press.

Moran, J. (2002). *Interdisciplinarity: The new critical idiom*. New York, NY: Routledge.

Morgan, J., & Sandage, S. J. (2016). A developmental model of interreligious competence. *Archive for the Psychology of Religion*, *38*(2), 129–158.

Moriarty, G. L. (Ed.). (2010). *Integrating faith and psychology: Twelve psychologists tell their stories*. Downers Grove, IL: IVP Academic.

Murphy, N. (1990). Theology and the social sciences—Discipline and antidiscipline. *Zygon*, *25*, 309–316.

Neville, R. C. (2006). *On the scope and truth of theology: Theology as symbolic engagement*. New York, NY: T & T Clark International.

Paine, D. R., Sandage, S. J., Rupert, D., Devor, N. G., & Bronstein, M. (2015). Humility as a psychotherapeutic virtue: Spiritual, philosophical, and psychological foundations. *Journal of Spirituality in Mental Health, 17*, 3–25.

Porter, S. L. (2010). Theology as queen and psychology as handmaid: The authority of theology in integrative endeavors. *Journal of Psychology and Christianity*, *29*, 5–16.

Pound, M. (2007). *Theology, psychoanalysis, and trauma*. London: SCM Press.

Raasch, C., Lee, V., Spaeth, S., & Herstatt, C. (2013). The rise and fall of interdisciplinary research: The case of open source innovation. *Research Policy*, *42*(5), 1138–1151.

Reno, R. R. (2004). Biblical theology and theological exegesis. In C. Bartholomew, M. Healy, K. Möller, & R. Parry (Eds.), *Out of Egypt: Biblical theology and Biblical interpretation, scripture and hermeneutics*, Series 5 (pp. 385–408). Grand Rapids, MI: Zondervan.

Reynhout, K. A. (2007). The hermeneutics of transdisciplinarity: A Gadamerian model of transversal reasoning. *Transdisciplinarity in Science and Religion*, *2*, 77–101.

Reynhout, K. A. (2013). *Interdisciplinary interpretation: Paul Ricoeur and the hermeneutics of theology and science*. Plymouth, UK: Lexington Books.

Rollins, W. G. (1983). *Jung and the Bible.* Atlanta: John Knox Press.

Sandage, S. J., & Brown, J. K. (2010). Monarchy or democracy in relation integration? A reply to Porter. *Journal of Psychology and Christianity, 29*(1), 20.

Sandage, S. J., & Brown, J. K. (2015). Relational integration, Part I: Differentiated relationality between psychology and theology. *Journal of Psychology & Theology, 43*(3).

Sharma, A. R., & Tummala-Narra, P. (2014). Psychotherapy with Hindus. In P. S. Richards, A. E. Bergin, P. S. Richards, & A. E. Bergin (Eds.), *Handbook of psychotherapy and religious diversity* (2nd ed., pp. 321–345). Washington, DC: American Psychological Association. doi:10.1037/14371-013

Sheppard, P. (2011). *Self, culture, and others in womanist practical theology.* New York, NY: Palgrave Macmillan.

Shults, F. L. (2003). *Reforming theological anthropology: After the philosophical turn to relationality.* Grand Rapids, MI: Eerdmans.

Shults, F. L., & Sandage, S. J. (2006). *Transforming spirituality: Integrating theology and psychology.* Grand Rapids, MI: Baker Academic.

Sorenson, R. L. (1996). The tenth leper. *Journal of Psychology and Theology, 24*, 197–211.

Sorenson, R. L. (1997). Doctoral students' integration of psychology and Christianity: Perspectives via attachment theory and multidimensional scaling. *Journal for the Scientific Study of Religion, 36*(4), 530–548. doi:10.2307/1387688

Sorenson, R. L. (2004). *Minding spirituality.* Hillsdale, NJ: The Analytic Press.

Spero, M. H. (1992). *Religious objects as psychological structures.* Chicago, IL: University of Chicago Press.

Stanton, G. (1992). *A gospel for a new people: Studies in Matthew.* Louisville: Westminster/ John Knox Press.

Starr, K. E., & Aron, L. (2008). *Repair of the soul: Metaphors of transformation in Jewish mysticism and psychoanalysis.* New York, NY: Routledge.

Stevenson, D. H., Eck, B. E., & Hill, P. C. (Eds.). (2007). *Psychology & Christianity integration: Seminal works that shaped the movement.* Batavia, IL: Christian Association for Psychological Studies.

Stokols, D., Hall, K. L., Taylor, B. K., & Moser, R. P. (2008). The science of team science: Overview of the field and introduction to the supplement. *American Journal of Preventative Medicine, 35*(2S), S77–S89.

Strawn, B. A. (Ed.). (2012). *The Bible and the pursuit of happiness.* New York, NY: Oxford University Press.

Strawn, B. D., Wright, R. W., & Jones, P. (2014). Tradition-based integration: Illuminating the stories and practices that shape our integrative imagination. *Journal of Psychology & Christianity, 33*(4), 37–54.

Unützer, J., Harbin, H., Schoenbaum, M., & Druss, B. (2013). The collaborative care model: An approach for integrating physical and mental health care in Medicaid health homes. *HEALTH HOME Information Resource Center.* Retrieved from www.chcs.org/media/ HH_IRC_Collaborative_Care_Model__052113_2.pdf

van Rijnsoever, F. J., & Hessels, L. K. (2011). Factors associated with disciplinary and interdisciplinary research collaboration. *Research Policy, 40*(3), 463–472.

Vanhoozer, K. J. (2005). *The drama of doctrine: A canonical linguistic approach to Christian theology.* Louisville: Westminster John Knox.

Wekell, W., Koenig, R. B., Walters, P., Steurer, B., Childress, V., Paine, D. S., . . . Roxin, A. (2015). *U.S. Patent No. 8,956,292.* Washington, DC: U.S. Patent and Trademark Office.

Whitehead, J. D., & Whitehead, E. E. (1995). *Method in ministry: Theological reflection and Christian ministry*. Lanham, MD: Rowman & Littlefield.

Wolters, A. (2007). No longer queen: The theological disciplines and their sisters. In D. L. Jeffrey & C. S. Evans (Eds.), *The Bible and the university* (pp. 59–79). Grand Rapids, MI: Zondervan.

Worthington, E. L. (1994). A blueprint for intradisciplinary integration. *Journal of Psychology and Theology, 22*, 79–86.

Wright, R., Jones, P., & Strawn, B. D. (2014). Tradition-based integration. In E. D. Bland & B. D. Strawn (Eds.), *Christianity and psychoanalysis: A new conversation* (pp. 37–54). Downers Grove, IL: InterVarsity Press.

2

WAYS OF RELATING PSYCHOLOGY AND THEOLOGY

Before moving to a more in depth expression of our model of relational integration (Chapter 3), in this chapter we offer a historical review of interdisciplinary currents between psychology and theology. We begin by summarizing how the term "integration" arose in relationship to psychology and theology. We then survey several major models for relating psychology and theology, drawing on a typology that highlights a relational spectrum, with any particular view representing a differing form of relationality. In the latter part of the chapter, we provide historical explorations of the ways each discipline has engaged the other, beginning with psychology's appropriations of theology and moving to theology's interactions with psychology. Our relational integration model is centered in a *differentiated* form of relationality, and the relevance of our argument will be clearer after we consider the historical moorings of integration and of the intersection of psychology and theology.

Historical Context for Scholarly Discussions of "Integration"

To provide context for our discussion, tracing the origins of the term "integration" can be useful. "Integration" came to be used to highlight the potential relationship between psychology and theology as academic disciplines in evangelical Christian scholarly literature over sixty years ago (for helpful overviews, see Johnson, 2010; Stevenson, Eck, & Hill, 2007). Vande Kemp and Houskamp (1986) suggest the first published use of the term "integration" in relation to psychology and religion may have occurred in 1953 in an article by Fritz Kunkel in the *Journal of Psychotherapy As a Religious Process*. Kunkel had come to the U.S. from Germany and started a counseling center in Los Angeles and a foundation for the advancement of "Religious Psychology" (p. 4; see also Stevenson et al., 2007; Strawn, 2016).

The term "integration" came into wider use in the 1960s in the context of continued tensions between fundamentalism and modernism—tensions still very much alive in evangelical communities at that time. These communities were typically suspicious that modern "secular" disciplines like psychology might undermine biblical authority or contaminate Christian faith. Some academics, however, became open to following the lead of Kunkel and others, such as Paul Tournier, by seeking to appropriate—or integrate—in rather selective fashion certain psychological theories, practices, and counseling strategies. Their method of integration involved filtering psychological ideas and practices through a religious lens, checking for consistency with the Bible and already established Christian theology. During the 1960s, evangelical Christian psychologists like Clyde Narramore and Gary Collins began advocating for the legitimacy of psychology for practical Christian living (e.g., parenting, marriage, and dealing with stress, depression, or crises in life) and heralded the concept of integration. Their success was probably due to a combination of scholarly credentials and practical spiritual acumen, combined with skills in making psychology accessible at popular levels through books, magazine articles, audio tapes, radio broadcasts, and seminars. This engagement represented a sociological movement of some Evangelicals toward more permeable relational boundaries with wider cultural and intellectual influences rather than expecting all helpful resources to come from within churches and from their Scriptures.

This initial interest in integration also unfolded during a time in U.S. history when many people were becoming spiritual *seekers* who wanted a "portable" spirituality they could integrate into their everyday lives—e.g., listening to a tape on the way to work—rather than only experiencing spirituality at a certain time and location, for example, at religious services (Wuthnow, 1998). The 1960s was also an era when traditional social norms and family structures were being challenged at multiple levels in U.S. society; and even within many conservative Christian communities there was a budding awareness that mental health problems were not always prevented by religious devotion, prosocial behavior, or family stability. Pastors and other religious leaders were often confronted by the realities of emotional and relational struggles among their congregants without having adequate training in psychology nor even sufficient time to counsel all the people seeking their help. While some progressive clergy may have been comfortable simply referring their congregants to competent mental health professionals of any religious orientation, evangelical and other conservative Christian leaders often desired some assurance of the theological consistency of the psychological inputs their congregants would receive. According to Worthen (2014), a central focus in Evangelicalism of the 1960s–1970s was addressing these questions of epistemological authority as well as developing a means for moving from their separatist (i.e., fundamentalist) heritage of biblical proof-texting toward intellectual engagement with disciplines like psychology. At the same time, more evangelical Christians were beginning to study psychology and engage in clinical practice and wanted to make their work consistent with a Christian worldview and Christian values. These factors generated an interest in forms of psychology that could be integrated with Christian theology.

The 1970s have been described as birthing the "Age of Evangelicalism" in U.S. religion (Miller, 2014), as well as being "a turning point for evangelicals in psychology" (Johnson, 2010, p. 31). Doctoral-level clinical psychology training programs had been started and were active at Rosemead of Biola University (1968) and Fuller Seminary (1965). The *Journal of Psychology and Theology* (1973) began to publish articles on integration, soon to be followed by the *Journal of Psychology and Christianity* (1982). Additionally, early leaders in the evangelical integration movement, such as Collins, Bruce Narramore, John Carter, Larry Crabb, Mary Stewart Van Leeuwen, Everett Worthington, Kirk Farnsworth, Charles Ridley, and Hendrika Vande Kemp, were articulating philosophical, sociocultural, and methodological issues related to integration. In the same decade, Jay Adams developed an alternative to integration with a biblical counseling organization that rejected most of psychology and argued for epistemological reliance on the Bible alone, as well as locating counseling within churches rather than mental health clinics. Adams's approach was originally called Nouthetic counseling (from the Greek word *noutheteō*, meaning to admonish) and focused on repentance from sin as the key pathway to change. Political scientist Alan Wolfe (2003) suggests the integration movement within evangelical schools like Fuller in the 1970s represented the movement of some Evangelicals to embrace psychology as a mode of healing in concert with the "larger therapeutic turn" in American society (Miller, 2014, p. 22). Alternately, fundamentalist communities and leaders like Adams remained less open to outside influences in their sociological relations. Debates about the language of "sin" and the legitimacy of singular or plural pathways toward change represented pivotal worldview tensions that eventually influenced views on how to relate psychology and theology (Wolfe, 2003).

The evangelical impetus toward integration and the development of distinctively Christian approaches to psychology and counseling practice and training during these decades proved to be sociologically successful. As of 2017, there are seven doctoral programs in clinical psychology accredited by the American Psychological Association (APA) at evangelical schools, far more than any other religious group. A 2015 Pew survey of religion in the U.S. found that 25.4% of respondents identified as evangelical Protestant, which suggests this is a substantial "niche" population for mental health providers. The American Association of Christian Counselors (AACC) is an evangelical organization with approximately 50,000 members and is similar in size to the more general American Counseling Association and is nearly half the membership size of the APA. Some healthcare insurers now list "Christian counseling" as one of their areas of clinical specialization (among others, such as PTSD, mood disorders, or family therapy) on application forms for mental health providers seeking to join their panels.

Donning a wider historical lens, however, illuminates various efforts across church history to engage psychology—understood broadly—and theology. Such work can be traced back to seminal figures, such as Augustine, Bernard of

Clairvaux, Theresa of Avila, St John of the Cross, Thomas Aquinas, Richard Baxter, John Wesley, and Soren Kierkegaard (Johnson, 2010). A great number of spiritual and theological writers have considered interior, emotional dynamics and relational issues within human experience that could be considered psychological. This historical horizon influences debates we describe below about definitions of what counts as "psychology" and whether a primary goal should be to integrate theology and contemporary psychology or to seek recovery of earlier psychological insights from key theologians and spiritual writers.

It is also noteworthy that the integration movement among Evangelicals in the U.S. arose during the turbulent 1960s–1970s, decades marked by significant social tensions about issues such as racial integration and gender equality (Sandage & Brown, 2012). Most of the schools that fostered discussions around the integration of psychology and theology during this time were predominantly Caucasian. The Christian Association of Psychological Studies (CAPS), which became the leading professional organization for discussions of integration, was started by a group of Dutch Calvinists. Broader diversity issues of racial or gender integration were rarely voiced in integration literature prior to the 1980s and were often neglected in the broader evangelical contexts of this time period. Yet the opening of Evangelicalism to psychology provided many women with a vocational pathway in Christian contexts that restricted the roles of women in ministry leadership (see Chapter 7).

A Heuristic Typology of Integration Models (Carter)

As the term "integration" was starting to gain momentum in the 1970s among Evangelicals interested in relating psychology and theology, Carter (1977) offered a seminal article drawing on a Reformed theological perspective to outline a four-fold typology of models for relating psychology and religion (see also Carter & Narramore, 1979). Related typologies have been offered by Entwistle (2010) on psychology and Christianity and by Barbour (1990) on religion and science (Table 2.1). We find Carter's fourfold typology to be a useful heuristic grid for framing our subsequent historical reviews of scholarly engagements

TABLE 2.1 Interdisciplinary Typologies

Carter (1977) Typology	Barbour (1990) Typology	Entwistle (2010) Typology	Examples of Defined Views for Psychology & Christianity
Against	Conflict	Enemies	Biblical Counseling
Of	n/a	Spies Colonialists	Psychology of Religion Christian Psychology
Parallels	Independence Dialogue	Neutral Parties	Levels of Explanation
Integrates	Integration	Allies	Integration

between psychology and theology. The four categories Carter offers for the relationship of theology and psychology are (1) *against* approaches; (2) *of* approaches; (3) *parallel* models; and (4) *integration* models.

"Against" Approaches

Carter begins his discussion with *against* approaches, which involve viewing psychology and religion as epistemologically incompatible and competing disciplines. Any potential tensions between psychology and religion (or theology) are alleviated by essentially de-legitimating and excluding one of the disciplines. For example, Freud's particular psychoanalytic interpretation of religion essentially viewed psychology or psychoanalysis as scientific and true and religious perspectives as immature, psychologically destructive, and false. Certain logical positivist perspectives in modern psychological science might also fit this vision of psychology as "debunking" scientifically the mythologies of religion. Alternately, Carter suggests that the Biblical Counseling movement (represented by Adams, and more recently David Powlison, 2010) tends toward an "against" position—in this case, by affirming biblical perspectives as true and psychology as generally deceptive, misleading, and contradictory to Scripture. Authors within the Biblical Counseling tradition also view the Bible as fully sufficient as a source of knowledge for counseling and claim the church as the central (and sometimes only) context for counseling. Theories of psychotherapy are construed as dangerous, superficial, and irrelevant for Christian counseling.

Thus, for those aligning with *against* models, psychology and theology are not simply offering differing perspectives. Rather, these "against" views assume a kind of hermeneutical splitting, with one of the disciplines understood through a *hermeneutic of suspicion* and the other through a *hermeneutic of trust* (Ricoeur, 1974). One discipline is helpful, and the other discipline is problematic or dangerous and so should be "cutoff" as a source of meaningful knowledge. Entwistle (2010) has used the relational metaphor of "enemies" for such views. Barbour, in his typology of approaches to science and religion, labels similar views as "conflict" models because they presume an inherent, unresolvable conflict between science and religion.

"Of" Approaches

Carter refers to a second set of approaches as *of* models. These approaches "solve" interdisciplinary tensions through the use of hierarchy, with one discipline "trumping" the other by assimilating pieces of information from that discipline interpreted through a grid provided by the first discipline. Carter offers as an example the psychology of religion. While the psychology of religion is a broad and diverse field involving many methodological and theoretical approaches, Carter is invoking specifically a reductionistic approach in which psychological explanations are offered for religious phenomena without integrating perspectives from the disciplines of religious studies or theology. In this perspective, religion is not viewed as a separate discipline that is antagonistic to psychology but rather becomes a psychological topic subsumed or assimilated into psychological methodologies and theories. In some cases, a particular theoretical orientation for psychology (e.g., evolutionary psychology, Jungian psychology, Object Relations theory, or cognitive-behaviorism) becomes a kind of hermeneutical grid for religion or theology, and only the aspects of the latter that readily fit the psychological theory are retained; other texts or teachings of religion and theology are discarded as irrelevant. Entwistle (2010) uses the relational metaphor of spies to describe this type of approach of plundering certain data that fit the other discipline. Or, to use another metaphor, this approach involves "cherry picking" parts of a discipline (or religion) considered useful while discarding what is considered extraneous. *Of* approaches selectively reject one disciplinary methodology while uncritically imposing the other. For example, a clinical focus on religious coping might fall into this category by merely trying to identify psychologically healthy religious practices, especially if the clinician or researcher does not also hold a curiosity and respect for contexts, traditions, and religious meanings that a person might associate with those religious practices or goals beyond psychological health.

Although Carter does not identify examples of a theology *of* psychology approach, any such method would privilege theology over psychology in hierarchical fashion by assimilating psychological concepts or data in piecemeal fashion into a theological framework without engaging psychological methodologies (or experts in those methodologies). For example, a popular evangelical systematic theology appears to subsume the task of psychological study under biblical or theological study, which is given decisive priority.

> We face problems of applying Scripture to life in many more contexts than formal doctrinal discussions. What principles does Scripture give us for studying psychology, or economics, or the natural sciences? . . . In every area of inquiry certain theological principles will come to bear.
>
> *(Grudem, 1994, p. 29)*

What Carter refers to as an *of* approach, Entwistle also calls *colonialist* because of its analogy to historical colonization, in which one country (read here, discipline) seeks to take over a "foreign" country (discipline) and bring it under their domination and control. The foreign entity is allowed to exist and function at a certain level of distinctiveness but only in ways determined in hegemonic fashion by the sovereign nation (discipline). *Postcolonial* approaches to theology (e.g., Dube, 2012; Haker et al., 2013) have raised the problem of ethnocentrism in theology and uses of theology to build empires of oppression. Movements of critical psychology and indigenous psychology have voiced parallel concerns about ethnocentrism and power dynamics within the field of psychology (Brown, Lomas, & Eiroa-Orosa, 2017; Kim, Yang, & Hwang, 2006). Thus, conversations in both theology and psychology involve questions about colonizing tendencies in those disciplines which could represent hierarchical and assimilationist forms of relationality. Below we consider certain voices representing the Christian psychology view as potentially fitting a theology of psychology approach; this view has been described by one advocate as "prophylactic: It is to bracket the *substance* of twentieth-century psychologies so that we can put the Christian tradition back in the psychological driver's seat" to prevent the "contaminating" influence of modern psychology on Christian faith (Roberts, 2000, pp. 155–156; see also Roberts & Watson, 2010).

"Parallel" Approaches

Carter refers to *parallels* as his third typological category, in which psychology and theology are understood as disciplines that do not interact much with each other—they simply run parallel to one another. One version of the *parallels* approach assumes the disciplines are hermetic and non-overlapping, allowing for *mutual respect* while remaining isolated from *mutual influence*. This category coheres with Entwistle's relational metaphor of "neutral parties" and with Barbour's "independence" category for viewing religion and science as autonomous domains. This category also fits the view that psychology and theology offer differing "levels of explanation" of a "multi-layered unity" (Myers, 2010, p. 51). Parallels or levels-of-explanation approaches manage interdisciplinary tensions through separation and autonomy, with each discipline having its distinct domain of knowledge. As an example, Myer's levels-of-explanation view assumes separate dimensions of reality and heralds the value of rigorous empirical research to complement or even revise theological understandings, although Myers does not address whether theology can revise psychological understandings. This approach can imply that theology and philosophy can somehow be completely bracketed from theories within psychology and psychotherapy. In fact, Plante (2012) represents the levels-of-explanation approach to counseling as utilizing a "biopsychosocialspiritual" framework (p. 67) to address distinct biological, psychological, social, and spiritual dimensions of clients' functioning and as an alternative to utilizing psychological theories (also see Melchert, 2013). This kind of purported atheoretical use of generic assessment of these multiple dimensions differs markedly from contemporary, post-positivistic and postcolonial frameworks (offered in both psychology and theology). For the latter, cultural, theoretical, and ethical assumptions are understood as inescapable, requiring conscious and explicit attention to one's commitments (Browning & Cooper, 2004) and the traditions that inform those commitments (Strawn et al., 2014).

Carter refers to another version of the *parallels* approach as *correlational*, in that it seeks to align similar concepts from psychology and theology (e.g., superego and conscience). Carter distinguishes this method from robust integration because it offers little attention to the broader worldview frameworks of the concepts utilized and ignores possible differences in understanding. Christians in psychology have sometimes been criticized by biblical scholars and theologians for citing Bible verses to offer "proof texts" for psychological concepts without a more comprehensive conceptual analysis of the relevant contexts (both historical and literary) and attention to differences between the two disciplines and the contrasting sociocultural contexts for the data. This might be considered a "sloppy" or premature form of integration which glosses over meaningful differences in conceptual frameworks, contexts, and methodologies. "Parallels" approaches deal with interdisciplinary tensions through what interculturalists would call *minimization*, namely, offering superficial points of connection while largely glossing over meaningful worldview and cultural differences (Bennett, 2004). Appreciation for both disciplines is routinely articulated in parallel approaches, but more substantive interaction between disciplines is neglected or minimized. Barbour's category of "dialogue" in religion and science seems similar to a correlational approach since the goal is more modest engagement of points of contact or methodological parallels rather than a comprehensive interdisciplinary synthesis.

"Integration" Approaches

Carter reserves the category of *integration* for approaches that assume God is the author of all truth and so seek to bring together psychology and theology for formulating congruent and unified understandings of human behavior. These approaches move beyond surface parallels toward deeper, multi-faceted engagement between psychology and theology with a goal of integrated knowledge and practice. Both Carter and Entwistle use the relational metaphor of *allies* to describe the roles of psychology and theology in integration, and Entwistle, like Carter, highlights the unity of truth assumption behind integrative approaches. Barbour also uses *integration* as a category of approaches within the religion and science dialogue (e.g., natural theology), by which he indicates approaches that assume direct connections between the content of science and the content of theology with some possibility of the disciplines reformulating theories between themselves. Jones (2010) also represents the integration view of psychology and Christianity, although he argues for a "fundamental loyalty being to the true teachings of the special revelation of the Bible" (p. 117). We discuss further these *integration* approaches below, but for now it is important to note the approaches to integration mentioned here (Carter, Entwistle, Jones) assumed a singular unity of knowledge *shaped by assumptions from Reformed theologies.* Stevenson et al. (2007) summarizes this type of understanding of integration among Evangelicals as

> the task of searching for the unity of truth, seeing things from a Christian perspective, and holistically attempting to relate elements of an objective real world given by God at creation. It is fundamentally a discovery, not a human creation.

> *(p. 5)*

This realist (rather than constructivist) and mono-cultural unity of truth world-view has been influenced by Euro-American intellectual currents of modernity and Western individualism, which also minimized the influences of cultural contexts, hermeneutical traditions, praxis, and interdisciplinary relational dynamics. We return to some implications of these omissions at the end of the chapter.

This typology for various approaches to psychology/theology integration illustrates a number of what we would call *relational stances* toward the intersection of the two disciplines. While some might seem more "relational" than others, each suggests a way of relating the disciplines and functions to provide a relational template for particular psychologists and theologians stepping into the terrain of integration. For example, *against* approaches take a more hostile and suspicious relational stance toward the other discipline, while *of* models tend toward an assimilationist relationship. We find such a relational lens to be profitable for our historical work below. Having introduced the language of "integration" and explored a typology for organizing various approaches to integration, we turn to historical and recent attempts to bring together psychology and theology, beginning with the vantage point of psychology.

Engagements With Theology in Psychology

During the past forty years, the fields of psychology and psychotherapy have experienced a profound shift on the topics of "religion" and "spirituality," even as the formal disciplines of theology and religious studies remain largely marginalized within psychology. Throughout most of the twentieth century, the dominant perspectives in North American and European psychology and psychoanalysis employed hostile (*against*), assimilationist (*of*), or minimizing (*parallels*) relational stances toward religion and spirituality. As we have described, Evangelicals began debating whether there was a legitimate place for integrating psychology with theology during the 1950s to the 1970s, in part, as a response to deconstructive and secularizing influences of modernity and as an opportunity to integrate Christian communities with the wider therapeutic ethos of U.S. society. The language of "integration" also emerged during that same time period in differing ways among several leading psychologists (e.g., Jung, Fairbairn, Winnicott, Maslow, Allport) who responded to the reductive naturalism and logical positivism of modernity with more holistic visions of human personhood that included integration of spirituality and religion with psychology (discussion follows).

Hostile views toward religion are apparent in the writings of some of the major theorists of psychotherapy, such as Sigmund Freud and Albert Ellis, who both argued that religiosity was incompatible with mental health. Freud (1925) described himself as having a "deep engrossment in the Bible story" while growing up (p. 8), probably through some conflicting influences from his Jewish father and Catholic nanny. Yet he came to view religion as regressive and an illusory defense against the psychological maturity of facing painful realities and inner conflicts. He appealed to psychoanalysis as a science despite the fact that his epistemological methodology more strongly reflected a hermeneutical, humanities-based approach, possibly rooted in his engagements with the Kabbalistic tradition of Jewish mysticism (Wulff, 1997). Despite his breadth of reading on various cultural and religious traditions (and the many religious icons that populated the desk in his study), Freud focused his psychoanalytic critique of religion and his Oedipal theory quite selectively on male- or father-centered expressions of religion while ignoring many other phenomena within the history of religions.

Ellis grounded his theory of Rational Emotive Therapy in Stoic philosophy and suggested religion as one of many irrational beliefs which contribute to neurotic anxiety and guilt, particularly in relation to sexuality. Like Freud, Ellis' early work on religion represented an "against" stance and focused on pathological expressions of religion with virtually no consideration of potentially salutary effects. Ellis did, however, moderate his view somewhat late in his career to acknowledge forms of religiosity he considered "rational" (Ellis, 2000). His embrace of Stoic philosophy shaped his valuing of equanimity—"accepting things as they are"—leading him to recommend the view that nothing is ultimately catastrophic nor salvific, a view that tends to relativize the importance of many religious narratives and values.

Carl Jung defected from his mentor Freud, in part, due to his more positive and humanistic view of spirituality as contributing to the quest for meaning and wholeness. In this way, Jung became an important theorist among psychology of religion approaches. He invoked the concept of integration as part of the developmental process of individuation and bringing together differing poles within the psyche (e.g., introversion and extraversion); and he considered spirituality and the search for meaning as key facets of adult individuation. However, Jung held a complicated view of religious and theological traditions and was troubled by the lack of authenticity of his father (a Swiss Reformed pastor) who masked his personal religious doubts. Jung frequently reinterpreted biblical texts, theological concepts and symbols, and religious rituals to assimilate them into his complex and highly individualistic psychological theory. This practice, which fits Carter's category of an "of" approach, created distance with some religious scholars and theologians. Unsurprisingly, these theologians valued the content of their traditions and the methodologies of their disciplines and considered Jung's biblical forays to be a kind of psychological "overreach." Alternately, others commended Jung's deep engagement with a variety of world religions, and some biblical scholars have sought to integrate Jungian psychology with biblical studies (e.g., Rollins, 1983). While Jung has proven influential among some psychoanalysts, psychologists, pastors, and spiritual directors, his intriguing symbolic and experiential approach to the psychology of religion has not catalyzed an influential body of empirical research on religious phenomena within mainstream psychology.

The post-Freudian "relational turn" in psychoanalysis during the 1950s–1970s emphasized the human drive for relatedness, and several Object Relations theorists (e.g., Fairbairn, Guntrip, Winnicott) held a positive, respectful stance toward religious traditions and the constructive potential of religion in human development. In fact, numerous Object Relations (Fairbairn, Klein, Winnicott) theorists invoked the explicit language of "integration" to reference an adaptive developmental process of reconciling part objects in the psyche to overcome fragmenting splits and to contain projections. Yet Object Relations theorists did not typically utilize much content from religious or theological sources of knowledge in building their theoretical models other than a few attempts at assimilation (i.e., Fairbairn's use of a theological concept like *Satan* to reference a primarily psychological reality). Thus, like Jung, their approaches could be considered psychology *of* religion rather than genuine interdisciplinary integration.[1] Nevertheless, Ana-Maria Rizzuto (1979, 2005, 2006), who belongs among these Object Relations theorists, fostered an important innovation with her classic contribution researching relational influences on the God concepts and God images of psychiatric patients. Rizzuto, while teaching psychology at Catholic schools and a seminary in her homeland of Argentina in the 1960s, developed an interest in psychological influences on religious belief. From her teaching context, she brought to her theorizing a respectful curiosity about the shaping influences of religious and theological traditions on the God concepts and sacred understandings of patients in psychoanalysis. By differentiating God concepts (more cognitive and shaped by traditions) from God images (more emotion-laden and shaped by relational experiences), she helped open the door to a more truly integrative paradigm in psychoanalysis. She argues there is a psychic need for belief and that religious "metanarratives" are an important complement to what she calls "the believing function." These relational schools of thought in psychoanalysis (e.g., ORT, Kohut, Intersubjectivity theorists, Relational Psychoanalysis) have been quite influential in the fields of pastoral psychology and pastoral counseling, which have been prominent in Mainline Protestant and Catholic traditions.

Many other psychological and psychotherapy theorists during the twentieth century, however, have neglected, dismissed, or minimized the importance of the topics of religion and spirituality. For example, behaviorists like B. F. Skinner adopted a logical positivistic approach to science that called for ignoring "non-observables" and internal mental states in favor of a focus on readily measurable behavior. This modernist philosophy of science contributed to a neglect of empirical research on religious or spiritual constructs during the middle part of the twentieth century, as many behaviorists considered religion and spirituality too ambiguous to operationalize and measure. When Skinner did consider religion, he interpreted religious phenomenon as resulting from operant conditioning and viewed religious institutions as primarily oriented toward the control of behavior through principles of reinforcement. Browning and Cooper (2004) have suggested Skinner's utopian vision of social cooperation involved accepting "the relentless power of natural selection" in a deterministic ethic that "takes on the proportions of a Calvinistic theory of predestination" (pp. 125–126), which is particularly interesting given the Presbyterian faith of Skinner's youth. Literature on behavioral approaches to therapy have tended to show little engagement with religious topics. However, the cognitive revolution in psychology and psychotherapy that started in the 1970s and became more influential in the 1980s did lead to greater integration with religion and theology. The cognitive-behavioral emphasis on how thoughts influence feelings and behaviors offered points of resonance with certain biblical texts for numerous theorists in evangelical integration circles (e.g., McMinn & Campbell, 2007; Tan, 2011).

Gordon Allport (1897–1967) was part of the "American Humanistic Synthesis" (Wulff, 1997, p. 582) in the psychology of religion and had been raised in "Protestant Piety" by a mother who "brought to her sons an eager sense of philosophical questing and the importance of searching for ultimate religious answers" (Allport, 1967, p. 4). Allport was a social and personality psychologist at Harvard and a devout Episcopalian who revived the earlier classic work by William James (*Varieties of Religious Experience*, 1958) on individual differences in religiosity. James's phenomenological or descriptive approach to the psychology of religion actually preceded Freud's work and offered a much more nuanced and sympathetic engagement of individual differences in religious temperaments and behaviors. James's pragmatism led him to focus on the "fruits" of religious experiences, which could range from the very negative to the exceedingly positive; and James' interest in religion was no doubt influenced by recovering from his own periods of depression, existential fear, and near "insanity" through clinging to certain "scripture-texts like 'The eternal God is my refuge'" (James, 1958, p. 136). Allport picked up this Jamesian interest in the range of religious sentiments expressing a person's perspective on meaning in life, and he significantly advanced quantitative research on individual differences in religious orientations. Like other humanistic and existential psychologists of religion and spirituality (e.g., Carl Rogers, Erich Fromm, Abraham Maslow, Victor Frankl), Allport believed some religious orientations would be more psychologically healthy and mature than others. Allport (1950) also suggested religion could serve an integrative function in personality if one's religiosity is characterized by humility, differentiation, and intrinsic motivation, all of which he related to the biblical concept of "single-mindedness" from the epistle of James and Kierkegaard's treatment of the "purity of heart to will one thing."

In contrast to Allport's respect for religion, Maslow moved away from what he called the "paraphernalia of organized religion," which he considered divisive, and drew upon transpersonal spirituality to describe the mature person as self-actualized, representing movement toward "an integrated, organized whole" (1970, p. 19). Wulff (1997) suggests Maslow identified with his atheist father and held contempt for his "religious" and "superstitious" mother (p. 605). Maslow's version of humanistic psychology attempted to minimize religious differences and integrate biology and mystical spirituality at a time when U.S. psychology was dominated by Skinnerian behaviorism.

Starting in the 1980s and 1990s, social scientists expanded the quantity, quality, and breadth of the empirical study of religion, spirituality, and health. Psychiatrist

David Larson was an important researcher in this area who helped advance the operationalization and measurement of religion and spirituality; he empirically demonstrated that many indices of religion and spirituality were positively associated with measures of mental and even physical health (Hill & Pargament, 2003). The scientific data now makes the case that Freud and Ellis were far too pessimistic in their global pathologizing of religion and spirituality. Psychological studies show that, for many people, spirituality and religion can be sources of meaning, purpose, hope, and coping, each of which is related to positive psychosocial functioning. A fairly recent research review has also concluded that a majority of therapists are open to discussing spiritual and religious issues in therapy and that many clients would like to discuss these issues, particularly those for whom spirituality or religion are personally salient (Post & Wade, 2009). A growing body of research is emerging around various spiritual practices (e.g., meditation, prayer, forgiveness) which might be employed effectively in psychotherapy (e.g., Aten, McMinn, & Worthington, 2011; Plante, 2009, 2012).

Marsha Linehan (1993) has been a key figure in the "mainstreaming" of spirituality and the practice of mindfulness in psychology with the development of her empirically supported Dialectical Behavior Therapy (DBT) to treat Borderline Personality Disorder (BPD) and other mental health problems. Her DBT approach gained momentum in the 1990s and represents a novel approach that combines individual therapy and skills groups. Linehan developed DBT by drawing upon personal meditative practices from Zen Buddhism and Contemplative Christian spirituality, in combination with cognitive-behavioral approaches to effectively treat BPD, which some had previously considered untreatable. (She has indicated that she chose the term "dialectical" because colleagues advised her it would be difficult to gain professional acceptance for "Zen Behavior Therapy.") More recently, Linehan has described her own healing from severe psychiatric problems through a religious experience as a college student sitting alone in a chapel at Loyola University contemplating a cross. Her DBT group skills workbook (Linehan, 2015) offers some information about differences in spiritual and religious traditions in relation to mindfulness meditation, and one handout instructs clients that:

> Spiritual words and concepts are often universal beliefs that, depending on one's own religion, are stated in vastly different words. It is important to see the commonalities across various practices and cultures. It is also important to be able to select the part of a practice that conforms to one's own beliefs and practices.
>
> *(p. 218)*

Linehan's emphasis on the commonalities across different traditions could imply a minimization of differences and would be objectionable to some religious scholars and theologians, however she is explicit in encouraging clients to find practices that can fit their own integrity.

Social psychologist Ignacio Martín-Baró (1996) has offered a unique contribution by developing a Latin American liberation psychology informed by liberation theology. Martín-Baró was a former Jesuit priest who had studied theology in Latin America prior to his psychology training at the University of Chicago. He wrote in his native Spanish and questioned many of the basic individualistic, positivistic, and ahistorical assumptions of North American psychology, while calling for a socially contextualized and praxis-oriented liberation psychology and theology that would work against oppression and embrace political solidarity with the poor to facilitate social justice (Goodman, Walling, & Ghali, 2010). His death at age 47 at the hands of a Salvadoran death squad was a result of his own integrative praxis and offers a sobering legacy of the sociopolitical risks inherent in psychologies and theologies that challenge systems of oppression.

Recently, Pargament and colleagues have called for an "integrative paradigm for the psychology of religion and spirituality" within the field of psychology (Pargament, Mahoney, Exline, Jones, & Shafranske, 2013, p. 5). While they do not explicitly suggest integrating the disciplines of theology, religious studies, or spirituality studies with psychology, they do call for awareness of multi-dimensionality and multiple valences of religion and spirituality and invite attention to social contexts and traditions. The two volume *APA Handbook of Psychology, Religion, and Spirituality* (2013), edited by Pargament and colleagues and published by the APA, is among the many contemporary scholarly and professional resources available which illuminate a more complex understanding of religion and spirituality in the field of psychology over the past thirty years. In the past decade, several clinical theorists have articulated approaches that "integrate" spirituality and psychotherapy in differing ways (e.g., Johnson, 2013; McMinn & Campbell, 2007; Pargament & Saunders, 2007; Sperry, 2012). For example, Sperry outlines an integrative approach to clinical assessment that seeks to attend to all relevant personality, family, cultural, and spiritual dynamics in a given case. Pargament and Saunder's (2007) spiritually integrated psychotherapy approach defines a "well-integrated spirituality" as "one whose component parts work together in synchrony with one another" (p. 34).

Nevertheless, if one searches specifically for thick engagement of theological and religious methodologies within psychological research and clinical literature, the findings will be quite modest. The growing acceptance of religion and spirituality as legitimate topics in the field of psychology also does not alleviate certain tensions created by the realities of human diversity, such as when a client and therapist differ in terms of spiritual or religious worldviews or the fact that some measures of religion and spirituality (e.g., spiritual instability; Hall & Edwards, 2002) can be associated with psychosocial distress.

Engagements With Psychology in Theology

Theology is an inherently multidisciplinary endeavor, as it attempts to speak holistically about God and humanity. As such, theology has had a long history of philosophical engagement for addressing various spheres of human knowledge and contemporary culture. Across this history, the ongoing claim of theology as "queen of the sciences" has resulted in an ordering of knowledge and inquiry that has prioritized the Bible as special revelation and theology as its guardian. As we will see, this historical prioritization has resulted in approaches to integration between theology and psychology that have tended toward Carter's "against" or "of" categories and fall short of what we are calling relational integration (Carter's "integration" category).

A caveat is in order for this historical review. In spite of theology's self-proclaimed priority and because of its inherent multidisciplinarity, it is difficult to clearly delineate theology from philosophy and various other precursors to the modern discipline of psychology. As Joel Green (2003) has suggested in his exploration of the seventeenth-century scientist Thomas Willis, in the history of the intersection of theology and science we cannot trace out fully distinct disciplinary boundaries. Instead, theology and science have had a mutually informing relationship, even if the mutuality and influence have not been (fully) acknowledged.

> [H]ow the world works and the constraints of our finitude [together] press for explanation, inevitably attracting the hermeneutical effects of both natural sciences and spirituality, with these providing sometimes competing, sometimes complementary, always inextricably related and mutually informing perspectives on these points.
>
> *(p. 178)*

Theological interactions with psychology are best understood from the vantage point of theology's engagement with philosophy, culture, the acquisition of human knowledge, and with the sciences conceived broadly. Given the development of psychology as a discreet discipline only within the last century or so, we will focus our attention of the theological currents of the early twentieth century that laid the groundwork for (or worked against) integration of theology and psychology. In the historical review that follows, we briefly explore Catholic and mainstream Protestant streams of the Christian tradition in their engagement with psychology. We also provide a note about the development of Reformed theology which provides the backstory for much of the impetus for the emergence of theology/psychology integration in evangelical circles (see previous discussion). To acknowledge the contested nature of history and history writing, we locate our interests and so our focus in what follows in the streams of tradition that emphasize the possibility of rich integration between theology and psychology. Consequently, we address these various traditions somewhat unevenly to highlight *correlative methods* most specifically.

Catholic theologians may have had the smoothest process for integrating insights from the newly emerging field of psychology, given that they already had what John McDargh (1985, p. 249) refers to as an "in-house psychology" (p. 249). This indigenous psychology had developed out of Thomistic reflection and was evident in the Catholic arenas of natural theology and mental philosophy (McDargh, 1985). As Paul Vitz (2011) notes, "Catholic tradition has always been able to defend itself at least in part in the language of philosophical and rational discourse" (p. 298). Catholic tradition included an emphasis on human wiring toward the transcendent, that is, human responsiveness "to the initiatives of the mystery of God" (McDargh, 1985, p. 250). Not surprisingly then, Catholic integration with psychology has accented anthropology, a theme evident in the work of Catholic theologians, Karl Rahner and Bernard Lonergan (Vitz, 2011; Rahner, 1968; Lonergan, 1972). "Every theology, as Karl Rahner asserted, is first an anthropology" (McDargh, 1985, p. 251; Rahner, 1961). David Tracy has been an important Catholic theologian whose work has impacted interdisciplinary methodology. As he had relied upon Paul Tillich's correlation method, we will discuss his work in concert with Tillich (below).

Protestant theology broadly conceived has been significantly influenced by Karl Barth in conversations about human knowledge generally, and so in theology's intersections with psychology more specifically. Although impacted by the existential thought of Kierkegaard, Barth came to expressly refute "natural theology"—that is, knowledge of God inferable apart from biblical revelation (see Chapter 4). This rejection derived, in part, from Barth's concern over the ways German nationalism was utilizing contemporary knowledge (e.g., science) and melding it with religion for its own devices. We might conceive of Barth's position, or at least the directions some have taken it, to illustrate an "against" stance in Carter's typology. Rudolf Bultmann represents a somewhat contrasting opinion in his ready use of existential philosophy and theological anthropology to illuminate and engage the biblical text. Yet Bultmann (1969) disavowed a naturally derived *knowledge of God*, limiting natural theology to (1) the *fact* of understanding; (2) the phenomenon of religion; and (3) the phenomenon of philosophy (pp. 313–314).

Barth's resistance to a natural theology helps to explain the ambivalence within various strands of twentieth-century Protestant theology toward interdisciplinary dialogue, at least without clear parameters in place, such as the prioritizing of theology over other disciplines and what each can or does contribute. For example, Wolfhart Pannenburg, whom Reynhout (2013) has referred to as a "post-Barthian disciplinarian," allowed for scientific disciplines to inform theology, including the provision of an undefined sense of "the infinite other" which still required special revelation for illumination. In this configuration which fits Carter's "of" approach, some accommodation is made for "natural theology," but theology's priority and even superiority over other disciplines remains clear. Yet even this stance was criticized by some as an inappropriate dependence upon non-theological disciplines (Placher & Nelson, 2013). And ambivalence to natural theology takes a more extreme form in the "Yale school" of post-liberal theology, where Barth has been interpreted in an even more exclusionary way.

Alternately, the "Chicago school" illustrates a more active interdisciplinary engagement with philosophy and culture. Paul Tillich, a key figure in that school, drew from existentialism and sought a compromise between the "conflicting theological epistemologies of Karl Barth and Rudolf Bultmann" (DeLashmutt, 2005, p. 749, n. 2). Tillich developed his "method of correlation" as an attempt to bridge interpretation of one's cultural situation with interpretation of the tradition. In Tillich's construal, this correlation is *unidirectional*; tradition (theology) provides the answers to the questions raised by culture. For Tillich, whatever psychology may be able to offer to human understanding, it "cannot trace the movement of the human being into the realm of graced living" (McDargh, 1985, p. 255). While the priority of theology continued to be clearly affirmed by Tillich, his "own wide interests in the arts, psychology, and intellectual history enabled him to arouse the interest of intellectuals in many fields who ordinarily dismissed Christianity as obsolete or meaningless" (Johnston, 2008, p. 258).

Catholic theologian, David Tracy, drawing on Tillich's correlational method along with the philosophical work of Paul Ricoeur, developed further the implications of Tillich's methodology for theology in its intersections with culture and society. Tracy's "revised correlational model" is *bidirectional*—both culture (including other disciplines, like psychology) and theology may provide questions as well as answers to one another. This implies that, for the theologian, the central sources for interdisciplinary work include both "Christian texts and . . . common human experience and language" (Reynhout, 2013, p. 16). Tracy proposed the exercise of "analogical imagination" as a bridge between theology and other disciplines by attending to the "similarities-in-difference" between disciplines (p. 18; cf. Tracy, 1981), an important contribution toward differentiation for interdisciplinarity. A key part of Tracy's understanding of how common ground is established between and among disciplines comes via hermeneutics. As Reynhout (2013) notes, "The universality of hermeneutics is . . . Tracy's way of establishing interdisciplinary common ground" (p. 20). Thus, neither theology nor psychology can, for Tracy, assume a place of superiority in attempts at interdisciplinarity. Tracy's understanding of disciplinary interaction with theology as bidirectional allows for and even encourages mutual influence among the disciplines and fits Carter's category of an "integration" approach. Not surprisingly, others have drawn on his methodology for integration between theology and psychology (e.g., McDargh, 1985) and theology and science (e.g., Reynhout, 2013).

From a different quarter (Protestant, though less Barthian), integration of psychology and theology has been a developing conversation in the evangelical, reformed tradition(s). As we have already noted, while there has been a historical tendency within "neo-evangelical" theological circles to eschew psychology, there have been those committed to the idea of the unity of truth who have pursued ways to bring psychology and theology (the Bible) together (McDargh, 1985, p. 254). The establishment of the *Journal of Psychology and Theology* provides an example of this trajectory, as seen in Narramore's (1973) inaugural article describing the need for the journal and its vision. Another example of bringing psychology and theology together comes from those who trace their theological lineage back to Abraham Kuyper, a nineteenth-century Dutch theologian. Kuyper emphasized what he called "sphere sovereignty"—the affirmation of Christ's reign over all areas of life and the world: "There is not a square inch in the whole domain of human existence over which Christ, who is sovereign over all, does not cry: 'Mine!'" (Kuyper, 1988, p. 488). Those who follow in the vein of Kuyperian theology have worked out this affirmation via a keen interest in interdisciplinary endeavor (e.g., Moreland, Plantinga, Wolters). This vantage point, with its accent on the priority of theology, has often led the conversation about theology/ psychology integration in evangelical circles. In fact, Strawn et al. (2014) have noted that integration literature in a broadly evangelical context often assumes this specific model, what they term "a generic . . . Reformed perspective" (p. 47).[2] Vitz (2011, p. 297) applies this problem to the multiple perspectives in Protestantism more broadly. Integration may then be unhelpfully "limited to an oversimplified 'mere Christianity'."

We have traced in quite broad strokes how various theological and ecclesial streams have interacted with what theologians have termed "natural theology" (corresponding to general revelation; see Chapter 4). This, in turn, has set the stage for the ways theologians have engaged psychology. As we conclude this particular discussion, we describe two specific conversations between theology and psychology that have emerged as the former has engaged the latter: the impact of psychology in biblical studies[3] and the discipline of practical theology.

Over the past forty years or so, the guild of biblical studies has moved from a more exclusive focus on historical-critical method to embracing multiple critical methodologies, including literary approaches (e.g., rhetorical criticism, narrative criticism) and various methods that highlight the usefulness of reading from particular locations (e.g., feminist criticism, post-colonial criticism). As Tolbert (2003) has described New Testament studies, "We are an interdisciplinary discipline." One particular intersection with psychological readings or readings with psychology has been provided by the "Psychology and the Biblical Studies" section of the Society of Biblical Literature, inaugurated in 1991 and founded by Wayne Rollins.[4] This inclusion of psychological perspectives on the Bible within the guild of biblical studies has, according to Underwood (2012), developed significantly and moved from a more simplistic level of analysis to become "more cognizant of historical, literary, and sociological studies of the Bible" (p. 72). In spite of these developments, much of the integrative work continues to be done by single disciplinarians, most of whom have by default greater expertise in one discipline than the other. For example, in *Psychological Hermeneutics for Biblical Themes and Texts*, a festschrift for Wayne Rollins (Ellens & Rollins, 2012), each chapter is written by a single author, with expertise either in biblical studies, psychology, and in some cases pastoral psychology.

A similar phenomenon is evidence in the emergence of social-scientific criticism in biblical studies, where there is great interest in exploring interdisciplinary approaches but often with the assumption and practice of a single-integrator model. Social science methodology is practiced by those trained in biblical studies and draws upon sociological modeling for understanding the original contexts of biblical material (Elliott and Via, 1993). Within the Society of Biblical Literature, there are program units devoted to the use of social sciences in both the Hebrew Bible and the New Testament. This methodology has proved a valuable addition to historical analysis of the biblical text and has illuminated ancient social dynamics, such as honor/shame, social stigma, and communal identity formation (e.g., Neyrey, 1998; Lawrence, 2013; Elliott, 2007). The infusion of cross-disciplinary methodologies into biblical studies—whether psychology or social science—can be understood as a microcosm of currents that had been at work in the wider arena of theological engagement with culture and science as described previously.

Practical Theology: A Bridging Discipline

Practical theology has emerged since the 1950s and 1960s as a distinct "integrative" and interdisciplinary field which has questioned the academic and curricular separation of theological knowing from embodied practice or lived religion (Miller-McLemore, 2014, p. 6). Cahalan (2014) notes that "integration appeared as a main topic in four subsequent meetings from 1950 to 1984" of the Association of Seminary Professors in Practical Fields in the United States (p. 387). Browning (1991) was an influential scholar in shaping the field of practical theology with the ancient idea of *phronesis* or practical knowledge and wisdom as the goal. The modernistic or foundationalist approach of organizing a seminary curriculum starting year one with a heavy emphasis on theoretical knowledge (e.g., biblical studies, systematic theology, church history) and then moving in linear fashion toward applied knowledge in subsequent years (e.g., preaching, pastoral care, religious education, leadership) is challenged by practical theologians who tend to view practice and theory as mutually informing. Liberative concerns for diversity, contextualization, and social justice—concerns both arising from and contributing to praxis—are more widely developed in the field of practical theology than in the evangelical integration literature (for examples, see contributions in Cahalan & Mikoski, 2014; Miller-McLemore, 2014). Practical theologians have also viewed processes of formation and hermeneutics as constitutive of theological knowledge—a perspective with which we resonate. The field of practical theology includes integration with a variety of empirical methodological approaches within the social sciences (Cahalan & Mikoski, 2014; Hermans & Moore, 2004). In fact, the rich and multi-dimensional concept of *practice* (Bass & Dykstra, 2008; Wolfteich, 2014) has served as a key interdisciplinary concept or even an integrative motif for many in the field of practical theology in ways that parallel our focus on relationality.

Pastoral theology can be understood as a sub-discipline of practical theology more specifically focused on pastoral care for persons who are suffering. A search of literature on pastoral theology, however, will show a variety of epistemological stances on relating psychology and theology. Pastoral theologians who locate themselves within the field of practical theology tend to come from Catholic or Mainline Protestant traditions and seek to develop models that *parallel* (i.e., correlate, based on Tracy, 2014) or *integrate* psychology and theology (e.g., Choi, 2015; Cooper-White, 2004; Doehring, 2015; Sheppard, 2011). Other writers in pastoral theology represent more conservative Christian perspectives and appear to hold *of* or *against* models for relating theology and psychology (Akin & Pace, 2017; Purves, 2004).

A Way Forward

Based on our historical exploration of interactions between theology and psychology, along with Carter's model for understanding these interactions, we are now able to suggest resources for integration that have either been missing or minimized in this history, allowing us to place our own relational integration model within this broader context. First, we would note that highly relational ways of pursuing collaboration have been rather sparsely represented in the history of interdisciplinary endeavors between psychology and theology. Specifically, the possibilities of reciprocal influence have been nominal given the ongoing assumption that interdisciplinarity will be accomplished primarily by single integrators. The paucity of collaborative examples in integration across psychology and theology has limited integrative possibilities arising from the relational space between and among multiple disciplinarians. A second lacuna that might be addressed by having psychologists and theologians at the same table is visualization of the richness of interdisciplinarity. Single integrator models tend to produce thin readings of at least one of the disciplines being integrated, a thinness most obvious to someone immersed in the field lesser known to that single integrator. Yet interdisciplinarity between psychology and theology at its best offers a thicker analysis drawn from differing traditions and models brought together in rich conversation. This greater depth and complexity will not be without conflict and negotiation, yet it is more able to avoid reducing one discipline or the other to its lowest common denominator.

Second, we suggest that Tracy's bi-directional correlational model is a productive integrative offering precisely because it presses toward mutual recognition and influence and so provides the basis for a hermeneutical and relational model of integration. Andrea Hollingsworth (2011), drawing upon Tracy to demonstrate the importance of what she calls "negation" in interdisciplinary work, argues that Tracy

> consistently challenges the pretension that the single subject can understand anything in a direct, transparent, unaffected, or controlling manner. Authentic understanding comes not through assertive presumption but through

vulnerable encounter and openness to transformation on ideological, ethical, and existential levels.

(p. 462)

This emphasis on vulnerability and openness provides an important trajectory for ongoing work between theology and psychology, especially a relational integration model that acknowledges the inevitability of conflict within interdisciplinary endeavors (Chapter 3) as well as the hermeneutical issues inherent in these endeavors (Chapter 5).

Third, a relational integration model offers a lens into contextual, diversity, and power dynamics, which have often been uncharted or left unaccounted for in the history of interdisciplinary engagement. While the history of psychology's engagement with theology or theology's interactions with psychology have illustrated power differentials, this very history has often ignored or even promoted these power dynamics in interdisciplinarity. It is vital to reflect on whose voices and which traditions are engaged or excluded in particular approaches to integration, and also to attend to relational dynamics involved in interaction with diverse perspectives. Too often, dominant-group scholars *appropriate* authors or texts outside their own traditions to "sprinkle in a little diversity" without engaging in meaningful and sustained dialogue with actual people who hold those perspectives.

A final gap we would mention relates to clinical and praxis integration arising from attempts to bring together psychology and theology in productive conversation. There has been limited influence from theological disciplines on mainstream approaches to counseling and psychotherapy, and several authors have suggested that evangelical Christian approaches to clinical practice have also been very thin theologically (e.g., Johnson, 2007; McMinn & Campbell, 2007; Strawn, Wright, & Jones, 2014). In the next chapter, we describe in more detail our relational integration model, in an attempt to address these underexplored resources for the integration of psychology and theology.

Notes

1 One exception is Ian Suttie who was quite conversant with theology and the history of religions, however, his early death limited his influence (Wulff, 1997).
2 Vitz (2011, p. 297) applies this problem to the multiple perspectives in Protestantism more broadly. Integration may then be unhelpfully "limited to an oversimplified 'mere Christianity'."
3 Typically in the book, we use "theology" to refer to "the *theological encyclopedia*, which includes biblical studies" (Craig Bartholomew, *Introducing Biblical Hermeneutics*, 475). In this particular discussion, we are addressing biblical studies as it is distinct from the discipline of theology.
4 Ellens (2012, p. 23) discusses early suspicion of psychology that entered the biblical studies guild through Wrede and Schweitzer, in their critique of nineteenth century historical Jesus scholarship. "Schweitzer had not intended to denounce psychology *carte blanche*,

only its 'amateurish' and 'faulty' instances. But his critique resulted in a demonization of psychology in the household of biblical scholarship" far into the twentieth century.

Bibliography

Adler, J. (2012). Sitting at the nexus of epistemological traditions: Narrative psychological perspectives on self-knowledge. In S. Vazire & T. D. Wilson (Eds.), *Handbook of self-knowledge* (pp. 327–347). New York, NY: The Guilford Press.

Akin, D. L., & Pace, R. S. (2017). *Pastoral theology: Theological foundations for who a pastor is and what he does*. Nashville, TN: B&H Academic.

Allport, G. W. (1950). *The individual and his religion: A psychological interpretation*. Oxford, UK: Palgrave Macmillan.

Allport, G. W. (1967). Gordon W. Allport. In E. G. Boring, G. Lindzey, E. G. Boring, G. Lindzey (Eds.), *A history of psychology in autobiography* (Vol. V, pp. 1–25). East Norwalk, CT: Appleton-Century-Crofts. doi:10.1037/11579-001

Association of Theological Schools. (2010). General institutional standards. *Association of Theological Schools*. Retrieved from www.ats.edu/uploads/accrediting/documents/general-institutional-standards.pdf

Aten, J. D., McMinn, M. R., & Worthington Jr, E. L. (2011). *Spiritually oriented interventions for counseling and psychotherapy*. Washington, DC: American Psychological Association.

Barbour, I. G. (1990). *Religion in an age of science*. San Francisco, CA: Harper & Row.

Bartholomew, C. (2015). *Introducing biblical hermeneutics: A comprehensive framework for hearing God in Scripture*. Grand Rapids, MI: Baker Academic.

Bass, D. C., & Dykstra, C. (Eds.). (2008). *For life abundant: Practical theology, theological education, and Christian ministry*. Grand Rapids, MI: Wm. B. Eerdmans Publishing.

Benjamin, J. (1988). *The bonds of love: Psychoanalysis, feminism, and the problem of domination*. New York, NY: Pantheon Books.

Benjamin, J. (1998). *Shadow of the other: Intersubjectivity and gender in psychoanalysis*. New York, NY: Routledge, Inc.

Bennett, M. J. (2004). Becoming interculturally competent. In J. Wurzel (Ed.), *Toward multiculturalism: A reader in multicultural education* (2nd ed., pp. 62–77). Newton, MA: Intercultural Resource Corporation.

Brown, N. J., Lomas, T., & Eiroa-Orosa, F. J. (Eds.). (2017). *The Routledge international handbook of critical positive psychology*. London: Routledge.

Browning, D. (1991). *A fundamental practical theology: Descriptive and strategic proposals*. Minneapolis, MN: Fortress Press.

Browning, D. S., & Cooper, T. D. (2004). *Religious thought and the modern psychologies* (2nd ed.). Minneapolis, MN: Fortress Press.

Bultmann, R. K. (1969). *Faith and understanding* (Vol. 1). New York, NY: Harper & Row.

Cahalan, K. A. (2012). Integration in theological education. In B. J. Miller-McLemore (Eds.), *Practical theology* (pp. 386–395). West Sussex, UK: Wiley Blackwell.

Cahalan, K. A., & Mikoski, G. S. (2014). *Opening the field of practical theology: An introduction*. Lanham, MD: Rowman & Littlefield.

Carter, J. D. (1977). Secular and sacred models of psychology and religion. *Journal of Psychology & Theology, 5*(3), 197–208.

Carter, J. D., & Narramore, B. (1979). *The integration of psychology and theology: An introduction*. Grand Rapids, MI: Zondervan.

Choi, H. A. (2015). *A postcolonial self: Korean immigrant theology and church.* Albany, NY: State University of New York Press.

Cooper-White, P. (2004). *Shared wisdom: Use of the self in pastoral care and counseling.* Grand Rapids, MI: Fortress Press.

DeLashmutt, M. W. (2005). Syncretism or correlation: Teilhard and Tillich's contrasting methodological approaches to science and theology. *Zygon, 40*(3), 739–750.

Doehring, C. (2015). *The practice of pastoral care: A postmodern approach.* Louisville, KY: Westminster John Knox Press.

Dube, M. (2012). *Postcolonial feminist interpretation of the Bible.* St Louis, MO: Chalice Press.

Ellens, J. H., & Rollins, W. G. (2012). *Psychological hermeneutics for biblical themes and texts: A festschrift in honor of Wayne G. Rollins.* London: T & T Clark Ltd.

Elliott, J. H. (2007). *Conflict, community, and honor: 1 Peter in social-scientific perspective* (Cascade companions). Eugene, OR: Cascade Books.

Elliott, J. H., & Via, D. O. (1993). *What is social-scientific criticism?* Minneapolis, MN: Fortress Press.

Ellis, A. (2000). Can rational emotive behavior therapy (REBT) be effectively used with people who have devout beliefs in God and religion? *Professional Psychology: Research and Practice, 31*(1), 29–33. doi:10.1037/0735–7028.31.1.29

Entwistle, D. N. (2010). *Integrative approaches to psychology and Christianity: An introduction to worldview issues, philosophical assumptions, and models of integration* (2nd ed.). Eugene, OR: Wipf and Stock.

Fisher, C. (2012). *Contemplative nation: A philosophical account of Jewish theological language.* Stanford, CA: Stanford University Press.

Freud, S. (1925). An autobiographical study. In *Standard edition* (Vol. 20, 1959, pp. 1–74). (First German edition, 1925).

Goodman, D. M., Walling, S., & Ghali, A. A. (2010). Psychology in pursuit of justice: The lives and works of Emmanuel Levinas and Ignacio Martín-Baró. *Pastoral Psychology, 59*(5), 585–602.

Green, J. B. (2003). Science, religion and the mind-brain problem—the case of Thomas Willis (1621–1675). *Science & Christian Belief, 15*(2), 165–185.

Green, J. B. (2008). *Body, soul, and human life (studies in theological interpretation): The nature of humanity in the Bible.* Grand Rapids, MI: Baker Academic.

Green, J. B. (Ed.). (2010). *In search of the soul: Perspectives on the mind-body problem.* Eugene, OR: Wipf and Stock Publishers.

Grudem, W. (1994). *Systematic theology: An introduction to Biblical theology.* Grand Rapids, MI: Zondervan.

Haker, H., Susin, L. C., & Metogo, E. M. (2013). *Postcolonial theology.* London: SCM Press.

Hall, T. W., & Edwards, K. J. (2002). The Spiritual Assessment Inventory: A theistic model and measure for assessing spiritual development. *Journal for the Scientific Study of Religion, 41*(2), 341–357.

Haskell, T. L. (2000). *Objectivity is not neutrality: Explanatory schemes in history.* Baltimore, MD: Johns Hopkins University Press.

Heitink, G. (1999). *Practical theology: History, theory, action domains: Manual for practical theology.* Grand Rapids, MI: Wm. B. Eerdmans Publishing.

Hermans, C. C. A., & Moore, M. E. (Eds.). (2004). *Hermeneutics and empirical research in practical theology: The contribution of empirical theology by Johannes A. van der Ven* (Vol. 11). Leiden: Brill.

Hill, P. C., & Pargament, K. I. (2003). Advances in the conceptualization and measurement of religion and spirituality: Implications for physical and mental health research. *American Psychologist, 58*, 64–74.

Hollingsworth, A. (2011). The ambiguity of interdisciplinarity. *Zygon, 46*(2), 461–470.

Jackson, R., & Makransky, J. (Eds.). (2000). *Buddhist theology: Critical reflections by contemporary Buddhist scholars*. New York, NY: Routledge.

James, W. (1958). *Varieties of religious experience: A study in human nature*. New York, NY: Modern Library.

Johnson, E. L. (2007). Towards a philosophy of science for Christian psychology. *Edification: Journal of the Society of Christian Psychology, 1*, 5–20.

Johnson, E. L. (Ed.). (2010). *Psychology & Christianity: Five views* (2nd ed.). Downers Grove, IL: InterVarsity Press.

Johnson, R. (2013). *Spirituality in counseling and psychotherapy: An integrative approach that empowers clients*. Hoboken, NJ: John Wiley & Sons, Inc.

Johnston, D. (2008). *A brief history of theology: From the new testament to feminist theology*. New York, NY: Bloomsbury Publishing.

Jones, S. L. (2010). An integration view. In E. L. Johnson (Ed.), *Psychology & Christianity: Five views* (pp. 101–128). Downers Grove, IL: InterVarsity Press.

Killen, P. O. C., & De Beer, J. (1994). *The art of theological reflection*. New York, NY: Crossroad.

Kim, U., Yang, K. S., & Hwang, K. K. (2006). *Indigenous and cultural psychology: Understanding people in context*. New York, NY: Springer.

Kuyper, A. (1988). *A centennial reader* (J. D. Bratt, Ed.). Grand Rapids, MI: Eerdmans.

Lawrence, L. J. (2013). *Sense and stigma in the gospels: Depictions of sensory-disabled characters*. Oxford: Oxford University Press.

Linehan, M. M. (1993). *Cognitive-behavioral treatment of borderline personality disorder*. New York, NY: Guilford Press.

Linehan, M. M. (2015). *DBT skills training manual* (2nd ed.). New York, NY: Guilford Press.

Lonergan, B. (1972). *Method in theology*. New York, NY: Herder and Herder.

Martín-Baró, I. (1996). *Writings for a liberation psychology*. Cambridge, MA: Harvard University Press.

Maslow, A. H., Frager, R., & Fadiman, J. (1970). *Motivation and personality* (Vol. 2, pp. 1887–1904). New York, NY: Harper & Row.

Mbuvi, A. M., & Mbuwayesango, D. R. (Eds.). (2012). *Postcolonial perspectives in African Biblical interpretations*. Atlanta, GA: Society of Biblical Literature.

McConville, J. (2016). *Being human in God's world: An Old Testament theology of humanity*. Grand Rapids, MI: Baker Academic.

McDargh, J. (1985). Theological uses of psychology: Retrospective and prospective. *Horizons, 12*(2), 247–264.

McMinn, M. R., & Campbell, C. D. (2007). *Integrative psychotherapy: Toward a comprehensive Christian approach*. Downers Grove, IL: InterVarsity Press.

Melchert, T. P. (2013). Beyond theoretical orientations: The emergence of a unified scientific framework in professional psychology. *Professional Psychology: Research and Practice, 44*(1), 11–19. doi:10.1037/a0028311

Miller, S. P. (2014). *The age of evangelicalism: America's born-again years*. New York, NY: Oxford University Press.

Miller-McLemore, B. J. (2014). Coming to our senses: Feeling and knowledge in theology and ministry. *Pastoral Psychology, 63*(5–6), 689–704.

Myers, D. G. (2010). A levels-of-explanation view. In E. L. Johnson (Ed.), *Psychology & Christianity: Five views* (pp. 49–78). Downers Grove, IL: InterVarsity Press.

Narramore, B. L. (1973). Perspectives on the integration of psychology and theology. *Journal of Psychology & Theology, 1*, 3–18.

Neyrey, J. H. (1998). *Honor and shame in the gospel of Matthew*. Louisville: Westminster John Knox Press.

Pargament, K. I., Exline, J. J., & Jones, J. W. (2013). *APA handbook of psychology, religion, and spirituality (Vol. 1): Context, theory, and research*. Washington, DC: American Psychological Association. doi:10.1037/14045–000

Pargament, K. I., Mahoney, A., Exline, J. J., Jones, J. W., & Shafranske, E. P. (2013). Envisioning an integrative paradigm for the psychology of religion and spirituality. In K. I. Pargament, J. J. Exline, J. W. Jones, K. I. Pargament, J. J. Exline, & J. W. Jones (Eds.), *APA handbook of psychology, religion, and spirituality (Vol. 1): Context, theory, and research* (pp. 3–19). Washington, DC: American Psychological Association. doi:10.1037/14045-001

Pargament, K. I., Mahoney, A., & Shafranske, E. P. (2013). *APA handbook of psychology, religion, and spirituality (Vol. 2): An applied psychology of religion and spirituality*. Washington, DC: American Psychological Association. doi:10.1037/14046–000

Pargament, K. I., & Saunders, S. M. (2007). Introduction to the special issue on spirituality and psychotherapy. *Journal of Clinical Psychology, 63*(10), 903–907.

Placher, W. C., & Nelson, D. R. (2013). *A history of Christian theology: An introduction* (2nd ed.). Louisville: Westminster John Knox.

Plante, T. G. (2009). *Spiritual practices in psychotherapy: Thirteen tools for enhancing psychological health*. Washington, DC: American Psychological Association.

Plante, T. G. (2012). A levels-of-explanation approach. In S. P. Greggo & T. A. Sisemore (Eds.), *Counseling and Christianity: Five approaches* (pp. 60–83). Donwers Grove, IL: InterVarsity Press.

Post, B. C., & Wade, N. G. (2009). Religion and spirituality in psychotherapy: A practice-friendly review of research. *Journal of Clinical Psychology, 65*(2), 131–146.

Powlison, D. (2010). A Biblical counseling view. In E. L. Johnson (Ed.), *Psychology & Christianity: Five views* (2nd ed., pp. 245–273). Downers Grove, IL: InterVarsity Press.

Purves, A. (2004). *Reconstructing pastoral theology: A Christological foundation*. Louisville, KY: Westminster John Knox Press.

Rahner, K. (1961). *Theological investigations* (Vol. 9). Baltimore: Helicon Press.

Rahner, K. (1968). *Spirit in the world*. New York, NY: Herder and Herder.

Reno, R. R. (2004). Biblical theology and theological exegesis. In C. Bartholomew, M. Healy, & K. Möller (Eds.), *Out of Egypt: Biblical theology and Biblical interpretation* (pp. 385–408). Grand Rapids, MI: Zondervan.

Reynhout, K. A. (2013). *Interdisciplinary interpretation: Paul Ricoeur and the hermeneutics of theology and science*. Plymouth, UK: Lexington Books.

Ricoeur, P. (1974). Metaphor and the main problem of hermeneutics. *New Literary History, 6*(1), 95–110.

Rizzuto, A. (1979). *The birth of the living God: A psychoanalytic study*. Chicago, IL: University of Chicago Press.

Rizzuto, A. (2005). Psychoanalytic considerations about spiritually oriented psychotherapy. In L. Sperry & E. P. Shafranske (Eds.), *Spiritually oriented psychotherapy* (pp. 31–50). Washington, DC, US: American Psychological Association. doi:10.1037/10886-002

Rizzuto, A. (2006). Psychoanalytic reflections about religious experiences: Description and dynamic understanding. *Archives De Psychologie, 72*(280–281), 81–96.

Roberts, R. C. (2000). A Christian psychology view. In E. L. Johnson & S. L. Jones (Eds.), *Psychology & Christianity: Four views* (pp. 148–177). Donwers Grove, IL: InterVarsity Press.

Roberts, R. C., & Watson, P. J. (2010). A Christian psychology view. In E. L. Johnson (Ed.), *Psychology & Christianity: Five views* (2nd ed., pp. 149–178). Downers Grove, IL: InterVarsity Press.

Rollins, W. G. (1983). *Jung and the Bible*. Atlanta: John Knox Press.

Sandage, S. J., & Brown, J. K. (2012). Converging horizons for relational integration: Differentiation-based collaboration. *Journal of Psychology and Theology, 40*, 72–76.

Sheppard, P. (2011). *Self, culture, and others in womanist practical theology*. New York, NY: Palgrave Macmillan.

Sperry, L. (2012). *Spirituality in clinical practice: Theory and practice of spiritually oriented psychotherapy*. New York, NY: Taylor & Francis Group.

Stevenson, D. H., Eck, B. E., & Hill, P. C. (Eds.). (2007). *Psychology & Christianity integration: Seminal works that shaped the movement*. Batavia, IL: Christian Association for Psychological Studies.

Strawn, B. D. (2016). Integration: What with what and with whom? *Fuller Magazine*, (5), 38–43.

Strawn, B. D., Wright, R. W., & Jones, P. (2014). Tradition-based integration: Illuminating the stories and practices that shape our integrative imagination. *Journal of Psychology & Christianity, 33*(4), 37–54.

Tan, S. (2011). Mindfulness and acceptance-based cognitive behavioral therapies: Empirical evidence and clinical applications from a Christian perspective. *Journal of Psychology and Christianity, 30*(3), 243–249.

Tolbert, M. A. (2003). Graduate Biblical studies: Ethos and discipline. *SBL Forum*. Retrieved August 28, 2017, from www.sbl-site.org/Article.aspx?ArticleId=195.

Tracy, D. (1981). The analogical imagination: Christian theology and the culture of pluralism. *Religious Studies Review, 7*(4), 281–332.

Tracy, D. (2014). A correlational model of practical theology revisited. In C. E. Wolfteich (Ed.), *Invitation to practical theology: Catholic voices and visions* (pp. 70–86). New York, NY: Paulist Press.

Underwood, R. (2012). Psychological insight into the Bible: Texts and readings. In H. J. Ellens & J. H. Ellens (Eds.), *Psychological hermeneutics for Biblical themes and texts: A Festschrift in honour of Wayne G. Rollins* (pp. 71–83). London: A&C Black.

Vande Kemp, H., & Houskamp, B. (1986). An early attempt at integration: The journal of psychotherapy as a religious process. *Journal of Psychology & Theology, 14*(1), 3–14.

Vitz, P. C. (2011). Christian and Catholic advantages for connecting psychology with the faith. *Journal of Psychology and Christianity, 30*(4), 294–307.

Wolfe, A. (2003). *The transformation of American religion: How we actually live our faith*. Chicago, IL: University of Chicago Press.

Wolfteich, C. E. (Ed.). (2014). *Invitation to practical theology: Catholic voices and visions*. New York, NY: Paulist Press.

Worthen, M. (2014). *Apostles of reason: The crisis of authority in American evangelicalism*. New York, NY: Oxford University Press.

Wright, N. T. (2003). *The resurrection of the Son of God* (Vol. 3). Minneapolis, MN: Fortress Press.

Wulff, D. M. (1997). *Psychology of religion: Classic and contemporary* (2nd ed.). New York, NY: John Wiley & Sons.

Wuthnow, R. (1998). *After heaven: Spirituality in America since the 1950s*. Berkeley, CA: University of California Press.

3

MUTUAL RECOGNITION AND RELATIONAL INTEGRATION

In their fascinating set of reflections on their experiences of scholarly inter-actions across the social sciences, neurosciences, and humanities, Callard and Fitzgerald (2015) ask probing questions about the relational dynamics of interdisciplinarity:

> What is this space? What forms of practice and ethics does it call us towards? What holds it together? What have its various analysts not told us? How does it end up deadening and closing down possibilities, even as it abounds in affirmations of its innovativeness and creativity? And how, if it is really as problematic as we think it is, might it be reimagined and practiced differently?
>
> *(p. 4)*

In this chapter, we will attempt our version of a relational integration answer to these complicated questions with respect to psychology and theology—one that addresses issues of anxiety, power and control, differentiated relationality, and third spaces that open "two-way streets" of mutual recognition. Before we do, we invite you to attend to relational dynamics in this hypothetical conversation on inter-disciplinary integration among a faculty and their dean at a Christian theological seminary.

A Case of Interdisciplinarity and Relational Tensions

DEAN ABERNATHY (Theologian): Welcome to our first official interdisciplinary colloquium. As a seminary, we have begun a new initiative to foster greater integration in our curriculum for our students. As we work on this curricular reform, we thought it would be helpful to begin a series of colloquia focusing on working across disciplines. To get us started, let's each share briefly some ways we have already been working on interdisciplinary integration in the classroom.

CHARLES (Theology Department; Theologian and Ethicist): The fields of theology and ethics are already integrative disciplines. So in my classes, I find it helpful to name some of the areas of contemporary thought that we will be addressing with various theological questions in mind . . . philosophy and social science, for example. We want to bring a theological worldview to all dimensions of life.

SONIA (Counseling Department; Psychologist): Charles, I'm interested to hear some of the ways you bring social science into your teaching, since this is an area our counseling students are immersed in throughout their studies.

CHARLES: In the second theology course, I use a text that brings some of the insights of sociology into theological reflection on ecclesia or what it means to be "church." It's written by a theologian who's done significant interdisciplinary work in social science. I can share the resource with you if you'd like.

PHIL (New Testament Department; Biblical Scholar): [interrupting] Dean Abernathy, can I clarify our process before going further? I'm concerned that we are getting the cart before the horse. I'd suggest that, as an institution that takes Scripture seriously, we evaluate such resources from other disciplines through the lens of the Bible. Don't we want our students to graduate with a biblical mindset rather than a secular one?

DEAN ABERNATHY: This is a valid question and one that we should address. I've actually drawn up some guidelines for conversation that I'll share with you at some point in our meeting. At this point we are just asking some of you to share a few examples of how you've been attending to interdisciplinary topics in your current teaching as a way to get the conversation going.

SANDY (Pastoral Theology Department, Homiletician): In our preaching courses, we are very centered on the biblical text but we also want students to interact with contemporary communication theory and rhetorical approaches that can help them be better preachers. I see these two areas working together quite nicely for student integration.

RAMON (Counseling Department, Psychologist): I find our counseling students frequently speak of wanting a kind of "practical integration" that helps them integrate theory and clinical practice. I get concerned that a lot of our curriculum is very conceptual and abstract and removed from "real life," and I want to help students deal with the personal challenges of sitting with people who are suffering. I hope we will talk here about these applied and personal kinds of integration. Some of the "theology" I interact with seems to be a privileged way of avoiding the need to honestly face suffering in the world.

PATRICK (Pastoral Theology Department, Leadership): Like Sandy mentioned, we also have a multi-disciplinary approach built into our leadership department

courses that moves beyond the purely affective level to the theoretical understandings that leaders need. One of my favorite class sessions is where I take a
look at the leadership models from the twelve New Testament apostles, with
each providing a key leadership quality for our class discussion. In fact, I've
thought of developing this lecture into some sort of interdisciplinary writing
project.

LATITIA (Old Testament Department, Biblical Scholar): *[hesitantly]* Patrick,
I would be interested in hearing about your method for "reading" leadership
in the text. Given that biblical characters are often more flawed than exem-
plary, how do you account for the full scope of their portrayals?

PATRICK: *[somewhat defensively]* I thought this was just about sharing what we do
in class, not an interrogation, Latitia. If you must know, I use case methodology, which is quite well established in my discipline. And I've read quite a
number of works in my field that highlight positive leadership qualities of,
for example, the apostle Peter. I think it's important that students consider
cases of biblical leaders along with the contemporary examples of leaders in
the course.

LATITIA: I didn't mean to offend. But if we are going to do integration or help
our students do so, don't we need to be able to talk as a faculty about methodological differences across our disciplines?

DEAN ABERNATHY: *[quickly inserting himself]* This might be a good time to move
to the next part of our colloquium and share the guidelines I've developed to
help us move toward integration among our disciplines.

Some might expect that this kind of interdisciplinary conversation among
educators would provide a stimulating opportunity for fresh learning among
professionals whose "trade" *is* learning. This vignette, however, depicts several
moments of escalation of tension and anxiety we have found common during
interdisciplinary conversations. The various contributions can be considered at
the level of content, but we want to also highlight relational process dynamics that
also shape this kind of interaction. We might begin by considering the role of the
Dean, who sets the table in an open fashion but seems to have a set of guidelines
ready at hand in case anything gets out of hand, as he perceives happening with
Patrick and Latitia (whose hesitancy in raising her question to Patrick may also
indicate some amount of anxiety). It might be interesting for the reader to reflect
upon their own internal response to the Dean's move—did it offer helpful structure to keep the conversation from spiraling out of control, or did it serve as a
pre-emptive, anxious response to a mild conflict that could have been productive?

Phil's interruption to clarify the parameters and role of Scripture—his discipline's specific purview—might evidence anxiety over disciplinary boundaries
and the relative hierarchy of disciplines. We have found this particular form of
anxiety to be fairly common in interdisciplinary forays, especially as it pertains to
the power that comes with hierarchy and concerns, implicit or explicit, to limit
or control the influence of other disciplines (see Callard & Fitzgerald, 2015). For

some, determining which disciplines or sources of authority take precedence over others is a purported means of lessening anxieties in what they take to be a kind "zero-sum" game of integration (i.e., a gain for any discipline means a loss for some other discipline). While Phil may contend that he is only arguing for an epistemological stance and not personal power in seeking to privilege the authority of Scripture over other disciplines, an integrative or multi-dimensional analysis of this debate about "integration" could likely reveal that numerous kinds of issues of power, control, and authority are at stake. These may include, for example, numbers of required courses in the curriculum, numbers of faculty positions in departments, the nature of funding and specialized scholarships available to students, research funds available to faculty, and/or merit raises.

We might also discern examples of disciplinary "overreach" (Reynhout's terminology)—moments where one disciplinarian transgresses (intentionally or not) methods or tenets of another "borrowed" discipline. Sonia's question to Charles might be understood as a query of the legitimacy or competency of his particular use of social science. His answer cites the work of a theologian who has "done significant interdisciplinary work" in the social sciences. While Charles offers a potentially promising resource and possible follow up conversation with Sonia (if he moves beyond simply sharing the resource to asking about Sonia's areas of expertise and her own assessment of the resource), his own work and the book he references provide a *single-integrator model* of interdisciplinarity. And his content-based response suggests he might have missed Sonia's implicit message about disciplinary boundaries. The conversation between Patrick and Latitia provides a more obvious example of disciplinary overreach. His reference to his own work in the New Testament on positive examples of leadership elicits Latitia's concern as a biblical scholar. Her sensitivity to selective use of the text (combined with analysis of narrative characters with little concern shown for authorial interests) illuminates a tension between the hermeneutical methodologies of her guild and the ways she perceives Patrick to be selectively and possibly unreflectively using the text for different purposes. Patrick's reference to scholars in his own field (Leadership) who have interpreted the biblical text as he does—a relational move we describe below as *triangulation* (Kerr & Bowen, 1988)—only exacerbates this disciplinary tension. As is often the case with disciplinary overreach, the transgressor (Patrick) is unaware of the transgression, even as Latitia is immediately and keenly cognizant of a sense of encroachment that undermines epistemological values and methodological practices of her discipline. Patrick may intend to be hospitable in engaging another discipline, while being oblivious to the methodological "trampling" Latitia experiences.

Ramon contributes additional practical, formation-based dimensions of integration to the discussion, ones we raise throughout this book. The rhetorical impact of his reference to "real life" might be off-putting to some of the other faculty who believe they also deal with real life in their classes, while Ramon may simply experience himself as advocating for student concerns. Notice that Patrick follows Ramon by minimizing and then ignoring the issues he raised, even offering what might be a subtle dig in talking about "moving beyond the purely affective" (i.e., emotional) level. His use of the language of "levels" in this context could also be experienced as a "one-up" power move that counters the critique offered by Ramon.

Although we have not touched on the gender, racial, and other diversity dynamics at play in this vignette, issues of *difference* and *power* are central to our model of relational integration. When we encounter one another in these types of discussions as faculty, professionals, or laypersons, we do not come as "blank slates" or neutral parties. Rather, we bring our social locations, our anxieties and concerns, and the relational dynamics of power and control in the structural systems we inhabit. Too often, these diversity and other relational dynamics become hidden or implicit factors that shape minefields of conflict, control, and cutoff within interdisciplinary relations rather than constructive resources that enrich the complexity of integrative collaboration.

Differentiation in Interdisciplinary Integration

Our overarching thesis in this chapter is that *differentiated relationality is the ontological foundation necessary for mutual recognition in optimal relational integration.* Central to this thesis is the concept of *differentiation of self.* In Bowenian family systems theory, differentiation of self (DoS) is a dialectical construct that involves an intrapsychic capacity to integrate thoughts and feelings, as well as an interpersonal capacity for both intimacy and autonomy in relationships. Those with high levels of DoS are generally capable of self-soothing the anxiety of being in close proximity with others, as well as the anxiety of being independent or alone. DoS is particularly useful for understanding the relational capacities necessary to "hold onto oneself" amidst the vulnerability of mature intimacy without excessive fears of engulfment or abandonment, a frequently underrated challenge (Schnarch, 2009). Empirically, DoS has been associated with numerous indices of relational health and maturity (Skowron & Dendy, 2004), as well as several measures of virtue and Christian spirituality, including: (a) forgiveness, (b) gratitude, (c) hope, (d) spiritual well-being, and (e) humility (for summaries, see Sandage & Jankowski, 2013; Worthington & Sandage, 2016).

A common concern about interdisciplinary integration is that it might necessitate, or at least encourage, a loss of disciplinary distinctiveness. The concept of differentiation answers this concern by highlighting the importance of maintaining an appropriately distinct stance grounded in one's own disciplinary methodologies and conceptualizations while engaging in authentic conversation for integration (Brown, Dahl, & Corbin Reuschling, 2011). DoS involves an appreciation for boundaries, perspective-taking, and acknowledging both one's strengths and limitations in competence.

Additionally, differentiation has been framed as an essential part of intercultural competence and a nuanced capacity to understand and respond effectively to cultural differences (Bennett, 2004). In empirical research, DoS has been positively associated with higher levels of intercultural competence or the ability to manage "stranger anxiety" by relating effectively across cultural differences (Sandage &

Jankowski, 2013). Differentiation involves neither a denial of differences nor an exclusive focus on difference. Rather, those with high levels of DoS can face and even value differences while also acknowledging points of similarity. The integration of capacities for both intimacy and alterity makes DoS a useful construct for conceptualizing the development of spiritual maturity (Majerus & Sandage, 2010); and differentiation promotes a willingness to tolerate anxiety and discomfort as part of a growth process (Schnarch, 2009; Shults & Sandage, 2006).

What might DoS offer to our opening vignette on interdisciplinary integration? We suggest that Dean Abernathy might have shown a more differentiated stance by introducing the conversation around integration as one that would highlight differences in the seminary disciplines as well as potential points of convergence. Setting up the conversation more realistically could have allowed him to highlight the dynamics of the conversation when conflicts began to surface. And such a differentiated stance could have offered a non-anxious presence for the group when conflict arose during the discussion. The group surfaced several important points of difference and tension, and it could have been useful for Dean Abernathy to allow the group to wrestle further with those tensions prior to offering his structured solution.

Our promotion of differentiated relationality for optimal interdisciplinary integration leads up to four affirmations, which we will explore before setting out a pathway for our relational integration model at the conclusion of the chapter. These affirmations have to do with the (a) inevitably of relational conflict; (b) the inadequacy of desegregation alone; (c) normalizing anxiety in interdisciplinary interactions; and (d) the influence of social hierarchy on models of interdisciplinary engagement.

Difference and the Inevitability of Conflict

The first affirmation stemming from our thesis that differentiated relationality is needed for optimal relational integration has to do with the inevitability of conflict: *If integration is understood as a relational process, it will inevitably lead to episodes of relational conflict even when pursued with positive intentions.* And we have found that a person's view of conflict influences their view of interdisciplinary relations between psychology and theology.

We have been influenced by numerous relational and systemic theorists from the social sciences that point to the inevitability of relational conflict even within constructive change processes. Stephen Mitchell (1988) suggests, "conflict is inherent in relatedness" (p. 160). And Robert Kegan (1994) writes, "differentiation precedes integration. Conflict precedes re-solution" (p. 326). Both of these theorists normalize the presence of conflict in systems and relationships and propose conflict as a potentially constructive aspect of human connections and personal agency. The goal is not to avoid conflict and deny differences but to achieve mutuality and intersubjectivity or a "meeting of minds" (Mitchell). Kegan invites a reconceptualization of conflict that *values* attending to differences in perspectives (his meaning of differentiation) and also moves from focusing on discrete parties in a conflict (e.g., persons or disciplines) toward intentional awareness of the relationship between the conflicted parties. He explains, "the relationship creates the parties; the parties do not create the relationship" (p. 320). Kegan offers the possibility of conflict as an impetus for transformation and suggests several reflective moves related to conflicts that are consistent with our approach to relational integration:

> (1) consider that your protracted conflict is a signal that you and your opponent have probably become identified with the poles of the conflict; (2) consider that the relationship in which you find yourself is not the inconvenient result of the existence of an opposing view but the expression of your own incompleteness taken as completeness; (3) value the relationship, miserable as it might feel, as an opportunity to live out your multiplicity; and thus (4) focus on ways to let the conflictual relationship transform the parties rather than on the parties resolving the conflict.
>
> *(p. 320)*

Other theorists have also explored the constructive contribution of relational conflict in personal and systemic transformation. For example, systems theorists typically view conflict as functioning to balance *stability* and *change* in systems. A systems theorist might ask, "What is the function of *this* particular conflict in *this* particular system in its quest to adapt, evolve, or integrate?" In Chapter 2, we suggested that the language of "integration" emerged in both evangelical discourse and among certain post-positivist psychologists, in part, as a response to the modern segregation of disciplines, including science and religion. In the opening vignette of this chapter, we might read Phil as representing a concern to hold onto their seminary's tradition of prioritizing Scripture, while Ramon may be oriented toward the need to attend to the personal formation of students and practical applications. From the perspective of relational integration, the initial question is not, "Which one of them is right?" but rather "What does this conflict represent within this overall system and its wider contexts?" (e.g., changes in higher education and changes in church practices). Transformation is possible when conflict is seen as a pathway to understanding more clearly these systemic realities and to navigating them with multiple perspectives and values held in dialectical tension (Ricoeur, 1970).

What might this possibility for transformation look like for the engagement of theology and psychology? First of all, for relational integration to be successful it will be important to normalize conflict in the integrative process. If, in our opening vignette, Dean Abernathy had called attention to the tensions emerging in the conversation and normalized the conflict among disciplines (or better yet, begun the conversation by introducing conflict as an integral part of the integrative process), the chances of pressing into real differences and moving toward mutual recognition would have increased. Additionally, highlighting the creative possibilities of interdisciplinary conversation because of and not in spite of conflict can move participants to reflect more carefully on their own perspectives and traditions. As Alasdair MacIntyre (1990) suggests about philosophical or religious traditions, interaction with a rival tradition can provide a creative encounter for adherents of a particular tradition if they are open to critique and reformulating their understanding. Applying MacIntyre to conflicts between psychological and theological traditions, Johnson (2010) observes, "Traditions sometimes discount and ignore each other, and typically only engage in dialogue when they are forced to, either out of social necessity or perhaps because of moral and intellectual integrity" (p. 24). Reimagining conflict as a catalyst for interdisciplinary integration rather than an impediment to it is a foundational affirmation for relational integration.

Inadequacy of Desegregation Alone

Our second affirmation about relational integration is that *interdisciplinary desegregation alone is not sufficient to achieve what we mean by collaborative relational integration*. It is common for efforts at interdisciplinary integration to start by bringing scholars or professionals from differing disciplines into contact and conversation, much like our opening faculty vignette. Yet this first step of disciplinary desegregation does not by itself guarantee interdisciplinary integration. In fact, based on our own experiences and conversations with many others who have participated in these kinds of interdisciplinary gatherings, constructive results emerging from interdisciplinary contact are not a given. Over seventy years of empirical research on intergroup relations in social psychology has shown that *contact* alone between groups does not predict progress in cooperative relations and can actually reinforce prejudice and stereotyping (Dovidio, Gaertner, & Kawakami, 2003). Rather, the "functional relations" between differing groups need to be altered (p. 7).

A useful analogy about the importance of equality and the limits of desegregation alone can be seen in efforts toward racial integration in schools and other social systems in the United States. Historically, there has often been idealism that simply desegregating and mixing different races will generate cooperative relationships or "integration." While desegregation is a crucial first step toward cultivating healthy and socially just multicultural societies, human finitude and fallenness contribute to both structural and interpersonal dynamics of exclusion even when contact across differences increases (Volf, 1996). Too often idealistic visions of integration, however well intentioned, have resulted in abandoning the effort once the difficult realities of conflict and resistance across differences emerge, particularly when dominant group members have opposed more personal forms of integration with minorities. In the U.S. context, neglecting racial integration leaves the unjust hierarchy of white supremacy in place. As Sheryll Cashin (2004) argues, the landmark 1954 decision in Brown v. Board of Education may have ended the legality of racial segregation in U.S. schools but the following fifty years have evidenced very little overall racial and class integration in a U.S. society that remains highly segregated. And as Martin Luther King, Jr. (1986a) so aptly put it,

> Integration is creative, and is therefore more profound and far-reaching than desegregation. Integration is the positive acceptance of desegregation and the welcomed participation of Negroes into the total range of human activities. Integration is genuine intergroup, interpersonal doing. Desegregation then, rightly, is only a short-range goal. Integration is the ultimate goal of our national community.
>
> *(p. 118)*

This relational vision for racial integration suggests the importance of building intentional and sustained *relationships* across racial and social differences, what Cashin calls "voluntary desegregration," that is, choosing to build personal, social, and neighborhood connections across racial and class lines. Elizabeth Anderson (2010) advocates a relational and structural model that addresses "intergroup processes or modes of interaction," i.e., relational dynamics (p. 10), while also focusing on systemic factors that sustain racial inequality (e.g., racist policies in access to housing). A facet of this relational perspective that both Cashin and Anderson identify is the toll that the conversation and work of racial integration takes on Blacks and other non-dominant groups. Anderson refers to the "psychological costs" (p. 180) involved, and Cashin notes that many African-Americans like herself have become "integration weary" (p. xii). Attitudes formed through segregation and racism are not easily undone by simple contact, and conflict may even escalate through intergroup contact or what Patterson (1998) calls "the ordeal of integration" (book title). This is a point that is often minimized by whites and other dominant group members whose privilege can blind them to these stressors of integration.

Certainly, racial integration in the U.S. is a much more dramatic, complicated, and violent story than the challenges of integrating theologians and psychologists, but we believe a very rough parallel holds, offering a dose of realism about the roles of conflict, difference, and inequality in relational integration. First, this analogy, rough as it may be, helps us to see that desegregation alone is not adequate for robust interdisciplinary integration. In the opening vignette, Dean Abernathy might have overestimated the trust, flexibility, and collaborative capacities of his faculty in electing to start the group conversation with so little structure about goals, expectations, and the status of various disciplines. It may be that the dean was assuming that integration would happen simply by inviting the conversation (an act of desegregation). The vignette highlights how anxiety and struggles of power and control often surface in interdisciplinary discussions, inviting further reflection on what needs to happen in addition to desegregation for productive and creative integration to occur.

Second, this analogy can illuminate the need to attend to both systemic and relational dynamics of interdisciplinary integration. Attention to *systemic issues* like imbalances of power across disciplines can explain why interdisciplinary conversations often resort to 'turf battles' and concerns about whose discipline should lead the conversation (Porter, 2010a). As King (1986b) said, "Integration is meaningless without the sharing of power. When I speak of integration, I don't mean a romantic mixing of colors, I mean a real sharing of power and responsibility" (p. 317). For some, the pursuit of integrative shared power and responsibility can involve a sacrificial loss of privileged status (Anderson, 2010). In addition to awareness of and attention to systemic issues, effectively relating across differences requires certain *relational virtues*, such as commitment, courage, humility, justice, and the highly differentiated capacity to take the perspective of others. It will also involve grappling with certain losses, including loss of comfort and familiarity of staying within the confines of one's own discipline group and the stability that adheres in such in-group associations. Such relational movement is often inherently anxiety-producing.

Normalizing Anxiety in Interdisciplinary Interactions

Our third affirmation about relational integration is that *interdisciplinary interactions will often involve anxiety, and anxiety can be productive for the integrative process*. The *Diagnostic and Statistical Manual of Mental Disorders* (APA, 2013; 5th ed.) defines anxiety as "the apprehensive anticipation of future danger or misfortune accompanied by a feeling of worry, distress, and/or somatic symptoms of tension. The focus of anticipated danger may be internal or external" (p. 818). Using a definition of anxiety from a taxonomy of mental disorders could reinforce the view that anxiety is always a pathology, and some theological perspectives view anxiety as sinful.

However, bringing an existential perspective to bear in both psychology and theology suggests anxiety as an ontological "given." Kierkegaard related anxiety to the German *angst*, which he suggested implies dread of human vulnerability to existential realities such as death. Christian theologians, such as Reinhold Niebuhr, have suggested anxiety is related to the human dialectic of finitude and freedom. Existential theologian Paul Tillich defines anxiety as "finitude with awareness" and suggests that the deepest ontological anxiety is about disintegrating or losing one's ontological structures in a fall into nothingness. For each of these existential theologians, anxiety is not sin but "readies us for sin" (Peters, 1994, p. 11); anxiety can press us to trust in idols rather than committing to trust in God's goodness even in the face of ambiguous outcomes and potential losses (Brueggemann, 2007). So, we would suggest that anxiety is not problematic in itself; it is to be expected when facing ambiguity and complex conflicts in making meaning of life. Yet under-developed capacities for anxiety management can lead to idolatry (the theological term) or maladaptive coping strategies (the psychological term), which will tend to perpetuate other problems.

In our approach to relational integration, we view anxiety as a dialectical phenomenon that is both stressful and potentially constructive. Much anxiety is unconscious and occurs at the cellular level to mobilize valuable immune functioning to protect against threats and maintain the stability of an organism or system (Kegan & Lahey, 2009; Kerr & Bowen, 1988). Overwhelming anxiety can lead to trauma and prove damaging to human well-being, while an optimal level of anxiety may be arousing and contribute energy to facing important issues, conflicts, or facets of non-integration and non-being (Tillich, 1952). If handled with a healthy balance of self-confrontation and emotional regulation in a supportive relational context, certain levels of anxiety can arouse or catalyze growth, creativity, and spiritual transformation (Sandage et al., 2008).

In the literature on interdisciplinarity and integration, anxiety is a much under-discussed topic. Callard and Fitzgerald (2015) are the only other authors we have found discussing the roles of anxiety (which they describe as "feeling fuzzy," p. 115) and emotional dysregulation in interdisciplinary work. They provide helpful analysis of interdisciplinary dynamics requiring affect regulation skills. Interdisciplinary work is quite often anxiety-provoking, in part, because certain phases of an interdisciplinary project often involve heavy doses of ambiguity of meaning and the dissonance of differing disciplinary languages and frameworks (cf. Dovidio et al., 2003). Those with a high need for epistemological clarity, structure, and organization will often be stretched by the interdisciplinary necessity to tolerate ambiguity and to be patient with the process of constructing new understandings. Anxiety regulation skills will be important in this regard, and leaders such as Dean Abernathy in our scenario would be wise to consider strategies for cultivating a cooperative relational environment prior to introducing significant ambiguity about interdisciplinary integration. When thinking about promoting various forms of interdisciplinary integration in a clinic, academic department, religious setting, or some other system, it is useful to attend to the overall level of anxiety in the system and whether it has been able to navigate successfully other recent changes involving new perspectives. Some systems with high levels of anxiety will have rigid boundaries and be impermeable to new inputs, while other systems might be overly porous to a cacophony of new inputs yet showing little capacity for integrative coherence.

Situations of interdisciplinary desegregation can also activate anxieties related to the ubiquitous systemic dynamics of power and control (Maddock and Larson, 2004). As with anxiety, power and control are not inherently good or bad but necessary parts of life. The key systemic and ethical questions involve various ways of seeking to balance power and control in relationships. Abuse is an extreme imbalance of power that over-rides others' boundaries of control. Neglect is an extreme imbalance of control that does not allow engagement or influence from another. Relational systems routinely engage in an ongoing process of seeking to balance power and control within shifting social contexts, but imbalances of power and control are far too common.

Within the practice of interdisciplinary integration, a significant lens for analysis is the distribution of power and control across disciplines. Important in this regard is a recognition of how disciplinary distinctions have arisen. One of the reasons for the modern creation (and segregation) of academic disciplines was to be able to construct the scholarly infrastructure and peer review process to regulate publically accepted knowledge in a field of study to enhance the quality (or power) of scholarly influence (Aldrich, 2014). Moran (2002) notes "From the beginning, the term 'discipline' was caught up in questions about the relationship between knowledge and power" (p. 2). Foucault (1979) brought a hermeneutic of suspicion in his tracing of the historical connections between disciplines broadly conceived, hierarchy, and social power and control. He explained, "Disciplines characterize, classify, specialize; they distribute along a scale, around a norm, hierarchize individuals in relation to one another and, if necessary, disqualify and invalidate" (p. 223). Though Foucault is addressing his skepticism toward the concept of disciplines more broadly than the academic, we find his overall point compelling as it relates to the academy: the power and control operations of disciplines do tend to be employed in hierarchical ways to regulate disciplinary norms. This can be seen in graduate education processes (e.g., admission, dissertations, and doctoral exams), the review process for publication, the ordination and licensing processes for clergy and therapists, and the tenure and promotion process at universities. The latter process usually involves soliciting letters from more advanced disciplinary experts to evaluate and rank candidates in direct comparison to others in the field already promoted. Our purpose here is not to suggest this hierarchical function of disciplines is inherently problematic. Rather, we propose that the move toward interdisciplinarity may be challenging, in part, because it requires different forms of relationality than the hierarchical ones that are normally used to regulate disciplines.

Gardner (2013) notes this kind of hierarchy in her insightful qualitative study interviewing twenty-five researchers involved in the interdisciplinary field of sustainability science. Paradigmatic differences in ontological and epistemological assumptions loom large in the reports of these researchers, particularly paradigm differences between "hard and soft" scientists (e.g., mathematics versus social psychology). Power and status also emerge as prominent issues, and numerous participants suggested humility and openness are needed for interdisciplinary collaboration. One participant offered the contrast between disciplinary and interdisciplinary dynamics, explaining:

> You have to have a high degree of humility. You have to be able to step back and say my way is not the only way or even the most important or even the best or even a good way of thinking about this, which is like the paradigmatic opposite of how we are trained as academics. We are trained to be big heads.
>
> *(p. 249)*

We could offer many practical illustrations of these dynamics of anxiety, power, and control and the need for humility in interdisciplinary contexts. For example,

I (Steve) was giving an invited presentation about empirical research on spirituality and religion in psychotherapy to psychological researchers in a secular venue when one of them voiced the perspective that spirituality and religion were outside the purview of scientific methods and thus psychological research could not investigate those topics. When other psychologists in the room noted that human experiences of spirituality and religion could be tracked just as easily as political views, feelings of depression or self-esteem, or a myriad of other variables studied empirically, the first psychologist became exasperated and exclaimed, "Then why even do science if it tells you the same information as religion?" This question and corresponding emotional valence suggest that the researcher may have felt threatened by what he perceived to be a loss of disciplinary distinctiveness and power. Perhaps he had felt more comfortable with a firmly boundaried control stance where psychology and religion could not influence one another (see our discussion of the parallels view in Chapter 2).

As I (Jeannine) teach a master's level seminar focused on integration, I often see students struggling with the place of social-scientific knowledge in their developing reflections on case dilemmas. Anxiety often attends questions raised of whether or how they should incorporate areas of learning outside of Bible and theology, even though they have taken seminary courses on leadership and spiritual and personal formation, which have drawn upon the social sciences. In this course, I attempt both to clarify what social science is and its predominant focus on description (over prescription) and also to demonstrate that they will inevitably bring what we might call a "lay social science" to their case studies. The question is not whether they'll make generalizations about human behavior (psychology) and human systems and institutions (sociology); instead, the issue is whether they will draw from research-based studies for these observations and generalizations or whether they will default to their own anecdotal testimony or to popular resources that assert the way things are without providing accompanying research support.

Hierarchy Expectations: From Social to Interdisciplinary

Our final affirmation related to relational integration has to do with the hierarchical privileging of disciplines in interdisciplinary relations that has been a point of debate, particularly among Evangelicals considering psychology and theology (see Chapter 2). Is theology "queen of the sciences," or does psychology deserve pride of place in interdisciplinary discussion? As we consider this important question, our affirmation is that *expectations about social hierarchy represent an important influence on models of interdisciplinary relationality or preferred disciplinary configurations.*

Prior empirical research has shown individuals differ in their expectations and preferences for interpersonal hierarchy (Mast, 2005); and preferences for hierarchical versus egalitarian (non-hierarchical) approaches to social relations represent a robust area of research on vertical and horizontal cultural orientations (Triandis,

2009). We have found an intriguing analogy between egalitarian and hierarchical approaches to gender and models of interdisciplinary relations, and especially various relational dynamics for integration. This analogy provides a particularly helpful heuristic, since approaches to gender are hotly debated in the same evangelical contexts that have given rise to questions about the integration of psychology and theology. Of course, genderqueer, transgender, and numerous other perspectives increasingly call into question gender binaries and diversify the options within gender orientations. For the sake of critical analogy here, we will focus on the contrast between egalitarian and complementarian views of gender which highlight social and relational assumptions about hierarchy, power, and control.

Egalitarian and complementarian views on gender represent a diverse array of perspectives, however a key difference involves ideals about the relational dynamics of power and authority. Complementarian (the term typically self-selected over the term "hierarchical") views tend to emphasize an understanding of male headship whereby men are to have more authority (power) in marriage, family life, and in the church than are women. As Ware (2007) explains: "Male and female were created by God as equal in dignity, value, essence and human nature, but also distinct in role whereby the male was given the responsibility of loving authority over the female, and the female was to offer willing, glad-hearted and submissive assistance to the man." He goes on to speak of "God's originally created and good hierarchical design." Egalitarian views tend to emphasize an ideal of women and men as equally authoritative dialogue partners in marriage, family life, and the church. Both genders can exercise leadership in these arenas based on gifting, with mutual submission characterizing the biblical model for such leadership.

These views on gender relations offer a striking parallel to preferred relational dynamics between theologians and psychologists. The parallel can be helpfully illuminated by considering some of the practical hopes and concerns behind these perspectives. Gender complementarians tend to be concerned about a lack of hierarchy in relational systems because of the ambiguity in decision-making that might result from a horizontal authority structure between men and women. In privileging male authority, gender complementarians often emphasize men having a "servant leadership" role they believe benefits rather than disadvantages women and the relationship between the sexes. These types of gender hierarchy involve a preferred imbalance of power and control in which men have greater power and control in relation to women.

In contrast, gender egalitarians (like the two of us) tend to believe that women and men can work cooperatively within an equal partnership without the necessity of privileging the authority of one gender. Gender egalitarians also express concern that power differentials are far from universally beneficial to those with lesser power and can, in fact, be oppressive. From an egalitarian perspective, the key barrier to healthy gender relations is not confusion about the lack of hierarchy or strict measures of control (i.e., limiting the influence of the other) but a lack of *differentiation of self*, which makes the anxiety of difference and intimacy too threatening to tolerate constructive and, at times, conflictual dialogue (Sandage, Jensen, & Jass, 2008). Adult relationships are challenging, in part, because in the absence of strict hierarchies there will often be higher levels of anxiety about power and control unless there are also higher levels of differentiation. Yet working through differences and conflict without having to default to preset hierarchies can be transformative, encouraging the development of mutual respect, courageous use of voice, intellectual flexibility, empathy, and humility.

We trust that the reader is already noting the potential connections between views of social hierarchy to perspectives on interdisciplinary relations. In circles where theology is perceived as the foundational discipline, there will be a tendency to privilege the voice of theologians and to express concern that theology maintains an upper hand in the discourse. In circles where psychology is the dominant discipline, e.g., perceived as the more rigorous science as in the psychology of religion school (see Chapter 2), the privilege and control issues will be reversed. One practical consequence of a hierarchical relationship is an avoidance of the potential constructive conflict that arises from a more open and cooperative relational stance. Our own experiences in team teaching integration courses and relating with other scholars and professionals in interdisciplinary settings have revealed that some people feel a strong preference for ordering a hierarchy of disciplines *prior* to bringing disciplinary perspectives into interaction. For example, someone might ask, "If there is a conflict between psychology and theology, which one wins?" We do not have related survey data, but it is interesting to note our experience that, if asked for a specific example of that type of conflict, the person is rarely able to give one. We are not suggesting these conflicts do not exist; we do wonder, however, if the chronic anxiety about an anticipated conflict may be so great that actual interdisciplinary exploration is hindered.

A more egalitarian perspective may do less to mitigate initial anxieties in interdisciplinary dialogue. In fact, a relational approach to integration between psychologists and theologians requires internalized growth in spiritual formation and Spirit-led constraints against one disciplinarian seeking hegemony over another (for further discussion of these issues, see Porter, 2010a, 2010b; Sandage & Brown, 2010). Yet a more equitable relationship offers transformative potential for both those engaged in the dialogue and for the outcomes of such collaboration, especially as theologians and psychologists pursue a differentiated posture toward each other and each other's discipline. This kind of conversation will require humility and continuing dialogue on differing ways of relating psychology and theology with an emphasis on listening carefully to those advocating positions other than one's own (Johnson, 2012). Johnson's point about "listening to others on *their own terms* in order to gain new understandings" (p. 27; italics his) is a hallmark of a more relational approach to interdisciplinary engagement.

Some preliminary empirical support for the connection between gender and views of interdisciplinary relations comes from a study with masters-level students at Bethel Seminary, an evangelical school in St. Paul, Minnesota (for details, see Sandage, Jankowski, Crabtree, & Schweer-Collins, 2017). Students completed measures of beliefs about gender, preferences related to social hierarchy, commitments to social justice and intercultural competence, their preferred view of the relationship between psychology and theology and the Defensive Theology Scale (DTS; Beck, 2006). Defensive theology as measured by the DTS is a theological stance (a) emphasizing a sense of God's special protection and provision for oneself and (b) oriented toward existential and epistemological closure. The measure of preferred ways of relating psychology and theology asked participants to respond to the following: "Which of the following positions best represents your view of the optimal relationship between theology and psychology?" Participants selected from a list of five statements, summarized here as follows: (a) A Biblical counseling view ("The Bible is sufficient as a complete source of knowledge for all counseling with the discipline of psychology being mostly deceptive and unnecessary."), (b) A Christian Psychology view ("Psychology can have some valid insights but needs to be brought under the authoritative headship of theology in pursuit of a distinctly Christian psychology."), (c) An Integration view ("Both theology and psychology are disciplines requiring responsible interpretation and can each contribute valid insights ideally brought together through a process of integration."), (d) A Levels of Explanation view ("Theology and psychology are very different disciplines offering separate methodologies and distinctive levels of explanation of the same phenomena."), and (e) A Psychology of Religion view ("As a science, psychology offers a more accurate picture of human nature than theology and should be used to evaluate theological validity.").

Nearly all students preferred either the integration view (65.9%) or the Christian psychology view (29.3%). In comparison to those preferring the Christian psychology view, those preferring the integration view scored higher in gender egalitarianism and commitments to social justice and intercultural competence and lower in gender complementarianism, preference for social hierarchy, and defensive theology. These results offer initial empirical evidence in a sample of emerging Christian leaders that there tends to be correspondence in worldview perspectives between views on social hierarchy and epistemological hierarchy or ordering of theology and psychology as disciplines. The higher levels of defensive theology among those also privileging theology over psychology suggest those who strongly believe that God protects them more than other people and that God controls and directs all the details of their lives may see less use for psychological perspectives than do those who have stronger views of (a) vulnerability to suffering among all people (i.e., "the rain falls on the just and the unjust;" Matt 5:45) and (b) human freedom or agency in life. Defensive theology has been associated with in-group bias among Christian undergraduate students (Beck, 2006), so these findings raise numerous questions about possible connections between preferred relational configurations of psychology and theology and a suite of diversity- and justice-related attitudes.

A Model for Relational Integration Between Disciplines

In the final section of this chapter, we describe our own model of relational integration built upon differentiated relationality and arising out of the four affirmations we have explored that prioritize relational capacities for navigating conflict, anxiety, and power dynamics in the interdisciplinary process.

"Third Space" and Mutual Recognition (Benjamin)

We draw a key construct for conceptualizing relational integration from the work of Jessica Benjamin (1998, 1999, 2004, 2006, 2018). Benjamin (1999) introduces the concept of a *third space* to account for the intersubjective "location" between the subjectivities of interacting persons (e.g., client and therapist). She explains:

> The third allows us to mediate between two differing points of view; a third line opens up a space where two points offer only a line back and forth between two poles. The intersubjective level aims to transform differences from the register of power, in which one partner asserts his or her meaning, will, need over the other . . . Here I agree with Lacan (1988) that the chief commitment of psychoanalysis is to release the psychic hold of the power struggle and to establish the commitment to recognition, the dialogic process itself.
>
> *(p. 204)*

We consider this conceptual *third space* to offer significant possibilities for interdisciplinary relational integration because it illuminates an often-neglected area for analysis and reflection—the relationship itself with its various dynamics and patterns. If we "envision the conversation itself as a third reality to be respected in its own right" (Sandage and Brown, 2015, p. 176), we will be more likely to be attentive to issues of process and more able to address the anxieties, conflict, and power dynamics that are a part of that 'third space.' To get a better feel for this construct, we will review Benjamin's use of it across her work.

Benjamin (1988) considers complementarity of power dynamics in traditional gender relations and other dominant-submissive relational pairings. Benjamin describes oppressive sides of gender complementarity which restrict the freedom of both genders. In Hegelian fashion, she argues master-slave power dynamics fail to achieve intersubjective recognition, in part, because these hierarchical forms of relational "twoness" lack a shared third dimension of understanding to which both parties have access. Thus, these types of hierarchical relations often collapse into a kind of "doer and a done to" (perpetrator, victim). Such relations are one-directional in terms of influence and "we can feel only the choice between control or submission" (Benjamin, 2006, p. 122).

In contrast, Benjamin views *mutual recognition* as a relational stance that represents a healthy alternative to discounting another person or seeking omnipotence over them. Benjamin (2004) defines mutual recognition as the intersubjective capacity to experience others as equal subjects and agents with differing perspectives, in conjunction with the reciprocal experience of the other's acknowledgement of oneself. Building upon relational theories of human development, Benjamin suggests mutual recognition can be challenging, since another person's differing subjectivity can confront one's own perspective with the anxiety-provoking reality of difference. She views human nature as involving a struggle with desires for narcissistic omnipotence (an interesting point of connection to many theologies of sin). The quest for omnipotence among dominant groups serves to perpetuate relational complementarities of master/slave or subject/object. In contrast, mutual recognition is grounded in more egalitarian and differentiated forms of relational reciprocity between two subjects.

Mutual recognition shapes a collaborative, bi-directional relationship (a "two-way street," Benjamin, 2006, p. 116) and dialogic process, which allows a shared third dimension to emerge, sustained by the actual differences between subjectivities. Benjamin (2004) describes this *thirdness* as correlated with highly differentiated internal mental space; yet the shared third must actually influence the relational interactions rather than remain an abstract ideal. Benjamin (1999) also likens the third dimension to music that two dance partners follow in patterned movements. "As in musical improvisation, there may not be one right way to go, but there are definitely wrong notes that can be anticipated or, more often, heard as soon as they are sounded" (p. 206).

Turning to the integration of theology and psychology, we would note that Hoffman (2011) utilizes Benjamin's notion of mutual recognition in seeking to integrate two traditions that have often been presented as rivals—psychoanalysis and Christian theology. The post-Cartesian, relational turn in psychoanalysis can facilitate an integration of relational psychology and theology through a realistic awareness of intersubjective conflict combined with the hope of mutual recognition. In this vein, we draw on Benjamin's constructs of a third space and mutual recognition for our own relational integration model. In our model, integration develops through intersubjective dialogue that periodically requires repair following destabilizing conflicts. By attending to the third space in which those conflicts and resulting anxieties "reside," patterns for addressing relational process emerge and an uncritical, unilateral privileging of one discipline over another can be avoided.

Triangulation

Attending to the relational third space also minimizes movement toward unhealthy triangulation to address relational conflict and anxieties. Family systems theorist

Murray Bowen developed the concept of triangles as "the basic molecule of an emotional system," such as a family, and considered triangles "the smallest stable relationship unit" (Kerr & Bowen, 1988, p. 134). Bowen's idea was that a relational dyad can often be destabilized due to the anxiety of differences, conflicts, abandonments, losses, and others sources of relational insecurity and threat. In Bowen theory, triangulation involves bringing in a third party to alleviate this relational anxiety. "When anxiety increases, a third person becomes involved in the tension of the twosome, creating a triangle" (p. 135).

Triangulation is actually a ubiquitous phenomenon in relational systems. And like anxiety, power, and control, triangulation is neither inherently good nor bad. Relational triangles can be helpful, even life-saving in certain situations. A triangulated third party might bring stability to a relational dyad in conflict, such as when an effective pastoral counselor or couple therapist meets with a distressed couple. However, a triangulated party can also contribute to the destabilization of a dyad, such as when a married person has an affair that gets revealed and leads to divorce. Importantly, when triangulated parties are driven by anxiety and an inflexible need to rescue, the relational patterns may limit the opportunities of the two initial parties to develop capacities for working through differences or resolving conflicts. For example, I (Steve) worked in therapy with a young heterosexual couple with the wife often turning to her father, a pastor they both idealized, whenever they had a significant conflict or a difficult decision to make. His calm and warm presence helped stabilize them, and they tried to follow the advice he gave. Over time, it became evident to the son-in-law that the pastor's advice tended to favor his daughter, so the source of triangulation introduced a power imbalance in the couple's relationship. Eventually, the couple needed to de-triangle and make their decisions as a collaborative dyad in order to develop their marriage.

We suggest that the concept of triangulation can illuminate our discussion of a model of relational integration between psychology and theology that takes seriously the need for mutual recognition and attention to the third space created by the relationship. One consequence of dyadic approaches to disciplinary integration is the ease with which unhealthy triangulation becomes a way of dealing with the inherent anxiety of the relationship. In other words, if we ignore the relational space between integrators (that *third space*), we can easily bring in a *third party* to mitigate our anxiety and 'solve the problem' of relational conflict. In interdisciplinary work, this "third party" may not be a person but an abstract category that allows for a shift in power between the disciplines (and the disciplinarians) in conversation. This coheres with a common feature of unhealthy triangulation, in which one or both parties are filled with anxiety over what feels like a zero-sum game. The unconscious assumption is that one person will win and one person will lose, so competition emerges to pull the triangulated source over to one's own side.

We can see epistemological versions of such triangulation in interdisciplinary discussions about psychology and theology. For example, framing the discussion as determining the relations between "Psychology & Christianity" (title of five views book; Johnson, 2010) rather than psychology and theology or psychology and biblical studies sets up a problematic triangulation since "Christianity" is neither a discipline nor a methodology. The import is to use a weighty category—as Christianity is for the intended audience of the book—to triangulate psychology and theology (the two disciplinary entities) in their perceived points of tension. By doing so, theology—in its alignment with Christianity—gains ascendency as the more powerful discipline in the conversation. Yet theology also loses its complexity, as the enmeshment of Christianity and theology implies a thin and monolithic version of the latter. We could also look at the example of practical theology, a field which tends to strongly value interdisciplinary work. Yet we can perceive a certain kind of triangulation in the name of the discipline itself. Practical *theology* points to an emphasis and potentially a greater allegiance to theological methodologies, with other disciplines like psychology engaged in secondary ways that tend to marginalize other disciplines. This triangulation of sorts, not surprisingly, creates intense debates in practical theology guilds.

Another example arises in some conservative Christian contexts, where theology as the study of God and God's word is privileged over and sometimes against psychology. An enmeshment between theology and God/Scripture gives epistemological privilege to theology and often sidelines psychology as a more "subjective" (human) enterprise. The order of privilege is reversed in some progressive Christian contexts or secular perspectives, in which psychology is assumed to hold greater validity because of its status as a science, whereas theology is assumed to be more or even purely subjective. In either of these cases, there is a "third" abstract dimension that is implicitly triangulated, such as truth, authority, reality, progress, or relevance. We say "implicitly" triangulated because the use of the third entity is often unacknowledged or taken for granted. And these unacknowledged assumptions often obscure the reality that theology and psychology are both human and hermeneutical disciplines and so individuals will need to grapple with their own subjectivities, assumptions, and interpretive strategies when engaging either discipline. And even though the triangulation involves epistemologies and abstract ideas, we can see in the opening vignette that there are relational dynamics and relational consequences in play.

Integration as Differentiated Relationality

We conclude by bringing together the various threads of this chapter into a summary of our model for relational integration. As we noted at the beginning of the chapter, we propose that *differentiated relationality is the ontological foundation necessary for mutual recognition in optimal relational integration.* In this frame, integration will prioritize relational connections of mutual recognition between differentiated integrators. This differentiation-based relational integration model highlights a dialectical balance for interdisciplinary work between (a) maintaining personal identity and disciplinary integrity and (b) fostering authentic relationship, dialogue, and mutual influence across disciplinary boundaries. As we have suggested elsewhere:

> Differentiated relationality allows for integration to happen in ways that honor . . . disciplinary parameters and distinctives, without requiring either a collapse of real differences between disciplines or withdrawal from the integrative conversation via authoritarian claims by one or another of the disciplines at the table.
>
> *(Sandage & Brown, 2015, pp. 170–71)*

Relational dynamics are constitutive rather than secondary in our model, which is why we move relationality to the foreground in our model and suggest that the relationship itself be understood as a "third space" between integrators. As we have proposed in this chapter's four affirmations, interdisciplinary integration arising from differentiated relationality is able to handle an array of relational challenges including the conflict, anxiety, and power dynamics that inevitably attend integrative efforts.

Although our model is fairly unique in the integration literature on psychology and theology, differentiation has been found to be a helpful direction in other integrative areas. For example, MacMynowski (2007) made *differentiation* the first stage in a three-stage process for interdisciplinary research in environmental science utilizing biophysical and social science disciplines. She describes differentiation as a stage of "specifying differences in approaches to knowledge, methods, research motivations, and the relationship between research and researcher" (p. 20). This differentiation stage addresses the need to communicate among researchers of differing disciplines about standards of reliability and validity, the nature of theory, and metaphors that signify epistemological assumptions, particularly at points of conflict or confusion. MacMynowski follows differentiation with stages of clarifying the purposes of research and then intellectual synthesis, and she likens the whole iterative process to the hermeneutical circle (citing Taylor, 1985). In her conclusion, she connects her differentiation-based approach to personal and relational dynamics, noting that the "social factors of trust, cooperation, patience, and openness are as key to interdisciplinary success as the ideas themselves" (p. 20).

The theoretical grounding for our model is a *relational ontology* in contrast to substance-dualist ontologies, and this means that "relations between entities are ontologically more fundamental than the entities themselves" (Wildman, 2010, p. 55; also, see Shults, 2003). However, a differentiated relational ontology indicates that both relations and entities are real, so we can still speak of differentiated entities in relation. Ultimate reality is not a singular thing (as implied in some versions of monism) and differences or differentiated entities do exist within a relational matrix, but relations are basic to *being* (both divine being and human being or personhood). This means relations are a central dynamic in understanding theology, psychology, and the connections between the two which exist prior to the formulation of disciplines.

In line with this relational ontological basis for our model, Sites and colleagues (2009) have suggested a neglected consideration in literature on the integration of psychology and theology has been the personal and spiritual "ontological foundations" of integrators (p. 28). This emerged as a key theme in their phenomenological study of student-nominated faculty at an evangelical liberal arts college whom students considered helpful for their own integration of faith and learning. They noted that all faculty members interviewed "described their faith in ontological terms, such as the essence of their being, inseparable in every way from every aspect of their life and work, the center of everything they do" (p. 32). This theme of ontological foundations is consistent with our desire to root our understanding of relational integration deeper than abstract academic ideas; and it fits with our emphases on relational and communal dynamics in spiritual formation, human development, and effective praxis.

As we turn to flesh out our model in the chapters ahead, we will pick up some central definitional categories for relational integration. In Chapters 4, 5, 6, and 7, we will propose and explore the themes of relational integration as *embodied*, as *hermeneutical*, as *developmental*, and as *intercultural*. We have, at numerous points, been circling around these themes in the present chapter, as they are inherent to our model of relational integration as differentiated relationality. To sum up, differentiated relationality allows for deep interaction between disciplines, including the integration of psychology and theology. This differentiated relationality can produce integrative conversations that prioritize the collaborative nature of integration without collapsing meaningful differences between persons, disciplines, and contexts. This relationality can foster the abilities of the scholars involved to remain personally and disciplinarily differentiated from one another while in productive conversation.

Bibliography

Aldrich, J. H. (2014). *Interdisciplinarity: Its role in a discipline-based academy.* Oxford: Oxford University Press.

American Psychiatric Association. (2013). *Diagnostic and statistical manual of mental disorders* (5th ed.). Arlington, VA: American Psychiatric Publishing.

Anderson, E. (2010). *The imperative of integration.* Princeton, NJ: Princeton University Press.

Beck, R. (2006). Defensive versus existential religion: Is religious defensiveness predictive of worldview defense? *Journal of Psychology and Theology, 34*(2), 143–153.

Benjamin, J. (1988). *The bonds of love: Psychoanalysis, feminism, and the problem of domination.* New York, NY: Pantheon Books.

Benjamin, J. (1998). *Shadow of the other: Intersubjectivity and gender in psychoanalysis.* New York, NY: Routledge.

Benjamin, J. (1999). Afterword to recognition and destruction. In S. Mitchell & L. Aron (Eds.), *Relational psychoanalysis: Emergence of a tradition* (pp. 201-210). Hillsdale, NJ: The Analytic Press.

Benjamin, J. (2004). Beyond doer and done to: An intersubjective view of thirdness. *The Psychoanalytic Quarterly, 73*, 5–46. doi:10.1002/j.2167–4086.2004.tb00151.x

Benjamin, J. (2006). Two-way streets: Recognition of difference and the intersubjective third. *Differences, 17*, 116–146.

Benjamin, J. (2018). *Beyond doer and done to: Recognition theory, intersubjectivity and the Third.* New York, NY: Routledge.

Bennett, M. J. (2004). Becoming interculturally competent. In J. Wurzel (Ed.), *Toward multiculturalism: A reader in multicultural education* (2nd ed., pp. 62–77). Newton, MA: Intercultural Resource Corporation.

Brown, J. K., Dahl, C. M., & Corbin Reuschling, W. (2011). *Becoming whole and holy: An integrative conversation about Christian formation.* Grand Rapids, MI: Brazos.

Brueggemann, W. (2007). Dialogic thickness in a monologic culture. *Theology Today, 64*, 322–339.

Callard, F., & Fitzgerald, D. (2015). Social science and neuroscience beyond interdisciplinarity: Experimental entanglements. *Theory, Culture & Society, 32*(1), 3–32.

Cashin, S. (2004). *The failures of integration: How race and class are undermining the American dream.* New York, NY: Public Affairs.

Dovidio, J. F., Gaertner, S. L., & Kawakami, K. (2003). Intergroup contact: The past, present, and the future. *Group Processes & Intergroup Relations, 6*(1), 5–21.

Foucault, M. (1979). *Discipline and punish: The birth of the prison* (A. Sheridan, Trans.). Harmondsworth: Penguin.

Gardner, S. (2013). Paradigmatic differences, power, and status: A qualitative investigation of faculty in one interdisciplinary research collaboration on sustainability science. *Sustainability Science, 8*(2), 241–252. doi:10.1007/s11625-012-0182-4

Hoffman, M. T. (2011). *Toward mutual recognition: Relational psychoanalysis and the Christian narrative.* New York, NY: Routledge.

Jankowski, P. J., Sandage, S. J., & Hill, P. C. (2013). Differentiation-based models of forgivingness, mental health and social justice commitment: Mediator effects for differentiation of self and humility. *The Journal of Positive Psychology, 8*(5), 412–424.

Johnson, E. L. (Ed.). (2010). *Psychology & Christianity: Five views* (2nd ed.). Downers Grove, IL: InterVarsity Press.

Johnson, E. L. (2012). Let's talk: Embeddedness, majority-minority relations, principled pluralism, and the importance of dialogue. *Journal of Psychology and Theology, 40*(1), 26–31.

Kegan, R. (1994). *In over our heads: The mental demands of modern life.* Cambridge, MA: Harvard University Press.

Kegan, R., & Lahey, L. L. (2009). *Immunity to change: How to overcome it and unlock the potential in yourself and your organization.* Boston, MA: Harvard Business Press.

Kerr, M. E., & Bowen, M. (1988). *Family evaluation: The role of the family as an emotional unit that governs individual behavior and development.* New York, NY: W.W. Norton & Company, Inc.

King, M. L., Jr. (1986a). The ethical demands for integration. In J. M. Washington (Ed.), *A testament of hope: The essential writings and speeches of Martin Luther King, Jr.* (pp. 117–125). New York, NY: HarperOne. (Original work published 1963)

King, M. L., Jr. (1986b). A testament of hope. In *A testament of hope: The essential writings and speeches of Martin Luther King, Jr.* (J. M. Washington, Ed.) (pp. 313–330). New York: HarperOne. (Original work published 1968).

Lacan, J. (1988). *The seminars of Jacques Lacan, Book I* (J. A. Miller, Ed., J. Forrester, Trans.). New York, NY: Norton Press.

MacIntyre, A. (1990). *Three rival versions of moral enquiry: Encyclopaedia, genealogy, and tradition.* Notre Dame, IN: University of Notre Dame Press.

MacMynowski, D. P. (2007). Pausing at the brink of interdisciplinarity: Power and knowledge at the meeting of social and biophysical science. *Ecology & Society, 12*(1), 1–14.

Maddock, J. W., & Larson, N. R. (2004). The ecological approach to incestuous families. In D. R. Catherall (Ed.), *Handbook of stress, trauma, and the family* (pp. 367–392). New York, NY: Brunner-Routledge.

Majerus, B., & Sandage, S. J. (2010). Differentiation of self and Christian spiritual maturity: Social science and theological integration. *Journal of Psychology and Theology, 38,* 41–51.

Mast, M. (2005). Interpersonal hierarchy expectation: Introduction of a new construct. *Journal of Personality Assessment, 84,* 287–295. doi:10.1207/s15327752jpa8403_08

Mitchell, S. A. (1988). *Relational concepts in psychoanalysis: An integration.* Cambridge, MA: Harvard University Press.

Moran, J. (2002). *Interdisciplinarity: The new critical idiom.* New York, NY: Routledge.

Myers, D. G. (2010). A levels-of-explanation view. In E. L. Johnson (Ed.), *Psychology & Christianity: Five views* (pp. 49–78). Downers Grove, IL: InterVarsity Press.

Patterson, O. (1998). *The ordeal of integration: Progress and Resentment in America's "racial" crisis.* New York, NY: Basic Civitas.

Peters, T. (1994). *Sin: Radical evil in soul and society.* Grand Rapids, MI: Eerdmans Publishing Company.

Porter, S. L. (2010a). Theology as queen and psychology as handmaid: The authority of theology in integrative endeavors. *Journal of Psychology and Christianity, 29,* 3–14.

Porter, S. L. (2010b). A reply to respondents of "Theology as queen and psychology as handmaid." *Journal of Psychology and Christianity, 29,* 33–40.

Ricoeur, P. (1970). *Freud and philosophy: An essay on interpretation* (D. Savage, Trans.). New Haven and London: Yale University Press.

Sandage, S. J., & Brown, J. K. (2010). Monarchy or democracy in relation integration? A reply to Porter. *Journal of Psychology and Christianity, 29*(1), 20.

Sandage, S. J., & Brown, J. K. (2015). Relational integration, part 1: Differentiated relationality between psychology and theology. *Journal of Psychology and Theology, 43,* 165–178.

Sandage, S. J., Cook, K. V., Hill, P. C., Strawn, B. D., & Reimer, K. S. (2008). Hermeneutics and psychology: A review and dialectical model. *Review of General Psychology, 12,* 344–364.

Sandage, S. J., & Jankowski, P. J. (2013). Spirituality, social justice, and intercultural competence: Mediator effects for differentiation of self. *International Journal for Intercultural Relations, 37,* 366–374.

Sandage, S. J., Jankowski, P. J., Crabtree, S. A., & Schweer-Collins, M. L. (2017). Calvinism, gender ideology, and relational spirituality: An empirical investigation of worldview differences. *Journal of Psychology & Theology, 45*(1).

Sandage, S. J., Jensen, M. L., & Jass, D. (2008). Relational spirituality and transformation: Risking intimacy and alterity. *Journal of Spiritual Formation and Soul Care, 1*(2), 182–206.

Schnarch, D. M. (2009). *Intimacy and desire: Awaken the passion in your relationship.* New York, NY: Beaufort Books.

Shults, F. L. (2003). *Reforming theological anthropology: After the philosophical turn.* Cambridge, MA: William B. Eerdmans Publishing Company.

Shults, F. L., & Sandage, S. J. (2006). *Transforming spirituality: Integrating theology and psychology.* Grand Rapids, MI: Baker Academic.

Sites, E. C., Garzon, F. L., Milacci, F. A., & Boothe, B. (2009). A phenomenology of the integration of faith and learning. *Journal of Psychology and Theology, 37*(1), 28–38.

Skowron, E. A., & Dendy, A. K. (2004). Differentiation of self and attachment in adulthood: Relational correlates of effortful control. *Contemporary Family Therapy: An International Journal, 26,* 337–357.

Taylor, C. (1985). Self-interpreting animals. In *Philosophical papers: Vol 1. Human agency and language* (pp. 45–76). Cambridge, UK: Cambridge University Press.

Tillich, P. (1952). *The courage to be.* New Haven, CT: Yale University Press.

Triandis, H. C. (2009). Ecological determinants of cultural variation. In R. S. Wyer, C. Chiu, Y. Hong, R. S. Wyer, C. Chiu, & Y. Hong (Eds.), *Understanding culture: Theory, research, and application* (pp. 189–210). New York, NY: Psychology Press.

Volf, M. (1996). *Exclusion & embrace: A theological exploration of identity, otherness, and reconciliation.* Nashville, TN: Abingdon.

Ware, B. (2007). *Summaries of the egalitarian and complementarian positions.* Retrieved August 28, 2017, from http://cbmw.org/uncategorized/summaries-of-the-egalitarian-and-complementarian-positions/.

Wildman, W. J. (2010). An introduction to relational ontology. In J. Polkinghorne & J. Zizioulas (Eds.), *The Trinity and an entangled world: Relationality in physical science and theology* (pp. 55–73). Grand Rapids, MI: Eerdmans.

Worthington Jr, E. L., & Sandage, S. J. (2016). *Forgiveness and spirituality in psychotherapy: A relational approach.* Washington, DC: American Psychological Association.

4

RELATIONAL INTEGRATION AS EMBODIED

A Case of Dis-Integration

Mee (age 32; Hmong-American) and Dan (age 34; Irish-American) are a couple in the midst of a marital crisis. They met through Christian friends and dated for a couple of years before marrying six years earlier. Mee had a daughter (age 10) from a previous marriage, and they have a son (age 5) together. Mee recently discovered Dan had been looking at pornography online when she borrowed his laptop. This had also happened two years before and Dan had vowed to not use pornography ever again, as Mee considered it immoral, disgusting, and dehumanizing of women. She confronted Dan and he tried to deny it briefly but eventually admitted he had fallen back into it in recent months. He apologized for hurting Mee and for compromising his own Christian values. Mee was initially shocked as she had trusted his earlier resolution to quit. But she also knew she and Dan had been drifting apart for some time and rarely had sex anymore. She was angry with Dan, but she was also battling disturbing internal questions— like "How did I miss the signs of this?" "What else has he been doing?" "Who is he, really?" and "How could God let this happen?"

Mee was so upset she considered asking Dan to move out for awhile, but they could not really afford separate rents and had a busy family life to try to maintain. She felt the need to try to see if they could work things out. Several days passed with Dan working hard to ingratiate himself to her, and Mee could feel herself wanting to try to forget about the problems and the disturbing images returning to her mind from what she saw online and simply try to move forward. But another part of her knew that things had not been good between them emotionally or sexually for a long time. She was not happy with their marriage and had raised counseling with Dan before, but he had not been motivated and so they never pursued it. She awoke in the middle of the night from a fearful dream. She couldn't remember the dream very well but knew they needed some kind of help as a couple and could not stay on the same track they had been on.

They were active in a large evangelical church where they met, which had been a departure from the religious backgrounds of both (Animistic for her; Catholic for him). They decided to reach out to Luis, the young Family Care Pastor who had joined the church staff the previous year after finishing seminary. Luis is a warm and caring pastor who believes strongly in the power of community to offer healing and support, and he has helped develop a marriage ministry at the church that offers large couple enrichment events, small groups, and mentors for young couples. He met with Mee and Dan, prayed for them, and told them he wants them to get involved in each of these components of the marriage ministry. He directs them to meet with Mary and Hal (ages 62 and 63; both Swedish-American), an energetic couple who have been active in marriage mentoring for a long time. Luis also explains to Dan that he wants him to meet with his supervisor, Pastor Randy (age 54; Euro-Am blend), who leads a support group at the church for men battling sexual addiction. Dan initially bristles internally and is not convinced the label "sex addict" applies to him, but he is trying to rebuild trust with Mee and agrees to go along with Luis' suggestions.

After the meeting, Luis feels a bit unsettled and walks down the hall to Randy's office, tells him about Mee and Dan, and then confesses, "Randy . . . this is one of those couples where I wonder if they need a professional therapist. They seem to have been struggling for a long time and . . ." "Nah," Randy interrupts (with an irritated tone), "A therapist would just blame it all on 'family of origin' problems and take a bunch of their money. Dan is in a spiritual battle against the Evil One and our group can help him fight against porn through accountability and prayer and help him work out his repentance with Mee." Luis nods, yielding to Randy's confidence.

Mee and Dan left the meeting with Luis feeling encouraged by the structure provided and the concrete steps they could take. But within hours Mee found herself thinking about her cousin who battled marital problems and said they were helped by working with a professional couple therapist. She decided to get the therapist's name (Arlenis; age 43; Caribbean) and within a week they were sitting in her clinical office. The next eight sessions with Arlenis felt like a roller coaster to both Mee and Dan, sometimes gaining moments of reassurance and insight while other sessions were filled with anger, hurt, and shame. Mee started session nine by saying, "I am still angry at Dan and feel like I can't trust him. But I have also been wondering if I am missing something . . . or if God wants me to learn something from this whole mess." Arlenis (sounding slightly impatient) responded, "Mee, this sounds like more of the pattern we discussed last time, where you tend to take a tremendous burden of responsibility onto yourself whenever problems arise. And it seems this leads you straight toward depression. In fact, I think you both end up depressed when this happens."

As we initially consider this case, we are struck that Luis, Randy, and Arlenis are each well intentioned and offer potentially constructive but partial interventions. Mee and Dan would also deserve credit for being active in seeking healing and growth from multiple sources. Yet we have also observed that people like Mee and Dan can begin to feel confused and pulled in different directions, experiencing the inputs they receive from the various helpers in their lives as fairly dis-integrated. The plurality of voices in this case study address different dimensions of their struggles, but it is up to Mee and Dan to do the integration on their own. This can be challenging to do under the best of circumstances but may seem nearly impossible in the throes of a marital crisis. In this chapter, we return to this case at a number of points to explore how the relational template we are introducing, and especially the concept of integration as embodied, could provide experiences of deeper integration for Mee and Dan, as well as for those who are seeking to support them.

In this chapter, we explore the first of four key themes in our model of relational integration: *embodiment*. We begin by problematizing the modern preference for abstraction—for what we might describe as disembodied cognition, a preference already noted in chapter two. Then we discuss theological and psychological resources for understanding the embodied reality of human existence and suggest embodiment serves as an integrative theme rather than being limited to a discrete level of analysis. Bringing these lines of study together, we then offer embodied ways for understanding relational integration between psychology and theology, including an understanding of the pursuit of human knowledge as a thoroughly embodied endeavor. Finally, we suggest the viability of a natural theology for supporting and amplifying the notion of embodiment in interdisciplinary integration.

Problematizing the Preference for Abstraction

Modernism in Western contexts has exhibited a marked preference for abstraction over particularity. As Reed (2002, p. 168) notes, "'Abstraction' occurs when we select out features or patterns that individual things have in common. This process pays attention to the generic and leaves behind, or even discards, the particular." Now a certain amount of abstraction—a move toward generalization—is necessary for second-order reflection and critical analysis; generalizing serves a certain heuristic purpose (Reno, 2004, p. 400). Yet modernism and the modern academy in particular have preferred what Mount Shoop refers to as "disembodied habits of thinking" (Mount Shoop, 2011, p. 238) over more embodied conceptualities. The phenomenological philosopher Merleu-Ponty, who is credited with the language of embodiment, was interested in developing an embodied epistemology; he focused the language of embodiment on the subjective and bodily aspects of perception and knowing (Morse & Mitcham, 1998). In this chapter on *relational integration as embodied*, we propose that the movement toward abstraction and the denial of embodied subjectivity significantly inhibit interdisciplinary integration.

As we consider theology as a set of disciplines (including biblical studies and systematic and constructive theologies), we observe that abstraction has routinely been employed to reflect on the religious significance of work being done. This move to abstraction seems to find its roots, at least in part, in the rationalism of the seventeenth and eighteenth centuries, coming into play in biblical studies through scholars such as Reimarus (1694–1768) and Paulus (1761–1851). The point of the move toward abstraction would be to arrive at a universal truth stripped of its cultural or historical specificity. For example, in historical Jesus studies many of those impacted by rationalism attempted to extract the universal "kernel" from the culturally located "husk." In his lecture, "What is Christianity?" (1900), Harnack uses this language to distinguish what is disposable from what is abiding in the Christian faith (p. 13). He speaks of "the [difficult] task of distinguishing what is permanent from what is fleeting, what is rudimentary from what is merely historical" (p. 15). In the process of his own work in this endeavor, Harnack himself essentially excised Jesus' Jewishness and thereby revealed his own location within German anti-Semitism of his day. "Jesus Christ's teaching will at once bring us by steps which, if few, will be great, to a height where its connexion with Judaism is seen to be only a loose one, and most of the threads leading from it into 'contemporary history' become of no importance at all" (p. 17).

Harnack provides just one concrete example of a theological preference for the generic that continues to the present. Mount Shoop (2011), exploring an embodied theological practice and purpose through the lens of motherhood, writes that "[t]heological conversations need space for deep dissonance and intuitive modes of doing theology to emerge. Legitimizing and authorizing this kind of dissonance and intuition in theology places a curious demand on our Western mentalities." A more disembodied and abstract hermeneutic has resulted in a context in which abstract principles are often preferred to textual specificities. As Reno (p. 401) observes, "modern theological readers drift toward abstraction, and their exegesis inscribes an eccentric move away from the biblical text."

Western psychology has also privileged efforts to develop abstract, universal (or "etic") knowledge that can generalize across populations. As in theology, this modernistic and Eurocentric approach has increasingly drawn prophetic critique from scholars within various streams of psychology. They have called for greater attention to sociocultural contexts and history, social power and oppression, indigenous (or "emic") forms of knowledge and healing practice, and narrative and qualitative epistemologies and methods of research. These prophetic voices in psychology include scholars representing multicultural psychologies, feminist psychologies, LGBTQ psychologies, indigenous and cultural psychologies, and critical psychologies, among others. Within the field of the integration of psychology and theology, Dueck and Reimer (2009) have argued that contemporary Western psychology tends to operate from modern foundationalism and a decontextualized reason-based epistemology that "generates an abstract morality" rather than multicultural sensitivities (p. 146). They note the lack of cultural and religious complexity and limited appreciation of diversity that often results from the "thin" or contextually minimalistic approach of abstract psychology: "Minimalism is a simplified and single-minded morality. It works with an elementary and undifferentiated understanding of society and self" (p. 148). Drawing on our understanding of differentiation described in previous chapters, we would suggest that Dueck and Reimer are pointing to limited differentiation and diversity in much of the modern psychological literature, as they wisely call for greater attention to particularity to counter the potential colonizing tendencies of Western institutional psychology.

There are now a growing number of dialectical perspectives in psychology that seek a more nuanced relationship between universals and particulars—between etic and emic forms of knowledge. Psychological constructs such as "attachment" or "differentiation" can be studied cross-culturally but with appropriate theoretical and methodological adaptations in differing contexts, resulting in more nuanced or diversified models. Rather than assuming constructs and models are universal, researchers can critically appraise needed modifications and disaggregate data to understand local patterns and exceptions to larger trends.

This kind of dialectical perspective was anticipated by Howard Thurman, a twentieth century minister and social justice activist who mentored Martin Luther King, Jr. Thurman's highly integrative writings show an impressive capacity for engaging many disciplines in the integration of spirituality, community, and social justice. In commenting on Thurman's work, Smith (2006, p. 26) explains:

> Thurman believed that a particular contains the universal, and the universal is composed of particulars. A proper understanding of the worth and significance of particulars is essential to realizing God's dream for universal community. If a particular race, ethnicity, gender, or nation is defined as the sole bearer of the universal, the conditions are established for dominion, oppression, and perhaps genocide. Particulars must be valued as bearers of the universal, but no particular can claim to be the sole proprietary expression of the universal.

Single Integrator Versus Collaborative Approaches

This fairly dominant preference for the abstract over the particular in both theology and psychology has also left its mark on interdisciplinary efforts and methodologies. We can see this in a rather prominent feature of this discourse—the commonplace individualistic assumption that interdisciplinary efforts will be carried out by single integrators rather than in conversations and collaborations between two or more scholars or practitioners of different disciplines. Moran (2002), for example, reflects this single integrator assumption as an intellectual limit to interdisciplinary efforts in the humanities.

> . . . given that most research in the humanities is undertaken by scholars working on their own, it may be difficult for these people to become conversant in the theories, methods and materials of two or more disciplines, without producing significant gaps in their knowledge.
>
> *(p. 184)*

Within the literature on theological engagement with the sciences, we have already highlighted Tracy's correlation method as an important and fruitful contribution. Yet even this helpful offering seems to imply a single integrator approach, at least as seen in the assessment that the correlation method involves "no third position from which to make the correlative comparisons that Tracy's method seems to require" (Reynhout, 2013, p. 21). Reynhout critiques the method as not fully correlational, if it assumes (as it seems to) that "one discipline (theology) seek[s] to appropriate meaning from a relatively foreign discipline (science)" (p. 21). In such a case the theologian is the single integrator, whose vantage point is the locus of integration.

Using an embodied and relational lens, we want to question this assumption that a single integrator offers the primary way forward for interdisciplinary integration. For this critique, we offer the helpful notion of a "third position" offered by Reynhout (theologian) and "third dimension" from Benjamin (psychologist), which offers a needed triangulation of the psychoanalytic relationship (2004). In any integrative endeavor, we can map out a theoretical space located between the relevant disciplines where resonance and integration occur (and where aspects of non-integration are clarified). In the integration of psychology and theology within a single disciplinarian, this space is interior to the person, which provides a challenge for reflection and assessment. Almost inevitably, the integrating person has more facility and level of comfort with one of the disciplines, which then functions as the primary lens for integration. When two or more disciplinarians embark on the task of integration, the "third space" moves exteriorly, allowing for more reflective critique and accountability in the process. As we have argued (Sandage & Brown, 2015), this third space "encourages a differentiated stance that invites both integrators to hold their views more loosely for the sake of the conversation [and for assessment of it] and to envision the conversation itself as a third reality to be respected in its own right" (pp. 175–176).

So we advocate for more interdisciplinary work in psychology and theology to be done by multiple persons, and we wonder what might be accomplished if this became the default rather than the exceptional position. Our relational model of integration presses for this kind of embodied collaboration, in which the full selves of psychologists and theologians are acknowledged as relevant to the integrative conversation. Our model also focuses attention on the importance of differentiation—both personal and professional—for those engaged in this conversation. As we note in Chapter 1, people do not bring disembodied thoughts to such interdisciplinary conversations; instead, they bring embodied perspectives, feelings (e.g., anxiety or excitement), and convictions. The more we are ready to acknowledge these realities, the better we may be able to navigate both pathways and barriers to integration.

To prepare the way for exploring a more embodied or "third-space" collaboration, we begin with discreet examinations of embodiment from theological, psychological, and sociocultural vantage points, before turning to describe embodiment as a resource for a more relational integration between psychology and theology—between psychologists and theologians.

Embodiment in Biblical and Theological Perspective

We have been exploring modern tendencies toward abstraction in the academy and in integrative endeavors specifically. This preference for the abstract can be correlated in part with more dualistic perspectives of the human person, tracing back to Descartes and beyond. As Leder (1990) notes,

> . . . a certain telos toward disembodiment is an abiding strain of Western intellectual history. The Platonic emphasis on the purified soul, the Cartesian focus on the "cogito" experience, pull us toward a vision of self within which an immaterial rationality is central. The body has frequently been relegated to a secondary or oppositional role, while an incorporeal reason is valorized.
>
> *(p. 3)*

A dualistic perspective on the human person is also affirmed within some streams of the Christian tradition, which often look to the New Testament (if not the Old) to support a body-soul duality. As Green (2005) notes, "given the pervasive influence of the Cartesian idea of a disembodied mind even today, it is no surprise that many readers of the Bible have found body-soul dualism in its pages" (p. 20). Murphy (2013) suggests that this perspective is more prominent among Christian laity than in scholarship, with dichotomous and even trichotomous (human as body, soul, and spirit) viewpoints regarding the human person being virtually assumed.

Yet Scripture tends toward a vision "of the human person as whole and singular, though integrally connected in a communal web of relationship" (Sandage & Brown, 2015, p. 171). As Bruckner (2005) writes with the Old Testament especially in mind, "Scripture and the tradition do not teach a doctrine of an inherently immortal soul or the persistence of a disembodied spirit beyond the grave" (p. 2). In fact, *nepeš*, the Hebrew term sometimes translated as "soul"—"means *to be alive* and *to be in relation*" (p. 10). Similarly, language of "body" and "soul" in Christian thought is not used to present a dichotomized human person but to describe the whole person from different angles. Much like their Old Testament counterparts, the New Testament authors draw on a variety of terms often rendered into English with language of spirit, soul, body, and mind. While there was a tendency in the Greek world toward dualistic anthropologies, the New Testament authors use Greek terminology in various combinations to *highlight the whole person*, without a corresponding sense of discreet parts. For example, in 1 Thessalonians, Paul writes, "May your *whole* spirit, soul, and body be kept blameless," in reference to the entire person who "will be kept blameless by God's power" (1 Thess 5:23; see Brown et al., 2011, pp. 93–96). As Green (2007) notes, "the monism of the Scriptures of Israel would have presented [for the NT writers] a significant counter-voice to dualism" from their Greco-Roman context (p. 27).

This anthropological monism arising from a biblical anthropology coheres well with the New Testament eschatological vision of bodily resurrection. While popular theology sometimes prioritizes a disembodied existence "in heaven," biblical authors like Paul and the author of Revelation are focused on *resurrection*, that is, some form of bodily existence at the time of God's final day restoration (e.g., Rom 8:23; Phil 3:11, 20–21; Heb 6:1–3; Rev 20:4–6). As Wright (2003, p. 31) speaks of it, these authors focus their attention, not on "life after death" (i.e., "disembodied bliss") but on "life *after* 'life after death'" (i.e., resurrection of the body). We see this embodiment concept most clearly in texts like 1 Corinthians 15, in which Paul argues for the resurrection of believers with a primarily Greek audience in mind that seems to be chaffing at the idea of final embodied existence (1 Cor 15:12, 35). Paul bases his argument for future resurrection on Christ's "already" bodily resurrection (1 Cor 15:20–23) and nuances the idea of embodiment by emphasizing the transformation that will occur between present and future bodies (1 Cor 15:35–49; Fee, 2014). As Paul sums up elsewhere:

> For our citizenship exists in heaven. It is from there that we wait for a savior, the Lord Jesus Christ. He will transform our lowly bodies to be like his glorious body . . .
>
> *(Phil 3:20–21a; our translation)*

This unified vision of the human person—located squarely in the context of relationship—goes hand-in-hand with affirmations of the goodness of the created order. While the early Genesis accounts accent the place of humanity in God's creative activity (e.g., 1:26–31; 2:1–25), their role in relation to the rest the created world is one of deep relatedness and mindful care (2:15; cf. 1:28). According to the storyline, the fall into sin produces a fissure between humankind and the land they work and tend (3:17–19). Paul addresses this cosmic disruption—the frustration of the original intention for the cosmos—in his eschatological vision of God's people as the firstfruits of the redemption that is promised for all creation (Rom 8:19–23). Creation's groaning matches the groaning of the people inhabited by God's Spirit and the Spirit's own "groaning with" for that final day restoration of all things (8:22–23, 26).

This motif of the renewal of all creation is not limited to Paul, even as he offers some of the most explicit references to God's work in Christ that is already bringing about "new creation" (*kainē ktisis*; 2 Cor 5:17; Gal 6:15). John's Gospel, for instance, foregrounds Genesis 1 and 2 in its opening (John 1:1–5) and provides hints of these chapters of Genesis at Jesus' passion and resurrection (e.g., 18:1, 26; 19:5, 41; 20:15, 22) to signal that creation's renewal has now begun (Brown, 2010). The fourth Gospel also accents Jesus' incarnation (1:14–18), which functions theologically as the ultimate affirmation of embodiment. As Johnson (2015) proposes, "the incarnation raises to the most explicit level possible the conviction implicit in creation, prophecy, and covenant: the human body not only can reveal God, it is the privileged medium of divine self-disclosure" (p. 57).

Theologically, humanity is called to embrace embodiment and conceive of God's purposes as leading toward rather than away from the restoration of creation and embodied existence. And we suggest that this eschatological vision can speak into interdisciplinary integration. We will explore what this vision might offer after turning our attention to embodiment from psychological and sociocultural perspectives.

Embodiment in Psychological Perspective

Human life is embodied, which means relational integration is neurobiological. Dan Siegel (2010; also see Cozolino, 2017), a leader in the field of interpersonal neurobiology, has shown that the *embodied integration* of differing neurobiological systems is necessary for healthy and coherent relational functioning. While Siegel speaks of various types of neurobiological integration (see Chapter 6), here we highlight his concept of a triangle of well-being involving the integration of brain, mind, and relationships and resting on a dialectic of differentiation and linkage, i.e., noting differences and making connections. While his use of the concept of "differentiation" as difference is less dialectical than our usage, his overall model of interpersonal neurobiology fits our emphases on embodied relational integration. A key implication is that constructive relational experiences are necessary to help people develop capacities for neurobiological integration, along with the reality that some neurobiological difficulties (e.g., brain injuries, autism, dementia, etc.) might place embodied limitations on certain capacities for integration.

The role of neurobiological embodiment has also been explored in relation to the integration of psychology and theology. Brown and Strawn (2012) have described how spirituality involves the relational coordination of neurobiological and other physiological functions rather than representing a state of a disembodied soul. They show how embodiment makes spirituality social and communal rather than individualistic and interior, fitting a relational understanding of human nature. While some dualists might fear that this non-reductive physicalist view somehow diminishes spirituality and soulcare, Brown and Strawn's model actually shows the necessity of integration by linking spiritual experience to physicality, communal or church practices and traditions, and theological frameworks.

Hall and Porter (2004) also have made a seminal contribution to the integration of theology and psychology on relational and symbolic aspects of neurobiological embodiment (also see Sandage & Brown, 2015). Drawing in Wilma Bucci's (1997) multiple code theory in cognitive science, they suggest that cognitive reflection always involves parallel levels of information processing that include implicit, pre-verbal levels of emotional experience based on internalized relationship dynamics (e.g., attachment). This serves to explain why we can see profound individual differences in emotional responses to theological statements such "God is loving" even among people who all share belief in this theological proposition. Relational images or representations of God, particularly personal ones, activate emotion-laden images at pre-verbal levels in the limbic brain related to relational experiences (Hall & Fujikawa, 2013). Individuals with securely attached internal working models of relationship can integrate verbal and pre-verbal levels of information quite consistently or cohesively. Thus, their unconscious or experiential theologies tend to integrate or fit with their conscious or reflective theologies, which attachment theorists call a correspondence effect (Hall, Fujikawa, Halcrow, Hill, & Delaney, 2009). Individuals with ambivalently attached internal working models of relationship may respond to a theological assertion that "God is loving" with agitation or tension in their limbic brains that generates emotions of frustration or sadness at the discrepancy between their experience and the ideal of God's love. They may seem emotionally reactive or lacking in stability of faith to others around them. Individuals with avoidantly attached internal working models of relationship are more likely to unconsciously mobilize deactivation of the limbic brain to shut down emotions and relational desires which can serve to keep their engagement of theology at verbal and neocortical levels. They may seem rather cold and overly rational in their approach to faith. A key point of this integration of attachment, psychoanalysis and cognitive science is that theology and psychology converge within individuals as part of an embodied neurobiological process linking emotions, symbols, and language (Sandage and Brown, 2015). An important implication of Hall and Porter's multi-level account involves the ways in which symbolic images potentially link affect-laden relational experiences and verbalized theological understandings. These kinds of connections between neuropsychological processes and theology have led Newberg (2010) to call for a field of *neurotheology*, with bi-directional interdisciplinary influence between these disciplines.

These contributions on the neurobiology of relational integration also underscore the important point that a psychology of embodiment involves the powerful role of emotions in consciousness, beliefs, values, and the formation of self (Damasio, 2010; M. Johnson, 2015). Beck (2012) has empirically studied the psychology of death anxiety and other emotions (e.g., disgust) that can be linked to theological beliefs and spiritual practices among Christians. He has noted dualistic and gnostic tendencies among many contemporary evangelical Christians which involves bifurcating the spiritual and material realms despite clear theological teaching to the contrary. Beck interprets this discomfort with human embodiment existentially by drawing on empirical research in Terror Management Theory (Greenberg, Koole, & Pyszcynski, 2004) as anxiety about bodily reminders of mortality and death. In one study, Beck (2012) measured Christian students' "ambivalence about the incarnation"—or the notion that Jesus was fully human—and found that such ambivalence was associated with higher levels of defensive theology based on a measure of the tendency to believe one is uniquely and specially protected by God's omnipotence from illnesses or other hardships. Interestingly, ambivalence about the incarnation was not correlated with a measure of theological or creedal orthodoxy, further suggesting an emotional process of discomfort with embodiment was influencing a psychological need for reassurance of God's total power and control and their own protection. Beck does not suggest theological beliefs are driven solely by anxiety and other emotions for everyone, as Freud implied, but his research does indicate emotions about embodiment can influence individual differences in how people employ their theologies.

Embodiment in Sociocultural Perspective

Embodiment also involves dynamics of "implacement," that is, our human situatedness in "certain social, cultural, historical, and geographical context[s]" (Hall & Thoennes, 2006, p. 30). Embodied subjectivity is influenced by these surrounding sociocultural attitudes regarding gender, race, sexuality, various aspects of size and appearance, ability, and other diversity dimensions. Hall and Jacobsen are psychologists who have developed a program of empirical research on embodiment, theology, and various aspects of behavior. Their research rests on the assumption that sociocultural contexts and theological interpretations shape interpretations about meanings of embodiment. They have noted the risk that radically dualistic views that separate the body and soul might lead to viewing the body as corrupt, as well as an "elevation of bodily sins" (e.g., sexual) as more serious than other kinds of sin (Jacobson, Hall, Anderson, & Willingham, 2016b, p. 2155). In contrast, other theological anthropologies view humans as a psychosomatic unity and sanctify the body as "holy, worthy of respect, and integral to one's being" (Jacobson, Hall, Anderson, & Willingham, 2016a, p. 52). The title of their 2016 article summarizes their overarching set of questions—"Temple or Prison: Religious Beliefs and Attitudes toward the Body" (p. 2154).

Hall and Jacobson have generated many clinically relevant findings associating individual differences in theological and religious beliefs about embodiment with psychological well-being and distress. In research with adult Protestants in the U.S. (Jacobson et al., 2016a, 2016b), they found radically dualistic beliefs were negatively associated with body appreciation and sexuality awareness and positively associated with a lack of body connectedness, body shame, and self-surveillance—the attempt to view one's body as an outside observer. Some participants held theological views that sanctified the body (e.g., "my body is a temple of God" or "my body is a gift from God"), and higher levels of belief in the sanctification of the body were associated with lower levels of body shame and higher levels of body connectedness. An earlier study (Jacobson, Hall, & Anderson, 2013) with undergraduate students found sanctification of the body was positively related to body satisfaction and negatively related to body objectification and depersonalization. Significant problems with body objectification can lead to mood disorders, eating disorders, and other psychological problems. Depersonalization can be driven by shame and involves a psychological process of emotional distancing or dissociating from one's own body and can be symptomatic of trauma. These findings do not mean theological understandings of the body cause certain positive or negative outcomes, but they do show that specific theological beliefs are implicated in psychological dynamics that connect embodiment, sexuality, and psychological suffering. Dualistic beliefs about the body are a risk factor for negative or dissociative ways of relating to one's body, whereas a theological sanctification of the body tends to be consistent with an integration of bodily awareness and connection.

In conversation with these studies, we would raise two issues from a theological point of view. First, an understanding of an individual's body as "God's temple" does emerge from the New Testament and expressly from 1 Cor 6:19. Yet all other occurrences of "temple" (*naos*) language in reference to Christians signals their *corporate existence*; it is the church that is predominantly identified as God's temple (1 Cor 3:16–17; 2 Cor 6:16; Eph 2:21–22; cf. 1 Pet 2:5). The second-person pronouns are uniformly plural in these texts, which is even the case in 1 Cor 6:19: "your [pl.] body [sg.] is a temple of the Holy Spirit who is in you [pl.]." Our Western context often leads us to place emphasis on the individual, when the New Testament writers are using this metaphor of God's temple to highlight the corporate reality of Christians gathered together in worship and mission. This fits with the social and communal emphases of Brown and Strawn (2012) cited above. Second, there are gender dynamics to the ways embodiment has been conceived in the Christian tradition. Within the philosophical tradition, which has exerted significant influence upon Christian theology, women have been tied to the body and men to the mind, with the superiority of the latter assumed as well as argued (Heikes, 2012). This dichotomizing of mind and body, male and female has often resulted in female ambivalence toward their bodies, something that needs to be factored into discussions of embodiment. It is not surprising then that embodiment has become a significant refrain in feminist theology.

Embodiment also has tremendous sociocultural and psychological significance in Womanist and other African-American spiritual traditions. Ethicist Peter Paris (1995) writes, "African spirituality is never disembodied but always integrally connected with the dynamic movement of life" (p. 22). Similarly, Womanist theologians such as M. Shawn Copeland (2010), Kelly Brown Douglas (2005), and Delores Williams (2013) have described the importance of the Black body and embodied spirituality for Black women in historically oppressive contexts of slavery, racism, and sexism, in which blackness and femaleness are associated with negative stereotypes. Racism and sexism are sociocultural dynamics that seek to disgrace Black women's bodies, and this point can be extended to oppressive forces against various races and non-dominant social groups. In the United States, this includes the aggressive violence inspired by White supremacy and also the more insidious ways certain types of embodiment are shamed or made invisible (i.e., erased). Phillis Sheppard's (2011) Womanist integration of psychoanalysis, culture, and practical theology starts with the centrality of embodiment as "integral to the epistemological positions" of her work (p. 14). Building on Williams' theological account of racism as defilement, Sheppard suggests healthy and liberative accounts of embodiment are particularly important for those who are seeking to heal from intergenerational social oppression; and she draws attention to constructive relational and systemic dynamics that can serve those goals. We would locate our account of relational integration as allied with these voices that draw attention to the ways the topic of embodiment can invite complex sociocultural awareness of violence and marginalization or healing and empowerment.

Case Analysis: Embodiment as a Lens

Drawing on themes of embodiment from the disciplines of psychology and theology, we suggest that sexuality and spirituality as illustrated in this case should not be conceived as different dimensions of the person or the relationship but as highly interactive aspects of experience. Through an embodiment lens, sexuality and spirituality do not require different levels of analysis. Instead, either or both can offer a specific lens to the case and neither should be excluded from the conversation. To begin, we invite consideration of the case by foregrounding sexuality as a "relational integrative window." In doing so, the following additional information becomes relevant:

Mee discloses that she has had "no libido" for most of their marriage. She says she was quite attracted to Dan during their dating and early marriage and still thinks he is "good looking." But she lost her desire for sex sometime during their first year of marriage. Mee says, "I would like to have more desire, but I just don't feel it." Dan goes on to admit he has been very resentful about Mee's lack of interest in sex and that when they do have intercourse "she doesn't seem into it," which causes him to feel like a failure. This seemed to get worse after his pornography use was discovered the first time. He says he went along with this for a while but eventually questioned whether it was "worth accepting mercy sex" and has mostly avoided the topic of sex with Mee for the past couple of years.

Mee, with reluctance, adds that she found intercourse with Dan difficult because he would often ejaculate very quickly (within 10–30 seconds of penetration by her estimate). This made it challenging for her to have an orgasm. Dan counters defensively, "It has gotten better. And what do you expect when we have sex so rarely? I don't know what I am supposed to do about it." He indicates Mee mentioned the problem of his quick ejaculation sometime back after he "badgered her for an explanation" and that he had "not really thought about it" before then. But he said he had been very nervous during sex since then, anticipating he will be a disappointment again. Mee explains the whole process of sex has come to feel like "an ordeal" to her and she never "looks forward to it" anymore. Upon further discussion of their sexual histories, she admits with visible shame that she greatly enjoyed sex with her daughter's father, whom she broke up with after the painful discovery of his repeated affairs. Dan adds that he and Mee had sex a couple times before marriage and that he wonders if their sexual problems might be "God's punishment for our lack of purity."

Deeper exploration of sexuality and embodiment for this case reveals the significant interactivity between this couple's experiences of sexuality and spirituality. Mee appears to be struggling with questions like, "Is it acceptable to want pleasure for myself or should I just take care of others?" "Does my own enjoyment inevitably lead to betrayal and rejection?" "Who actually cares about my desires?" and "What is God trying to teach me?" Dan is wrestling with questions like, "Am I just a disappointment?" "What does it take to be wanted?" "How can I control myself?" and "Am I contaminated by past sins?" We could also identify several implicit themes that are both psychological and theological, such as guilt, mistrust, anxiety, self-control, desire, hiding, and forgiveness.

As we will explore below, these multifaceted questions and themes hint at a number of assumptions about the relationship between spirituality and sexuality which could be helpfully explored by those who are counseling and guiding Dan and Mee, as well as by psychologists and theologians seeking to understand how relational integration is an embodied endeavor. It is also important to recognize there are empirically supported treatments available for premature ejaculation and low sexual desire. Some counselors or therapists might tend to focus on emotional and relational dynamics, such as guilt, betrayal, or forgiveness to the neglect of sexuality, while others might prioritize symptoms of sexual dysfunctions. Our relational integration approach suggests making use of empirical wisdom related to embodiment within integrative thematic frameworks that fit clients' worldviews. In this case, it might be hard for Mee and Dan to move toward forgiveness and reconciliation without some shared understanding of their history of sexual struggles that shaped and is shaped by relational contexts of betrayal. On the other hand, it would also be important to assess their spiritual, theological, and sociocultural assumptions about sexuality and embodiment before proceeding toward sex therapy interventions. They may not be motivated to work on improving their sexual relationship until some level of forgiveness emerges, but underlying beliefs and feelings of shame about sexuality could also limit their motivations for change.

Bringing Theology and Psychology Together in Embodied Ways

As we have seen, both theological and psychological perspectives offer strong affirmations of human embodiment and the importance of conceiving of the human person in holistic ways. What might these affirmations offer for conceptualizing interdisciplinary integration within a relational model?

Grounding Relational Integration in Disciplinary Particulars

Understanding the integration of psychology and theology as embodied endeavors means addressing the disciplines, and more so those practicing these disciplines, in *grounded* ways. By this we mean locating disciplines and disciplinarians *on the ground*, in all their particularity and specificity. If, as we have argued, the modern academy exhibits a marked preference for abstraction, then one response toward embodiment is to explore *the value of the particular*.

In theology, this might involve reversing a trend toward the "most abstractive and de-particularized formulations" (Reno, 2004, p. 389) in a movement toward embracing the "blessed messiness of the text" (Gaventa, 2011, p. 3). As Gaventa argues, "there is a deep connection between the details of the biblical text" and "what Scripture has to say about God" (i.e., its theology). We might also take our cues from scholars like Rambo, whose work on trauma thematizes embodiment: "We are grounded in the world through our bodies" (Rambo, 2010, p. 20). The field of trauma theology exposes the tendency among many theologians to avoid the messy, dysregulating, and painful realities of embodiment, which can result in highly sanitized theologies.

In line with these themes, we suggest that the integration of psychology and theology might look more like an engagement between the particulars of one discipline and specifics of the other than the derivation of an abstracted, generalized set of principles arrived at far above the ground level of each discipline. To provide an analogy, integration between and among disciplines has been for us more like the traversal of a low flying helicopter than of an airplane at 30,000 feet. Rather than moving away from particularity in a preference for higher and higher levels of abstraction, we have found it productive to foster a conversation that allows each of us to share from our own work and discipline in quite specific areas and with very particular insights. What we have found is that commonalities and differences emerge quite freely and unexpectedly in these "on the ground" conversations. In language we have introduced above, the "third space" of integration offers a place of particularity that allows for a kind of "blessed messiness" of both disciplinary realities and lived experience.

For example, while teaching a master's level course on integration, we decided to address integratively the topic of narrative or story. During our pre-class conversations, I (Jeannine) was mentioning the narrative-critical task of reading a Gospel as a coherent story, with the expectation that students would attend to and offer narrative coherence in assignments on the Gospels. I (Steve) suggested that some students might not be able to offer a coherent reading of, say, Mark's Gospel, if they had experienced life trauma. In fact, these students might not be able to tell the story of their own life in a coherent fashion due to the embodied effects of trauma they had experienced. This conversation began an ongoing interest in our own collaboration on narrative and its interdisciplinary potential, since narrative criticism (in biblical studies), narrative theology, narrative therapy, and narrative psychology are growing areas within our respective disciplines.

More recently, I (Jeannine) have drawn on resources suggested by Steve for an essay on storied forms of biblical theology. Specifically, I drew upon insights from Adler (2012, p. 329) on the function of stories to "bind"—that is, to "hold together a sequence of moments" and prevent "the utter dispersion of experience." Adler points to the concept of narrative coherence as the basis for this binding function of stories, yet also notes the potential for being "imprisoned by too-coherent narratives" and suggests a middle position that navigates between "glossing over . . . potentially incongruous detail(s)" and "a rigid adherence to a tight story line" (p. 330). Picking up on this caution, I argued against pursing the project of a kind of storied biblical theology that "creates coherence at the expense of authorial particularities" (Brown, 2015, p. 21).

Bringing together insights from psychology and theology in relational integration allows the integrity of each discipline (its discreetness) to be maintained, while offering integrative insights from the dialogue between disciplines as well as illuminating disciplinary specifics that may lack integrative potential. Both kinds of knowledge—insights from integration and non-integration—are valuable. As we have noted in our definitional work on relational integration, this kind of both/and derives from a differentiated stance of each person in the conversation. As differentiation of self creates the possibility in human relationships for both connectedness and autonomy—or intimacy and alterity, so a differentiated interdisciplinarity potentially offers insights deeply rooted in disciplinary specifics while maintaining disciplinary integrity. "By attending to what fits and what does not, we are better able to foster truly integrative work that allows each discipline to speak from its own standpoint without sacrificing its distinctives or attempting to trump another discipline" (Brown, Dahl & Corbin Reuschling, 2011, p. 13).

Embodied Integration and Human Finitude

Understanding integration as embodied also foregrounds human finitude, another necessary corrective to the modern preference for abstraction. Viewing our disciplines as abstract systems only or primarily subtly shifts us away from the reality that the quest for knowledge is always undertaken by concrete persons who live with limitations. Individuals are finite, suggesting that their academic, disciplinary work also participates in finitude, even while stretching to answer profound questions of human existence. To grapple with this finitude is to face squarely the truth that our particular discipline cannot do it all in the quest for human knowledge. Theology needs psychology and vice versa. Or to frame it more relationally, theologians and psychologists need one another. As we consider this inherent tension between limitations and questing, Kierkegaard's dialectic of the self as a relational synthesis of "infinitude and finitude" provides a helpful analogy (1849/1980, p. 29). By holding these together we might, in his terms, avoid both "the fantastic" and "reductionism" (pp. 32–33). For Kierkegaard, the fantastic represents the grandiose desire to be infinite or unlimited and to transcend human embodiment in a kind of spiritual intoxication. Reductionism represents the opposite tendency toward narrowness of purpose and becoming absorbed in temporal concerns, which robs us of the uniqueness of selfhood and the need for existential commitments.

The importance of acknowledging the finitude of embodied integration can be seen in the connections between several broad areas of interdisciplinary research, such as sexuality, health psychology and psychoanalytic research on coping with illness and trauma, and embodiment theology and pastoral care related to disability. For example, Parton and colleagues (2016) have investigated the ways women construct a sense of their bodies and sexual "selves" in the context of cancer. They found the "abject body" or bodies defined outside the bounds of physical and feminine "normalcy" often created a liminal crisis of meaning that pulled for transformed understandings of female embodiment, beauty, sexuality, and belonging. English (2016) raises parallel points about the theological and psychological dynamics of caring for those with disabilities and avoidance of facing our shared finitude or excluding parts of their embodied experience. More specifically, English prophetically warns against presuming that persons with disabilities are disinterested in sexuality. Interdisciplinary research on trauma also illuminates the ways "the body remembers" traumatic experiences and threats to existence in ways that are often ruptured and dis-integrative—they do not readily integrate with dualistic or polished, positive-minded theologies (Jones, 2009; Rambo, 2010; van Deusen Hunsinger, 2015). Each of these lines of finitude research points to a similar theme: suffering bodies or struggles with embodiment reveal important truths of dis-integration and ambiguities of meaning that can potentially set the stage for more textured and differentiated forms of relational integration.

The finitude of embodied integration also has implications for the relational stance of integrators. If any particular discipline is a finite perspective on reality and an embodied attempt to speak into the development of human knowledge reflectively and productively, then a great measure of humility is required for disciplinary work and interdisciplinary efforts (Hall & Thoennes, 2006). Additionally, we may need to grapple with and grieve the loss of control that this kind of mutuality invites.

I (Jeannine) have had the experience of embarking on an integrative conversation and project across disciplines, only to find that the other scholar had a vested interest in a particular method and specific conclusions for the work of biblical interpretation. In spite of a surface (and expressed) respect for my discipline, this person whose discipline intersects with the social sciences had difficulty relinquishing control of the work of my discipline (New Testament studies). This situation arose, in part, from the use of the Christian Scriptures as a common resource and repository across the seminary curriculum. While every Christian, including a seminary professor, may appropriately claim the biblical text as a resource for their work and their teaching in the seminary classroom, an interdisciplinary approach that draws on biblical studies will need to grapple with the realities of disciplinary boundaries—an awareness necessary for all interdisciplinary work. "To be interdisciplinary you need to be disciplinary first" (Foster, 1998, p. 162). The integrative work in which I had initially engaged with my colleague lost its momentum when disciplinary boundaries were not maintained. Multiple-person interdisciplinary integration can only succeed if such boundaries are owned, recognized, and honored.

Embodied Integration as an Exercise in "Pacing and Leading"

While it may seem that we have been highlighting some challenges of holding an embodied perspective on interdisciplinary integration, we would suggest that an awareness of location and finitude—both for ourselves and for our disciplines—can offer quite positive outcomes. One such outcome is a deeper appreciation for the particular strengths offered by a discipline (and so a disciplinarian) to interdisciplinary conversation. A heightened sense of the limits or boundaries of one's own discipline can invite greater recognition of the strengths and contributions of other disciplines and encourage interdisciplinarity.

In true relational style, however, this recognition of the strengths of other disciplines does not require minimizing the strengths of one's own discipline. Instead, it invites a kind of conversation that might be characterized by therapeutic language of "pacing and leading" (from Erickson; see Haley, 1993; Worthington & Sandage, 2016). While this language refers in therapy to the work of the therapist toward client, it has been adapted for use in teaching and leading contexts. We suggest it offers a helpful framing for what two or more disciplinarians do in interdisciplinary work. Pacing would involve careful listening to understand a person and "join them" in their own disciplinary location. This learning posture releases the leadership role in the interdisciplinary conversation to the other disciplinarian. Careful listening allows the strengths of the other to emerge more clearly. In such conversation, there are often frequent and agile shifts between who is pacing and who is leading. The conversation is "a two-way process," characterized by mutuality (Beaver, 2011, p. 44), yet with appropriate leadership exercised in areas of strength. What is lacking is any significant exertion of control of one person over another (i.e., one discipline over the other).

In interdisciplinarity between psychology and theology, we have found it helpful to accent their complementary strengths in the area of descriptive and prescriptive knowledge. Theology tends to focus on prescriptive knowledge—the "oughts" of human existence—and therefore may lead the way in framing questions about the nature of the good life or human flourishing. Psychology, and the social sciences more broadly, emphasizes descriptive knowledge—the "is" of human existence—and so may lead the way in framing questions and providing insight toward what people actually do in their lives. Yet we would be shortsighted if we did not notice that theology also offers descriptive formulations, often in its historical inquiry (e.g., analysis of the history of Christian thought); and psychology is also at times prescriptive, especially as it offers perspectives—explicitly or implicitly—about ultimate concerns (Browning & Cooper, 2004). In a model that recognizes the complexity of this set of strengths as well as limitations, we might envision the disciplines of psychology and theology in a dialectic relationship, with each discipline offering from their areas of strength toward a conversation that does not impose rigid guidelines for what may be offered by any particular disciplinarian. In this view, influence and insight flow in multiple directions, without the need for high control and with respect for disciplinary boundaries and corresponding strengths.

This interactivity between descriptive and prescriptive forms of knowledge point to primary source material for psychology and theology, respectively.

Theology draws its reflections primarily from special revelation, focused on divine revelation in the Christian Scriptures, and climactically in the person of Jesus Christ. Psychology centers on what can be discerned from descriptive study of general revelation and, particularly, the created order. The inherent embodiment recognized by a relational integration approach suggests that both kinds of revelation are important areas of study.

(Sandage and Brown, 2015, pp. 172–173)

Reference to revelation leads us to a final topic of exploration for our discussion of embodiment, namely, the viability of the category of natural theology.

Case Analysis: Integration of Spirituality and Sexuality

Our development of an embodied integration of psychology and theology leads us to suggest a deep connectivity between sexuality and spirituality in human experience. As we have noted previously, these are not so much discrete dimensions as highly interactive aspects of experience. This interactivity emerges in the questions that we have suggested that Mee and Dan are holding, which involve a fluid movement between what we might characterize as sexual and spiritual concerns. So, we suggest it might be fruitful to consider these questions from embodied and relational angles.

> Mee: "Is it ok to want pleasure for myself or should I just take care of others?" "Does my own enjoyment inevitably lead to betrayal and rejection?" "Who actually cares about my desires?" "What is God trying to teach me?"
> Dan: "Am I just a disappointment?" "What does it take to be wanted?" "How can I control myself?" "Am I contaminated by past sins?"

A first observation relates to both Mee and Dan's assumptions that God has very strong feelings about sex. A common proof-text for this view is 1 Cor 6:18, which reads: "Flee from sexual immorality. All other sins a person commits are outside the body, but whoever sins sexually, sins against their own body." Yet Paul's seeming point in this admonition is to encourage his readers to understand sexual immorality as harming their own selves (bodies) and so to discourage them from it (why do something that harms yourself?). The rather commonplace assumption that God really doesn't like sex or at least that sexual sin is the worst kind of sin doesn't square with any number of New Testament authors, whose use of the genre of vice lists often highlight other transgressions more than or as well as sexual ones (see Matt 15:17–20). Paul's infamous vice list in Romans 1, for example, though beginning with sexual sin common outside of Jewish circles (1:24–27), culminates and so places emphasis on *the absence of understanding, fidelity, love, and mercy* (1:31).

Helping Mee and Dan to understand better their current ways of integrating God and sex could be a step toward addressing unhelpful assumptions.

Religious communities, like the one in which Mee and Dan participated, too often focus most of their discussions of sexuality on prohibitions and problems, which we could call a "sex-negative approach." Thus, sexuality comes to be viewed in a rather un-differentiated fashion primarily as something dangerous, sinful, and problematic. In the United States, it is probably easier to find a group on sexual addiction meeting at a church than a church-based group or class on how couples can improve their sexual intimacy. A sex-positive approach tends to focus on sexuality as a positive, growth-enhancing aspect of human development which requires the cultivation of certain relational virtues (e.g., love, generosity, self-control, humility, confidence, etc.) and an appreciation for relational boundaries. One can hold a sex-positive attitude and still be realistically concerned about the damage and exploitation that can be done through sexuality. In fact, our experience has been that sex-negative approaches often implicitly rest on a rather naïve assumption that as long as people do not violate certain moral boundaries then couples will have good sexual relationships. Sex-positive approaches are more realistic about both the challenges and potentialities of embodiment and the need for educational and developmental supports to help individuals and couples grow through sexuality. From a relational perspective, it may be helpful for Dan and Mee to eventually encounter others in their religious tradition working on integrating spirituality and healthy sexual development through some type of group, retreat, or workshop experience that encourages appropriate boundaries. However, they will also likely need more personalized therapeutic attention, and empirical studies have shown that highly distressed couples often experience intensification of their problems in large couple enrichment groups as Luis recommended.

A Place for Natural Theology: God "Shines in All That's Fair"

General Revelation

To assess the viability of a "natural theology"—that is, knowledge of God inferable from nature or human reason and apart from revelation in Scripture specifically—we will first need to explore the theological category of general revelation. Traditionally, general revelation has been defined as what God discloses about Godself apart from special disclosure in Scripture or quite specific human experience (e.g., visions, dreams). The vehicles for general revelation are typically understood to be nature, the human conscience, and reason. The question of natural theology is whether knowledge of God is discernable in general revelation—whether humans after the fall are able to "read" general revelation rightly or whether the noetic effects of sin cloud the human capacity to see God's handprint in nature or to derive divine knowledge from human moral and intellectual capacities.

In the traditional view, the use of "general" (sometimes referred to as "natural") in general revelation is meant to highlight something about both its content and its audience: "a knowledge of "God-in-general" to all people (Sproul et al., 1984, p. 26). Recently, Johnston has helpfully expanded our vision in this area by arguing that general revelation should not be reduced to "those general truths that are communicated by God to all persons at all times and in all places" (2014, p. 8). Instead, a more helpful definition of general revelation would take account of revelation of God "through creation, conscience, and culture" that could involve the metacognitive, what Johnston calls "a numinous encounter" that may very well transform as well as inform (p. 9).

In his biblical exploration of general revelation illuminated, Johnston widens the scope of what has traditionally been studied—for example, Psalm 19, Romans 1–2, and Acts 17. He adds to these usual loci in-depth discussions of Old Testament wisdom literature as well as examples of general revelation from historical narrative (e.g., non-Israelites kings, like Cyrus, portrayed as hearing from Yahweh in 2 Chron 36:22–23) and the prophets (e.g., Habakkuk's interest in showing God's message to Israel coming via Babylon's armies). We have argued elsewhere for something like this wider view of general revelation (Sandage & Brown, 2015, p. 173). There, we mention Old Testament wisdom literature and Paul's use of the categories of Greco-Roman moral discourse (Phil 4:8–9) as examples of this engagement. Both examples fit nicely with Johnston's emphasis on human culture as a potential means of divine revelation.

Such an expansive definition of general revelation contributes to a robust vision for interdisciplinary work between theology and psychology. Specifically, the inclusion of human culture or creativity as a possible avenue for God's revelation signals an affirmation of social science disciplines, which seek to study the human person and human societies as epistemological sources as they exist in the real world. From this perspective, an expansive definition of general revelation opens up conceptions of natural theology to include human culture and creativity as ways of understanding God and God's world.

Natural Theology

As we have already noted in Chapter 2, natural theology has been a contested category in the history of theology. And where the possibility of natural theology has been significantly questioned, there has been a corresponding hesitancy to embrace mutual influence between psychology (or other disciplines) and theology. An important factor in these misgivings about the viability of natural theology is a pessimism about humanity's receptivity to the truths of general revelation due to sin's noetic effects (Johnston, 2014, p. 11).

While granting that distortion of what God reveals about God, humanity, and the world in creation, conscience, and culture is a real possibility, we would affirm two corresponding truths. First, potential distortions should not be understood or used to discount the entire endeavor of learning from sources of general revelation. Moreover, an embodied perspective, as we have been highlighting in this chapter, will need to take account of lived human experience. Johnson, in *The Revelatory Body* (2015, p. 231), argues for "the human body [as] the preeminent place of God's continuing revelation in the world, and that theology must pay close attention to what is happening in actual human experience, which is always in some way somatic."

Second, the possibility of human distortion should also be acknowledged for the study of *special revelation*. As humans are thoroughly hermeneutical in relation to general revelation, they also do not have unmediated access to Scripture, for example. Interpretation of both spheres of revelation is inevitable and will, no doubt, result in some amount of distortion, whether because of sin or finitude (as we discuss in the next chapter). For this reason, "[w]e need a hermeneutic that includes not only Scripture and the tradition of the church but also cultural receptivity and human experience . . . A robust, two-way conversation is called for" (Johnston, 2014, p. 15). Our model of relational integration, with its focus on mutual influence between theology and psychology, provides a framework for the conversation that involves both spheres—Scripture and tradition *and* cultural receptivity and human experience.

Conclusion

In this chapter, we have proposed embodiment as a crucial theme for relational integration. We have defined embodiment from a multidisciplinary perspective and have suggested some avenues for pursuing a relational integration between psychology and theology that is attuned to human embodiment. The search for integration always takes place in embodied form (in bodies), as people seek coherence and integrity among the diverse facets of their lived experience. Throughout this chapter, we have used the case study of Mee and Dan to explore and illustrate the importance of attending to embodiment. We conclude by returning to the case for bringing together various threads from this chapter.

Case Analysis: Luis's Role

In a final return to the case dilemma, we would like to explore the role of Luis particularly, given his seeming capacity to see Mee and Dan and their marriage in multifaceted ways that provide a potential bridge between what

Randy and what Arlenis offered to the couple. The church ministries that Luis had developed had the potential to provide solid relational support to Dan and Mee. Additionally, his inclination to recommend professional counseling for Mee and Dan was a move we would endorse. Yet, in the face of comments by Randy, his superior at the church, Luis begins to distrust his own voice—what we might think of as his embodied wisdom—and he struggles to find the differentiation necessary to offer a different perspective to Randy. And, unfortunately, Randy did not seem curious enough to dialogue with Luis in a collaborative manner but took an authoritative stance that shut down exploration.

Luis is also the helper in the case who seems best poised to hold together the sexual and spiritual lives of Mee and Dan in this particular case. Randy and Arlenis exhibit a certain kind of reductionism, with Randy exhibiting a perspective that sexual problems (simply) need spiritual answers. Alternately, Arlenis seems to experience some amount of discomfort or at least impatience with Mee's own spiritual self-diagnosis of her sexual dilemma. It may be that Arlenis demonstrates a reductionism in which Mee's spiritual concerns are subsumable to her sexual and emotional struggles. Kierkegaard might say Randy and Arlenis are imbalanced toward infinitude and finitude, respectively.

If we propose a more integrated and complex view of the sexual, emotional, and spiritual aspects of the case, Luis's multi-pronged strategy for supporting Dan and Mee in their marriage suggests he has an intuition about the need for wholeness and integration. After meeting with the couple to pray with them and integrate them into the marriage enrichment opportunities the church offers, he connects them with a more seasoned couple for mentoring. He also presses for Dan to meet with Pastor Randy about his pornography use. We would suggest each of these strategies has certain advantages but also important limitations from an integrative perspective, and it is unclear whether Luis has a well-conceptualized practical strategy or if he is more simply wanting to try several different things to see what might work. Perhaps sensing his own integrative limits, Luis wonders whether Dan and Mee might need to see a professional therapist, recognizing that there may be resources that their church isn't able to provide. From a relational integration perspective, we want to highlight the potential value of Luis's sense of tension and his concern as to whether other resources might be needed.

Although it is commendable that Randy has developed a support group for men dealing with sexual addition, it might be that the church is not fully prepared to provide a theology and psychology of sexuality that could help couples like Mee and Dan navigate the complex layers of their sexual relationship. This could easily arise from the historical tendency toward a deep suspicion of pleasure within Greco-Roman moral discourse (e.g., Aristotle), which has significantly impacted the Christian tradition (L.T. Johnson, 2015). In response, Johnson speaks of "resist[ing] at all costs the tendency to disembody sexual desire in order to make it 'spiritual'" (p. 149).

There is not space to consider all pastoral or clinical considerations in a case like this, but we want to mention a few key areas for assessment and possible exploration and intervention from our relational integration perspective. First, we would want to explore the gender and cultural identities of Mee and Dan to see (a) if there are influences on assumptions they might hold related to sexuality and relationships and (b) if there are strengths that might be mobilized. This will involve exploring differences between them, so well-paced therapeutic work could facilitate differentiation (i.e., the appreciation of differences). In terms of gender, it could be helpful to know if Mee has internalized certain social or religious messages that females should not be particularly interested in or knowledgeable about sexuality. For Dan, we might be listening for whether he has bought into certain shaming stereotypes that men should always be masterful in sexual performance (emphasis here on *performance* in contrast to attachment). If these hypotheses prove valid, Mee and Dan might have been too preoccupied with defending against shame and anxiety to actually be physically, emotionally, and spiritually grounded (or embodied) during sex or even discussions about sex. A relationally attuned counselor or therapist might help them differentiate and integrate parts of themselves and their relationship through pacing and leading.

Second, we would wonder how Mee and Dan understand dynamics of suffering and transformation. They seem to be interpreting their suffering as a stigmatizing punishment, and yet social science data would suggest their sexual and marital struggles are quite common. It is also common for clients like Dan and Mee to either hope there is a quick, pain-free solution to their problems or to begin to despair they will have a lifetime of chronic pain and unhappiness. Sadly, religious communities sometimes reinforce this with theologies of prosperity or theologies of resigned masochism. We would hope Mee and Dan could somehow gain influence from more integrated theological and psychological perspectives that suggest temporary suffering is often part of a painful growth process but that also illuminate pathways toward healing and well-being.

Third, we would be interested in exploring Dan and Mee's understandings of intimacy in its various interacting dimensions (e.g., sexual intimacy, emotional intimacy, spiritual intimacy, intercultural intimacy) amidst the embodied anxieties they may experience about differences. Intimacy is sometimes idealized as an anxiety-free state, but we have found this perspective to not be spiritually or psychologically realistic. Temptations toward "hiding" versus taking risks of intimacy (knowing and being known) could emerge as important symbolic and integrative themes in a case like this. We would want to also understand how Mee and Dan have related around their cultural differences (i.e., differentiation) and whether there are ways they might better connect and support each other as a biracial couple (see Chapter 7).

Bibliography

Adler, J. (2012). Sitting at the nexus of epistemological traditions: Narrative psychological perspectives on self-knowledge. In S. Vazire & T. D. Wilson (Eds.), *Handbook of self-knowledge* (pp. 327–347). New York, NY: Guilford Press.

Bartholomew, C., Healy, M., & Möller, K. (Eds.). *Out of Egypt: Biblical theology and biblical interpretation* (pp. 385–408). Grand Rapids, MI: Zondervan.

Beaver, R. (2011). *Educational psychology casework: A practice guide* (2nd ed.). Philadelphia, PA: Jessica Kingsley Publishers.

Beck, R. (2012). *The authenticity of faith: The varieties and illusions of religious experience.* Abilene, TX: Abilene Christian University Press.

Benjamin, J. (2004). Beyond doer and done to: An intersubjective view of thirdness. *The Psychoanalytic Quarterly, 73*, 5–46. doi:10.1002/j.2167–4086.2004.tb00151.x

Brown, J. K. (2010). Creation's renewal in the Gospel of John. *Catholic Biblical Quarterly, 72*, 275–290.

Brown, J. K. (2015). Is the future of Biblical theology story-shaped? *Horizons in Biblical Theology, 37*, 13–31.

Brown, J. K., Dahl, C. M., & Corbin Reuschling, W. (2011). *Becoming whole and holy: An integrative conversation about Christian formation.* Grand Rapids, MI: Brazos.

Brown, W. S., & Strawn, B. D. (2012). *The physical nature of Christian life: Neuroscience, psychology, and the church.* New York, NY: Cambridge University Press.

Browning, D. S., & Cooper, T. D. (2004). *Religious thought & the modern psychologies* (2nd ed.). Minneapolis, MN: Fortress Press.

Bruckner, J. K. (2005). A theological description of human wholeness in Deuteronomy 6. *Ex Auditu, 21*, 1–19.

Bucci, W. (1997). Psychoanalysis & cognitive science: A multiple code theory. New York, NY: Guilford Press.

Copeland, M. S. (2010). *Enfleshing freedom: Body, race, and being.* Minneapolis, MN: Augsburg Press.

Cozolino, L. (2017). *The neuroscience of psychotherapy: Healing the social brain.* New York, NY: W. W. Norton & Company, Inc.

Damasio, A. (2010). *Self comes to mind: Constructing the conscious brain.* New York: Pantheon.

Douglas, K. B. (2005). *What's faith got to do with it? Black bodies, Christian souls.* Maryknoll, NY: Orbis Books.

Dueck, A., & Reimer, K. (2009). *A peaceable psychology: Christian therapy in a world of many cultures.* Grand Rapids, MI: Brazos Press.

English, T. (2016). How pastoral care providers can help people with disability in claiming their sexuality. *Sexuality and Disability, 34*(1), 89–95. doi:10.1007/s11195-015-9418-4

Fee, G. D. (2014). *1 Corinthians*. Revised edition. Grand Rapids, MI: Eerdmans.

Foster, H. (1998). Trauma studies and the interdisciplinary: An interview. In A. Coles & A. Defert (Eds.), *The anxiety of interdisciplinarity* (pp. 157–168). London: Blackdog Publishing.

Gaventa, B. R. (2011). Reading for the subject: The paradox of power in Romans 14:1–15:6. *Journal of Theological Interpretation, 5*(1), 1–12.

Green, J. B. (2005). Body and soul, mind and brain: Critical issues. In J. B. Green & S. L. Palmer (Eds.), *In search of the soul: Four views of the mind-body problem* (pp. 7–32). Downers Grove, IL: InterVarsity Press.

Green, J. B. (2007). *Seized by truth: Reading the Bible as scripture*. Nashville, TN: Abingdon Press.

Greenberg, J., Koole, S. L., & Pyszczynski, T. (2004). *Handbook of experimental existential psychology*. New York, NY: Guilford Press.

Haley, J. (1993). *Uncommon therapy: The psychiatric techniques of Milton H. Erickson, MD*. New York, NY: W. W. Norton & Company.

Hall, M. E., & Thoennes, E. (2006). At home in our bodies: Implications of the incarnation for embodiment and Christian higher education. *Christian Scholar's Review, 36*, 21–37.

Hall, T. W., & Fujikawa, A. M. (2013). God image and the sacred. In K. I. Pargament, J. J. Exline, & J. W. Jones (Eds.), *APA handbook of psychology, religion, and spirituality (Vol. 1): Context, theory, and research* (pp. 277–292). Washington, DC: American Psychological Association.

Hall, T. W., Fujikawa, A., Halcrow, S. R., Hill, P. C., & Delaney, H. (2009). Attachment to God and implicit spirituality: Clarifying correspondence and compensation models. *Journal of Psychology and Theology, 37*(4), 227–242.

Hall, T. W., & Porter, S. L. (2004). Referential integration: An emotional information processing perspective on the process of integration. *Journal of Psychology and Theology, 32*, 167–180.

Harnack, A., & Saunders, T. B. (1900). *Christianity and history*. London: A&C Black.

Harnack, A. von. (1902). *What is Christianity?* (2nd ed.). London: Williams and Norgate.

Heikes, D. K. (2012). *The virtue of feminist rationality*. New York, NY: Continuum International Publishing Group.

Jacobson, H. L., Hall, M. L., & Anderson, T. L. (2013). Theology and the body: Sanctification and bodily experiences. *Psychology of Religion and Spirituality, 5*(1), 41–50. doi:10.1037/a0028042

Jacobson, H. L., Hall, M. L., Anderson, T. L., & Willingham, M. M. (2016a). Religious beliefs and experiences of the body: An extension of the developmental theory of embodiment. *Mental Health, Religion & Culture, 19*(1), 52–67. doi:10.1080/13674676. 2015.1115473

Jacobson, H. L., Hall, M. L., Anderson, T. L., & Willingham, M. M. (2016b). Temple or prison: Religious beliefs and attitudes toward the body. *Journal of Religion and Health, 55*(6), 2154–2173. doi:10.1007/s10943–016–0266-z

Johnson, L. T. (2015). *The Revelatory body: Theology as inductive art*. Grand Rapids, MI: Wm. B. Eerdmans Publishing.

Johnson, M. (2015). Embodied understanding. *Frontiers of Psychology, 6*, 1–8.

Johnston, R. (2014). *God's wider presence: Reconsidering general revelation*. Grand Rapids, MI: Baker Academic.

Jones, S. (2009). *Trauma and grace: Theology in a ruptured world*. Louisville, KY: Westminster John Knox Press.

Kierkegaard, S. (1980). *The sickness unto death: A Christian psychological exploration for upbuilding and awakening* (H. V. Hong & E. H. Hong, Eds. & Trans.). Princeton, NJ: Princeton University Press. (Original work 1849)

Leder, D. (1990). *The absent body*. Chicago: University of Chicago Press.

Moran, J. (2002). *Interdisciplinarity: The new critical idiom*. New York, NY: Routledge.

Morse, J. M., & Mitcham, C. (1998). The experience of agonizing pain and signals of disembodiment. *Journal of Psychosomatic Research, 44*(6), 667–680. doi:10.1016/S0022-3999(97)00301-2

Mount Shoop, M. W. (2011). Embodying theology: Motherhood as metaphor/method. In *Women, writing, theology: Transforming a tradition of exclusion* (pp. 233–252). Waco, TX: Baylor University Press.

Murphy, N. (1990). Theology and the social sciences—Discipline and antidiscipline. *Zygon, 25*, 309–316.

Murphy, N. (2013). When Jesus said 'Love your enemies' I think he probably meant don't kill them. *Perspectives in Religious Studies, 40*, 123–129.

Newberg, A. B. (2010). *Principles of neurotheology*. Burlington, VT: Ashgate Publishing Company.

Paris, P. J. (1995). *The spirituality of African people: The search for a common moral discourse*. Minneapolis, MN: Fortress Press.

Parton, C. M., Ussher, J. M., & Perz, J. (2016). Women's construction of embodiment and the abject sexual body after cancer. *Qualitative Health Research, 26*(4), 490–503. doi:10.1177/1049732315570130

Rambo, S. (2010). *Spirit and trauma: A theology of remaining*. Louisville, KY: Westminster John Knox Press.

Reed, T. I. (2002). Time in relation to self, world, and God. In A. Ramos & M. I. George (Eds.), *Faith, scholarship, and culture in the 21st century* (pp. 166–180). Washington, DC: American Maritain Association.

Reno, R. R. (2004). Biblical theology and theological exegesis. In C. Bartholomew, M. Healy, & K. Möller (Eds.), *Out of Egypt: Biblical theology and Biblical interpretation* (pp. 385–408). Grand Rapids, MI: Zondervan.

Reynhout, K. A. (2013). *Interdisciplinary interpretation: Paul Ricoeur and the hermeneutics of theology and science*. Plymouth, UK: Lexington Books.

Sandage, S. J., & Brown, J. K. (2015). Relational integration, part 1: Differentiated relationality between psychology and theology. *Journal of Psychology and Theology, 43*, 165–178.

Sheppard, P. (2011). *Self, culture, and others in womanist practical theology*. New York, NY: Palgrave Macmillan.

Siegel, D. (2010). *Mindsight: The new science of personal transformation*. New York, NY: Bantam Books.

Smith, L. E. (2006). *Howard Thurman: Essential writings*. Maryknoll, NY: Orbis Books.

Sproul, R., Gerstner, J., & Lindsley, A. (1984). *Classical apologetics: A rational defense of the Christian faith and a critique of presuppositional apologetics*. Grand Rapids, MI: Zondervan.

van Deusen Hunsinger, D. (2015). *Bearing the unbearable: Trauma, gospel, and pastoral care*. Grand Rapids, MI: Eerdmans.

Williams, D. (2013). *Sisters in the wilderness: The challenge of Womanist God-talk*. Maryknoll, NY: Orbis Books.

Worthington, E. L., Jr., & Sandage, S. J. (2016). *Forgiveness and spirituality: A relational approach*. Washington, DC: American Psychological Association.

Wright, N. T. (2003). *The resurrection of the Son of God*. Grand Rapids, MI: Fortress Press.

5

RELATIONAL INTEGRATION AS HERMENEUTICAL

In the previous chapter, we have defined relational integration as embodied. This quality of physicality and concrete location leads inexorably to the hermeneutical or interpretive character of relational integration. As Taylor (1985) has noted, humans are "self-interpreting animals" and typically engage in an ongoing hermeneutical process of seeking to make meaning out of life at levels that can range from the concrete (e.g., "What is causing my headache?") to the reflective (e.g., "What should I do with my life?"). In this chapter, we explore the hermeneutical facet of a relational interdisciplinarity between psychology and theology (or any two disciplines). We begin by giving attention to questions of objectivity and subjectivity in the quest for knowledge, before offering a *hermeneutical realism* for our understanding of the possibilities of human knowledge. We then turn to explore more fully the notion of hermeneutical "locatedness" in the academic enterprise. We conclude by highlighting the relational dynamics of hermeneutics as a lens for integration. Throughout the chapter, we engage a case study to illuminate our discussions and to press toward deeper integration.

Lost in Translation

Ruth—a theology professor at a seminary—was invited to be a participant at an interreligious conference held at a state university. The conference hosted visiting Islamic scholars from United Arab Emirates working in religious educational institutions in their country. These scholars were joined by local scholars teaching in Christian higher education, all of whom were asked to participate in the week leading up to the conference. The focus of the conversation was on the sacred texts of Islam and Christianity. There was an interpreter present to translate, since only the hosting scholar was fully conversant in both English and Arabic.

Ruth prepared a paper on the variety of ways that Christians appropriate the Bible as scripture for its use in theology, ethics, and church life today. Her hope was to stimulate dialogue around similar or different methods of appropriation within Islam, a subject about which she was not conversant. Other presenters from Christian schools presented papers on a variety of topics. For example, Carl, a teacher of Old Testament studies at a Christian college, presented a paper on a single-meaning approach to biblical interpretation. To elaborate this theme, Carl shared his analysis of a specific Hebrew word used in consistent ways across the Pentateuch, suggesting that his results paved the way for a literalist interpretation of the Bible.

Khalid, one of the Islamic scholars, used linguistics to argue for the superiority of the Qur'an over the Bible, contending that the Qur'an's infallibility confirmed its superiority. Another Islamic scholar, Nadia, focused her paper on the impact of linguistics for Qur'an interpretation and noted how this area of study affirms the truthfulness of the Qur'an. At this point, Ruth made a side-comment to John, a colleague from her own seminary, "I had no idea this conference would be about ideology rather than based on scholarly conversation and comparative studies." She realized that her paper was not particularly suited to these contours but hoped it would provide an interesting stimulus for conversation, even though there proved to be very little time for discussion after each paper due to the additional time required for translation during the papers.

Hamza, one of the Islamic scholars, didn't directly address the issue of the Qur'an's authority as others had. Instead, he provided an analysis of a particular early commentary on the Qur'an to illuminate Islamic interpretive method, suggesting that the history of interpretation opens the way for something of a contextual approach to hearing and applying the sacred text. Ruth was intrigued by Hamza's thesis, but there was only time for one or two questions after his presentation and she was concerned about asking a follow up question through the interpreter when she knew so little about Islam.

The scholars walked as a group to the faculty cafeteria, but ate in groups very much based on their language barrier. After the conference concluded, Ruth reflected on the day. She was struck by the common points of interest during the conference. Carl's paper, for example, engendered much interest from Khalid, who was affirming of Carl's lexical analysis for a literal reading of the Old Testament. Ruth herself was drawn to Hamza's work with its themes of interpretative traditions and the role of context in interpretation.

Ruth and John discussed their impressions of the conference the next day at the seminary. Ruth said, "I was surprised at what seemed to be areas of some agreement across religious lines. In fact, I felt like I had more in common with Hamza than with Carl."

We begin our case analysis around Ruth's comment to John, her colleague, that she was surprised by the ideological nature of the conference when she had expected a scholarly conversation. In this setting, the apologetic aims of various presenters were certainly more explicit than in the contexts Ruth usually participated in (e.g., the American Academy of Religion). In fact, we might characterize the work of Carl, Khalid, and Nadia as being prescriptive rather than descriptive. Yet we wonder if Ruth is aware of the "ideology" that may be more implicit but which informs even her more descriptive work (on "ways that Christians appropriate the Bible . . ."). How easily is any scholar able to separate their scholarship from their own interests?

We also would highlight the number of junctures in the case where *relational factors* contribute to a breakdown in collegiality, communication, and possibilities for integration. While we will discuss these in more detail at the end of the chapter, we would delineate here these relational missteps: (1) the provision of only one translator for the conference when only the host is bilingual, including during informal times like breaks and lunch; (2) Ruth's (and others'?) lack of knowledge about the religion and culture they are coming to engage; (3) seeming "power plays" from scholars on both sides to "demonstrate" the superiority of their faith; (4) Ruth at least considering the possibility that her take on the "power plays" might be a cultural difference in communication style; and (5) fear, at least on Ruth's part, of appearing incompetent ("she was concerned about asking a follow up question through the interpreter when she knew so little about Islam"), which functioned to inhibit curiosity and conversation.

Objectivity and Subjectivity

Objectivity and Scientific Inquiry in the Academy

In the modern era, objectivity had been tied to the legitimacy of the academic endeavor. While the natural sciences have been the vanguard of such claims, each of the disciplines has sought in its own way to authenticate its work through identification as science or assertions of scholarly objectivity. Many of the "non-scientific" disciplines (e.g., the humanities) evolved in the nineteenth century along the lines of the scientific method being used in the natural sciences (Moran, 2002, p. 151). In the latter part of that century, Dilthey proposed a theoretical foundation for the "human sciences" (with the term, *Geisteswissenschaften*, corresponding roughly to the social sciences and humanities) "that could support assertions of scientific objectivity while retaining a fundamental distinction from the natural sciences" (Reynhout, 2013, p. 11).

This concern for objectivity made its way into the disciplines of theology and psychology. The idea of theology *as a science* can be traced as far back as Aquinas, who used Aristotelian categories to claim theology as science in terms of drawing out through reason the implications of theology's first principles (Turner, 1997). Nevertheless, the late nineteenth and twentieth centuries saw intensified interest in framing theology and its various sub disciplines as "scientific," pressing further toward a norm of objectivity for theological inquiry, in part to work against the assignment of religion to the domain of symbolic (versus literal) language (Watts, 2012). This led to definitions of theology as merely descriptive, in which "the theologian is an investigator engaged in research, and his [sic] sole task is to give an objective account of the content of the Christian faith" (Nygren, 1972, p. 248). In the area of biblical studies, in spite of important currents that affirm the hermeneutical nature of all textual interpretation, Schneiders (1982) has opined that the "temptation in biblical criticism . . . to slip into a quasi-positivistic approach to the text has never been fully overcome" (pp. 54–55; for an example, see Baird, 1976).

The tensions between objectivity and subjectivity in psychology have been turbulent over the past century. Freud claimed his creation of psychoanalysis to be a science even though his interpretive methodology actually drew heavily on the humanities, highlighted the role of personal subjectivity, and lacked empirical testing. The logical positivist paradigm of science behind behaviorism in psychology emphasized the objectivist pole of epistemology and the study of tightly defined observable behaviors rather than mental states. At present in North America, it seems fair to say the dominant scientific philosophy in psychology is post-positivism which seeks a more dialectical perspective "beyond objectivism and relativism," to use the title of Bernstein's (1983) excellent book on science and hermeneutics. Post-positivists generally accept insights from the sociology of knowledge that observations of data are theory-laden and influenced by the personhood of the scientist, that scientific theories are located within historical contexts, and that scientific advances are often influenced not by the raw accumulation of more data but through shifts in interpretive perspectives or "broader conceptual webs" (Jones, 1994, p. 188). Nevertheless, debates continue in psychology between those holding constructivist frameworks emphasizing subjectivity, historical contexts, and qualitative research methodologies and those holding on to vestiges of positivism by privileging quantitative research over qualitative and discounting the role of theory (Melchert, 2013).

The topic of hermeneutics has been given some relatively limited engagement in psychology and psychoanalysis (for a review, see Sandage, Cook, Hill, Strawn, & Reimer, 2008). Examples include Cushman's (2007) work comparing Jewish Midrash hermeneutics with relational psychoanalysis and efforts by Richardson (Richardson, 2011; Richardson & Bishop, 2015) to argue for the benefits of psychologists owning certain social, moral, and narrative commitments in the interpretive research process. When "hermeneutics" is invoked in psychological literature, there is a strong tendency to associate hermeneutics with constructivist, non-realist epistemologies and qualitative or purely theoretical methods rather than quantitative methods, despite the fact that the diverse traditions of philosophical hermeneutics offer a range of perspectives on levels of objectivity and subjectivity in interpretation (Sandage et al., 2008). This imbalanced leaning toward subjectivity has limited the incorporation of hermeneutical thinking into psychological discourse since the major organizations that sustain and fund psychology research emphasize its empirical and scientific orientation toward generalizable knowledge.

The split between the objective and subjective dimensions of knowing and the limited recognition of more dialectical approaches to hermeneutics may be influenced by the modernistic segregation of academic disciplines. While many scholars acknowledge in theory the role of subjectivity and interpretation in their fields and work, it is precisely in the modern academy, with its *high degree of specialization*, where illusions of pure objectivity could be, at least temporarily, maintained and actualized. When we remain safely ensconced in our disciplines and among those in our discipline who are like-minded, it can be relatively easy to think we can achieve scientific objectivity. For example, Moran (2002) notes that

> [s]cience's self-confidence has traditionally stemmed from its self-limitations, its refusal to deal with those metaphysical or subjective concerns on which there are grounds for skepticism, confining itself to aspects of the biological or mechanical world that can be known "objectively" and "neutrally."
>
> *(p. 152)*

It is when we move into interdisciplinary dialogue that we often wonder more deeply about our own work. *Interdisciplinarity reveals the located-ness of ourselves and the disciplines we engage.* This is, in part, because someone outside of our own discreet discipline is often able to discern more easily the basic assumptions of our discipline than we ourselves can. This also happens within a single discipline across quite different methodologies. A scholar employing a different method is often able to reveal more easily the presuppositions of our own methodology, while we are able to grasp what invigorates their method. This kind of cross-disciplinary (and cross-method) illumination spotlights the traditions that sustain our disciplines and methods. It is in this space between disciplines (and between methods) that the role of subjectivity in the quest of knowledge becomes quite apparent.

Subjectivity and Tradition

We suggest that understanding how subjectivity functions in relation to objectivity comes by way of recognizing the role of tradition in human inquiry. Gadamer used the language of *tradition* for the history of a person or a discipline, and we find it helpful language to employ for our discussion. Rather than viewing tradition as anathema to the academic endeavor, we suggest understanding tradition as a situational given. Grappling with the inevitability of tradition can lead to deeper, critical analysis of the assumptions, canons, and methods of our own disciplines. In fact, we would suggest that eschewing the role of tradition in a discipline already betrays the presence of a specific tradition—what we might call the "I don't have a tradition" tradition.

As we have already noted, neither theology nor psychology is immune to this notion of bringing a "clean slate" to academic work. In theology, Hart (2000, p. 191) writes that such "a 'naked' reading of Scripture . . . is in practice a convenient fiction since even an initial approach to the text is already shaped by all manner of things which we bring to it." For those of us in theology and biblical studies, this "convenient fiction" then masks the realities of the reading locations of ourselves and our disciplines. Hart (1996) addresses how this "fiction" keeps us from critical assessment of our presuppositions.

> The Bible must be read and made sense of, by the traditions (theological and otherwise) within which we stand as interpreters. The idea that it is possible to step back entirely from these influences and achieve a pure reading of the text, therefore, is one which must be shown up for the self-deception that it is . . . Simple appeals to "what the Bible says" are always the sign of (no doubt unconscious) subservience to an interpretative tradition, not liberation from it. That which we mistakenly think we have escaped from is in reality free to exercise all the more influence over us, and is therefore all the more potentially dangerous.
>
> *(p. 167)*

It is often the "pre-theoretical commitments" of our tradition(s) that are most difficult to recognize and yet that energize our work most deeply (Wolters, 2007).

Nevertheless, traditions, once recognized, are ideally not chains but guides. As Gregersen (2015) argues,

> Traditions are inescapable as our epistemic starting points—they are boundaries from which we address the world. But traditions are not inevitably our final destination—we can both extend our traditions by entering into trans-communal dialogues and also take leave of traditions, even if we continue to be marked by them.
>
> *(p. 150)*

Recognizing how our traditions continue to leave their mark on us, even as we might move beyond a certain tradition or into another one, helps us to reflect critically on traditions even as we seek to understand what they might illuminate for us.

Strawn and colleagues (Strawn, Wright, & Jones, 2014; Wright, Jones, & Strawn, 2014) have argued for tradition-based integration, noting much of the integration literature has attempted to employ relatively generic versions of Christian theology without acknowledging the particular theological and moral traditions that inform their views (see a similar argument in Dueck & Reimer, 2009). This is essentially a hermeneutical argument for greater differentiation of interpretive frameworks, building on the arguments of MacIntyre (1990) and Taylor (1985) that hermeneutical traditions shape our views of virtue and "the good life." Certainly, theories of counseling and psychotherapy typically include implicit conceptions of the goals or telos of mature human functioning; and Browning and Cooper (2004) have done a masterful job of interpreting such values and metaphors of ultimacy (or ultimate concerns) in their work. We agree with the hermeneutical and integration benefits of acknowledging our traditions, and we each locate our own traditions in greater detail later in this chapter. We have also tried to be explicit throughout this book about our ideals of relational functioning and the theological and psychological grounding for those ideals. This is an important part of hermeneutical work in our relational integration model. For those of us who are clinicians or educators, this kind of hermeneutical, tradition-based self-awareness can also be part of differentiated understanding of distinctions between our own perspectives and those of clients or students with whom we work.

The importance of hermeneutical self-awareness is related to the psychotherapy topic of countertransference or the subjectivity of therapists. Older, modernistic perspectives in psychology largely viewed countertransference as problematic, generated by client transference dynamics, and something to be bracketed from the clinical process. This assessment was based on an objectivist orientation, in which the therapist was supposed to be objective to help correct problematic subjectivity in clients. Contemporary relational perspectives view countertransference more dialectically, as potentially helpful or problematic depending upon various factors (for an overview, see Cooper-White, 2004). Personal or subjective reactions to clinical experiences might be either informative or distorting. Relational models of psychotherapy and psychoanalysis also tend to view the therapists' subjectivity as inevitably influencing the intersubjective process of interaction between clients and therapists. This more relational approach requires therapists to be self-aware and reflective to decide how to make use of countertransference reactions, which might range from metabolizing their own reactions privately to avoid unhelpful projections or biases to disclosing certain responses that might offer useful interpersonal feedback and connection for clients.

Hermeneutical Realism

We recognize the importance of reckoning with both objectivity and subjectivity in academic pursuit, and we consider every discipline and disciplinarian to be situated in particular locations or traditions. We propose a dialectical version of *hermeneutical realism* that holds in tension the role of the objective and the subjective in epistemology and ethics (Browning & Cooper, 2004; Sandage et al., 2008; Schweiker, p. 1995). A dialectical approach is able to affirm that there is such a thing as (objective) reality that may be sought, while recognizing that human understanding is always subjective and partial. We pursue knowledge from particular locations and with particular assumptions, interests, and goals, influenced by our effective histories (Gadamer, 1989). Several scholars inform our view of hermeneutical realism, but the theological ethicist Don Browning (2003), drawing on Schweiker and Ricoeur, offers a particularly helpful overview:

> Hermeneutic realism . . . acknowledges that all understanding—including scientific understanding—is historically and linguistically shaped. But it also holds that it is possible, through various methodological maneuvers, to gain degrees of what Ricoeur calls "distanciation" (1981, 64–65). The concept of distanciation is Ricoeur's happy substitute for the positivist concept of objectivity. The idea of objectivity holds that understanding must begin with a cognitive self-emptying of one's prejudices and, through controlled experiment, conclude with objective propositions of states of affairs. Hermeneutic realism argues against the possibility of these positivistic assumptions about objectivity but contends that the inquirer can gain enough *distance* from his or her historically conditioned beginning point to achieve glimpses of the stable structures of reality (kinds of regularities within the human and natural world), even though one can never grasp them completely unsullied by culturally and historically shaped prejudgments.
>
> *(p. 319)*

While we derive our understanding of hermeneutical realism from a number of theorists working in our own disciplines as well as from philosophical currents, we believe that we offer something novel in our application of hermeneutical realism *to interdisciplinary relational integration between psychology and theology.* As suggested above, most psychological theorists who engage hermeneutical philosophy tend toward the subjectivist pole more exclusively. In theology (and in biblical studies particularly), there has been important work in the area of "critical realism," which we will elaborate below, but there continues to be something of a divide between those who consider their approaches more objectively scientific (e.g., sometimes claimed for historical criticism) and those who expressly advocate for hermeneutical awareness and approaches and rightly argue that all interpretations are located (Schüssler Fiorenza, 1988).

Hermeneutical Realism From the Angle of Theology

There are a number of theologians who propose a methodology of hermeneutical realism, although the language they suggest has typically been "critical realism."

Ben Meyer, for example, has drawn on this concept to forge a middle path between positivism and dogmatism in biblical studies. He argues that true biblical theology "conceives of the critical spirit not as closing off religious allegiances in favor of the objectivity of positivism but as serving them in accord with the objectivity of critical realism" (Meyer, 1989, p. 197). N. T. Wright (1992), addressing historical investigation of the New Testament, has suggested that critical realism forms a middle road between positivism (or "naïve realism") and phenomenalism (pp. 32–35). Wright defines critical realism as

> a way of describing the process of "knowing" that acknowledges the *reality of the thing known, as something other than the knower* (hence, "realism"), while also fully acknowledging that the only access we have to this reality lies along the spiralling path of *appropriate dialogue or conversation between the knower and the thing known* (hence, "critical"). This path leads to critical reflection on the products of our enquiry into "reality", so that our assertions about "reality" acknowledge their own provisionality. Knowledge, in other words, although in principle concerning realities independent of the knower, is never itself independent of the knower.
>
> *(p. 35)*

A critical realist approach does not simply assume that knowledge comes from the collection and organizing of empirical data; rather, it takes account of the ways data find coherence within particular worldviews, i.e., sets of stories, theories, and assumptions about the way things are (Wright, 1992, p. 37–44). And it is precisely these latter worldview categories that must be acknowledged and accounted for to avoid naïve forms of empiricism.

From another angle in the work of theology, critical realism has found traction in the *dialogue between theology and the natural sciences.* Ian Barbour, a physicist with theological training, introduced this concept to interdisciplinary work between science and theology (Barbour, 1966; see Reynhout, 2013). For Barbour, "the *meaning* of truth is correspondence with reality" (1990, p. 110). But because human beings lack direct access to reality, attention must be paid to the criteria of truth. Barbour identifies these criteria as (1) agreement with data; (2) coherence; (3) scope (comprehensiveness or generality); and (4) fertility or generativity (p. 109). "Because correspondence is taken as the definition of truth, this is a form of realism, but it is a *critical realism* because a combination of criteria is used" (p. 110). As Reynhout (2013) describes Barbour's view, a critical realist stance "can acknowledge *both* the independent existence of a real world and the creativity of the human mind" (p. 5). One of the strengths of Barbour's theoretical work was his eschewing of abstraction and the grounding of his theory in the actual practices of religious and scientific communities (p. 3; see Barbour, 1966). This coheres with our emphasis in the previous chapter on embodiment over a kind of disembodied abstraction frequently preferred in scholarly communities.

For Barbour, like Wright, a critical realist perspective navigates between the poles of positivism (that "theories are mere summaries of data;" Reynhout, 2013, p. 3) and idealism, defined similarly to Wright's phenomenalism. Reynhout (2013) sums up Barbour's expression of critical realism in this way:

> Notice that for Barbour a realist not only believes that there is a real world external to the scientist's theoretical constructs, but that there is also a potential connection between theories and the objects they represent. Realism is thus both a metaphysical and an epistemological position. Even if "being is prior to knowing," as Barbour contends, there must be a link between knowing and being in order for science to work, and it is the nature of that link at stake in the move from realism to *critical* realism.
>
> *(p. 5)*

Reynhout (2016) has provided an even more finely tuned perspective on critical realism by proposing a movement from a primarily epistemological framework to a hermeneutical one. He argues, in concert with other voices like Coleman (2014), that epistemology provides an inadequate bridge between theology and the natural sciences (the particular dialogue he is involved in), in part because of the long history of associating natural sciences with the explanatory and human sciences (including theology) with interpretation. Reynhout's (2013) alternative proposal toward interdisciplinary dialogue is to highlight how theology and science each engage in both *explanation*—"a 'bottom up' operation"—and interpretation or *understanding*, which proceeds "in a 'top-down' fashion" (p. 83). Reynhout (2013, 2016) delineates an inner and outer hermeneutic of scientific practice, both of which include the work of understanding, that is, acts of interpretation. He (2016) concludes,

> All scientific disciplines use interpretation—understanding through explanation—in different ways and to varying degrees, as I have described. This doesn't necessarily level the playing field, since the hermeneutical distinctions between disciplines can be profound, but the universality of hermeneutical practice does imply that the natural sciences cannot claim any kind of pristine, interpretation-free zone of inquiry.
>
> *(p. 89)*

In application to the dialogue between psychology and theology, we would affirm that there is no "pristine, interpretation-free zone of inquiry" for either of our disciplines. Rather, both are engaged in explanatory and interpretive inquiry, even as the ways these areas of inquiry are practiced and interact in either discipline will vary, often significantly. As such, we suggest that a method of *hermeneutical realism* might be fruitfully engaged for an interdisciplinary method for psychology and theology.

Hermeneutical Realism From the Angle of Psychology

The splits in theology and biblical studies between those advocating for more objective, scientific approaches and those suggesting all hermeneutical orientations as located are paralleled by debates in psychology over degrees of objectivity and subjectivity in research. These tensions play out in dramatic fashion in the clinical applications of psychology (counseling, psychotherapy, psychoanalysis), in which arguments occur about the need and appropriateness of empirical research. At one extreme (objectivist) focused on scientific explanation is the argument that treatments should be based on empirical evidence in randomized clinical trials, and those treatments should be manualized to foster high levels of treatment adherence. Interestingly, I (Steve) heard an advocate of this view suggest that one of the benefits of manualization of treatments is that therapists do not need to be highly skilled—they can just follow the manual. A better argument for manualization is to try to enhance the fidelity of treatments for research purposes and to contribute to the thoughtful use of clinical strategies and interventions. At the other extreme are those who focus on relational understanding and view psychotherapy or psychoanalysis as a practice that is too dynamic, complex, and non-linear for empirical methodologies and a scientific paradigm (e.g., Stern, 2015), or they object to the privileging of systematic empirical research over the more traditional case study methods of knowing in psychoanalysis (Hoffman, 2009). It is worth noting that psychoanalysis is the area of psychology that has made the greatest use of hermeneutical philosophy (Saks, 1999; Sandage et al., 2008); Stern and Hoffman are among those constructivists offering a strong contrast between empirical and hermeneutical ways of knowing and a preference for the humanities in their theorizing.

We would affirm that there are valid concerns on both sides of this debate. Naïve forms of empiricism can be reductionistic with respect to subjective, relational, contextual, and non-linear aspects of psychotherapy, although a careful reading of contemporary empirical research on psychotherapy will show more nuanced and sophisticated attention to these dynamics than some critics acknowledge. Alternatively, ignoring empirical research altogether carries some risk of authoritarianism and hierarchical power dynamics where clinicians are the ones who determine in a unilateral way what is effective without boundaried feedback from clients. It is interesting to note that certain psychoanalysts relativizing the importance of empirical research, such as Hoffman and Stern, find company with Biblical counselors like Powlison (2010) who consider empirical research a "second-tier priority" (p. 198) and have not yet published outcome research on the effectiveness of Biblical counseling. Despite the limits of empirical research, it does provide a means for clients' voices and confidential evaluations to be recognized in the assessments of treatments, even if those voices are translated into numbers. Research has shown that clinicians often over-estimate the effectiveness of the treatments they provide, which also highlights the need for a feedback loop from clients (Wampold & Imel, 2015). Ethically speaking, it also seems problematic to ignore the vast empirical literatures available in so many crucial areas, such as reducing depression and suicidality, treating problems of sexual functioning or marital conflict, enhancing interpersonal forgiveness, and many other areas.

In our relational integration view, hermeneutical realism offers a framework that acknowledges we do make theory- and tradition-based interpretations of meaning that mediate our access to data (Slife & Christensen, 2013). Yet it also suggests there is a real world that offers constraints on the coherence of interpretations that can be developed and effectively applied (Slife & Christensen, 2013). Hermeneutical realism also goes beyond most critical realist views that focus on our imperfect and mediated access to reality, and does so by building on the dialectical views of ontology and epistemology among certain scholars who have contended that reality is both discovered and constructed (e.g., Bernstein, 1983; Gadamer, 1989; Mangis, 1999; Ricoeur, 1981; Sandage et al., 2008). Systems theorists Maddock and Larson (1995) have explained, "humans simultaneously perceive and create their own experiences" (p. 105). Cushman (1995) applied Gadamer's ontological hermeneutics to psychotherapy and argued for a dialogical view of reality as co-constructed: "There is a very subtle and complex dialectic at work in human life: the world we are thrown into constructs us and then we must continually reconstruct it" (p. 310). Richardson and colleagues (1999) offer a similar understanding in their approach to psychology based on Heidegger's ontological hermeneutics: "Our nature or being as humans is not just something we *find* (as in deterministic theories) nor is it something we just *make* (as in existentialist and constructivist views); instead, it is *what we make of what we find*" (p. 212; italics original). This "constructing" aspect of the hermeneutical process also fits Gadamer's notion of effective history and the influence of historical contexts on knowing. For example, when we seek to hermeneutically integrate contemporary psychological research on forgiveness with ancient understandings of forgiveness in biblical texts (e.g., Shults & Sandage, 2003), the result will be a new construction influenced by the historical and social context of that integrative work.

Sandage and colleagues (2008) have developed a hermeneutical realist process model for research in psychology based on these ideas above and oriented toward both *explanation* and *understanding* (see also Ricoeur, 1981). The goal of explanation fits with the analytic, objectivist pole in science in an attempt to gain some distance from a phenomenon and identify parts within a structure, causal relations, or other patterns (Grassie, 1994). Quantitative approaches in psychological research tend to orient toward a goal of explanation. Understanding represents inferential and synthetic thinking of putting things together in meaningful wholes and drawing implications, especially practical ones. Explanation and understanding are often held as separate goals in different social science methodologies, with qualitative methods focused on understanding. However, Ricoeur (1981) differentiated explanation and understanding but also brought them together in an overarching hermeneutical process: "understanding is entirely mediated by the whole explanatory procedures which precede and accompany it" (p. 220).

Figure 5.1 depicts the hermeneutical realist process model developed by Sandage et al. (2008; adapted from Grassie, 1994 and based on Ricoeur, 1981). Both Ricoeur and Gadamer suggested our tradition-based knowing starts with pre-understandings or what Gadamer called "prejudice" (i.e., pre-judgements). Gadamer did not use the term "prejudice" in overtly negative terms; rather, he meant by it a kind of initial bias. This fits with theory-driven approaches to empirical science; the phase of explanation or distanciation (see below) is a moment of distance in the process that allows for viewing data from a different vantage point and challenges one's pre-understanding. Both Gadamer and Ricoeur also emphasized that the hermeneutical process should lead to comprehension and practical appropriation: "to make one's own what was initially 'alien'" (Ricoeur, 1981, p. 185), and this can potentially lead to revised understanding. This insight about practical appropriation and "making one's own" in an overall hermeneutical process of understanding *and* explanation is consistent with our relational integration emphases on both formation and practical integration through case study methods (see also Chapter 8 of this book).

Hermeneutical Realism From Philosophy: Paul Ricoeur

Much of our theoretical work throughout this book is focused on and derived from psychology and theology (and at times biblical studies more particularly). This should come as no surprise given our own disciplinary locations as a psychologist and a biblical scholar (which we describe below). Yet we think it important to acknowledge that we are also influenced by voices from other disciplines, including philosophy. Certainly, in some cases philosophy has already left its mark

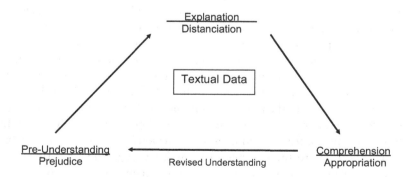

FIGURE 5.1   Hermeneutical Process Model

Source: Adapted from Grassie, 1994; based on Ricoeur, 1981. Reprinted with permission from Sandage et al., 2008.

on our respective disciplines, as, for example, in Bultmann's engagement with existentialism for biblical studies (Bultmann & Ogden, 1960) or Stoic philosophical influences on cognitive-behavioral therapies (Robertson, 2010) In other cases, our own reading interests have carried us into ancillary or related disciplines like philosophy, where we sojourn as respectful laypersons and guests.

As indicated at several points above, both of us have been influenced in our thinking on hermeneutics by philosopher Paul Ricoeur, whose work suggests holding in dialectical tension objectivity and subjectivity. Ricoeur was an exemplar of interdisciplinary fluency as he traversed philosophy, linguistics, theology, psychology, biblical studies, history, literature, neurobiology, and many other disciplines. While his work is sophisticated and complex, many have noted the humanness of Ricoeur and a dialectical commitment to love and justice that comes across in his writings. He conveyed both a hopefulness and a capacity for pathos, the latter no doubt formed through the many personal losses he experienced and the five years he spent as a prisoner of war during World War II.

One of Ricoeur's main contributions can be understood as implicitly integrating hermeneutics and development, as he proposed that the interpreter initially begins with a certain naïveté in relation to what is being interpreted. In this early stage, the interpreter experiences a phenomenon without much awareness of or attention to the act of interpretation that they are performing. In theology, this might look like the claim that "I just believe what the Bible says," as if the reading process was not already interpretative in nature. Ricoeur then offers the concept of "distanciation," which is the experience of distance between the interpreter and that which is being interpreted. This experience of difference, which we would relate to differentiation of self, allows the "object" of interpretation to be understood on its own terms to a greater extent than previously was the case. For Ricoeur, with distanciation comes the possibility of a return to proximity—what he calls a "second naïveté"—without the loss of what was gained in the movement of distanciation. After distance is experienced, "[t]hen, and only then the hermeneutical concept par excellence, *appropriation*, would appear as the dialectical counterpart of distanciation which ought to remain the first and the last word . . ." (Ricoeur, 1978, p. 319). In this return to proximity, object becomes subject in its own right and interpretation becomes a kind of conversation (Brown, 2007).

Ricoeur's concept of distanciation offers for our model of hermeneutical realism the possibility of a kind of frame shifting. "Moments of distanciation," as Ricoeur (1981) refers to them, allow an interpreter to shift perspectives and view the landscape from a different perspective. This alternate perspective or frameshifting offers the partial bracketing of some previously held assumptions, which in turn contributes to the possibility of new knowledge and explanation. The hermeneutical process in this dialectical model can then move to appropriation— i.e., testing the fruits of explanation. Tests of appropriation can lead to revised understandings and the re-forming of integrative models (Sandage & Brown, 2015, p. 174).

We find Ricoeur's framework of movements—from an initial naïveté to distanciation to second naïveté—valuable for an interdisciplinary hermeneutical realism between psychology and theology, not least because it holds together "subject" and "object" in interpretation both dialectically and relationally. A second naïveté also speaks to the potential, and also to the challenges, of returning to the language, practices, and meanings that can be found in cultural and religious traditions following our moments (or seasons) of distanciation and growth in critical awareness. The differentiated integration and appropriation of a second naïveté can involve "making one's own" certain aspects of a tradition that have been questioned or reframed toward a new understanding. Sometimes it may feel safer to maintain or jettison a tradition altogether rather than come back into proximity and reengagement. Bowen has noted a parallel dynamic of reducing anxiety about one's family of origin through emotional cutoff and geographic distancing (Kerr & Bowen, 1988).

Maintaining a dialectic of proximity and distance also allows the interpreter to both listen *and* suspect, to use Ricoeur's language (see below), allowing critique to function precisely as a means toward (and not necessarily a movement away from) appropriation. Ricoeur is also known for his dialectic of a hermeneutics of suspicion and a hermeneutic of faith—a dialectic that involves holding the differing and conflictual hermeneutical poles of both suspicion (e.g., the uncovering of hidden dynamics from Nietzsche, Freud, and Marx) and the eventual restoration of meaning. For Ricoeur, interpretation means suspicion *and* listening, or rigor *and* obedience—all highly relational terms, we would note.

In his discussion regarding "The Conflict of Interpretations," Ricoeur (1970) names this dialectical tension among the interdisciplinary sets of interpretive disciplines that make up the field of hermeneutics.

> The difficulty . . . is this: there is no general hermeneutics, no universal canon for exegesis but only disparate and opposed theories concerning the rules of interpretation . . . According to one pole, hermeneutics is understood as the manifestation and restoration of a meaning addressed to me in the manner of a message, a proclamation, or as is sometimes said, a kerygma; according to the other pole, it is understood as a demystification, as a reduction of illusion. Psychoanalysis, at least on the first reading, aligns itself with the second understanding of hermeneutics . . . Hermeneutics seems to be animated by this double motivation: willingness to suspect, willingness to listen; vow to rigor, vow to obedience.
>
> *(pp. 26–27)*

Ricoeur was on target with his emphasis on a hermeneutics of suspicion and a kind of prophetic, deconstructive unmasking in Freudian theory, although in recent decades certain psychoanalytic theorists have also emphasized a hermeneutics of trust that assumes truthfulness and common goodwill between client and therapist (Orange, 2011, p. 38). Yet Ricoeur's unique dialectical hermeneutics of suspicion and faith speaks to a relationally integrative process that resonates with the insights of certain relational psychoanalysts (e.g., Benjamin, 2004; Mitchell, 1988) and relational psychotherapists (e.g., Kegan, 1994; Safran & Muran, 2000), who hold a dialectical mindset and normalize the developmental functions of relational ruptures. The integrative goal for each of these theorists is hardly to avoid relational or intellectual conflict nor to seek a superficial harmonizing of perspectives. Rather, the client-therapist relational process is understood as dialectical and dialogical and involves making use of ruptures and conflicts productively in order to construct something transformative. This requires a kind of hermeneutical openness to new understanding, but not so open or "over-incorporative" that tensions or conflicts are dissociated and unengaged.

Hermeneutical Realism for Interdisciplinarity

We find hermeneutical realism a helpful framework for interdisciplinarity within our relational integration model for several reasons. First, the key metaphors of dialogue and conversation in the ontological hermeneutics of Gadamer, Ricoeur, and Habermas foreground the transformational dynamics of relationality in the process of knowing; and these metaphors are consistent with our relational integration emphasis on interdisciplinary dialogue and conversation between psychologists and theologians as real, located persons. Second, the positive valuing of interpretive traditions *and* the questioning of our traditions are helpful as we have come together as scholars representing different traditions (or collections of traditions) and disciplines, providing needed dialogue that helps us see our own traditions and disciplines from a different perspective. Third, the dialectical emphases on both understanding and explanation in hermeneutical realism fit nicely with both our own hermeneutical assumptions about our respective disciplines and what actually happens when we enter deeply into interdisciplinary dialogue, namely, our pre-understandings are challenged or stretched by gaining the distance offered by interdisciplinary relations. In this light, the differences between our disciplines are less obstacles to be overcome and instead serve to benefit the overall goal of differentiation in the relational integration process. Fourth, the *realism* in hermeneutical realism leads us to believe there is a real world to study from our differing vantage points, however partially we may be able to access it. A relationally integrative fusion of different personal and disciplinary horizons can help us more richly understand and respond to that world. Finally, the practical appropriation edge of hermeneutical realism is consistent with our experience that engagement with real world problems and cases pull for relational integration and can enhance the quality of relationally integrative reflection and application.

A hermeneutical realist ontological paradigm for interdisciplinarity also resonates with the dialectical and differentiated relationality approach to the disciplines of psychology and theology we have discussed in Chapter 1, namely that psychology and theology can be meaningfully differentiated as disciplines yet they are mutually embedded in human experience. There is a dialectical tension between description and prescription that cannot be completely collapsed or segregated (Browning & Cooper, 2004; Sandage et al., 2008). This fits with empirical evidence that personality traits can influence theological beliefs among Christians in an area as central as Christology (Piedmont, Williams, & Ciarrocchi, 1997; Strawn & Alexander, 2008). There are also implicit moral, ethical, and ontological or religious assumptions in many psychological and psychotherapeutic theories (Browning & Cooper, 2004). For example, in Linehan's (2015) skills training manual for Dialectical Behavior Therapy—probably one of the most widely used forms of psychotherapy in the world—she claims the following metaphysical or theological belief in a handout for clients:

> *Everything in the universe is interconnected.* This is a major finding of modern physics. It is also a tenet of all major religious and spiritual paths. Given this reality, each of us is also interconnected with the entire universe. *There are no outsiders or strangers.*
>
> *(italics hers; p. 215)*

If psychology and theology cannot be completely segregated, as hermeneutical realism suggests, it seems important to engage the disciplines responsibly, reflectively, and relationally through interdisciplinary dialogue.

"Locatedness" in the Search for Knowledge

If all human inquiry involves interpretation (i.e., is hermeneutical), then it is essential to attend to location in the quest for knowledge. And locations—disciplinary, personal, social—matter for integration. "Integrators cannot separate fully their ideas from their social locations, conscious and unconscious assumptions, and relational experiences" (Sandage & Brown, 2015, p. 172). By affirming that location matters in interpretation and interdisciplinarity, we highlight the importance of reckoning with tradition, experience, and other particulars of location in these processes.

Yet as we have suggested in our discussion of hermeneutical realism, the reality of location does not mean that humans are locked into a single perspective, without the means of transcending that specific location for interpretation and interdisciplinarity. Instead, increased awareness of location allows one to intentionally move toward "distanciation," bringing with it the ability to assess more carefully one's assumptions and frame of reference. As I (Jeannine) have noted in relation to interpretation of the Bible (2007), "by engaging in dialogue with others who do not think exactly as we do, we increase the likelihood of having our own interpretive blind spots clarified" (p. 133).

And we have found that awareness of "locatedness" is often heightened during interdisciplinary dialogue, allowing for greater critical engagement with and appreciation for that location. For example, in a cross-listed course between family therapy and theology that I (Steve) taught, a school counseling student remarked at the end of the class that she had initially considered theology as irrelevant to her work as a school counselor due to perceived boundaries against the promotion of religion in public schools. But after a semester of class dialogue with theology students, she had come to understand theology as a broader discipline that could not be completely segregated from her own discipline. She also mentioned her own personal ambivalence about religion and her resolution to revisit her beliefs, which underscores our emphases on personal influences upon relational integration. As Moran (2002) suggests, "[i]nterdisciplinarity could . . . be seen as a way of living with the disciplines more critically and self-consciously, recognizing that their most basic assumptions can always be challenged or reinvigorated by new ways of thinking from elsewhere" (p. 187). In this way, recognition of location can be a potential strength rather than a drawback for integration.

Yet there is often resistance to understanding integration in located ways, and examples of such resistance can be found in both psychology and theology. In psychological practice, it is not uncommon to hear case presentations where the ethnicities or social locations of the clients and the therapist involved are left unstated or only mentioned if the clients are persons of color. In theology, sidelining of or even resistance to so called "contextual theologies" belies assumptions of an objective high ground for those doing "classic" or "mainstream" theology. The claim of contextual theologians—those who name their location and argue that theology be done with a view to one's present context as well as Scripture and tradition—is that all theology is contextual; it is located and situated. As much as possible, we should account for how our locations impact our scholarship (for an example, see Brown & Roberts, in press, Chapter 1).

A relational approach to integration that accounts for location differs from other integrative approaches and has been relatively scarce in the integration literature. While Johnson (2010) describes five views relating psychology and Christianity, none of them expressly acknowledges social location in their epistemology. Yet a more relational and located view of knowledge coheres quite well with Christian theology, as it finds its source in the biblical witness. Paul in 1 Corinthians, for example, views knowledge alone or as the highest goal to actually work against its acquisition. To his Corinthian audience fixated on *gnosis*, Paul points instead to love as a framework for truly knowing.

> If anyone presumes to have knowledge, they do not yet know as they ought to know. But the one who loves, that person truly knows.
>
> *(1 Cor 8:2–3; our translation; see Brown, Dahl, &*
> *Corbin Reuschling, 2011, p. 69)*

As Scott, in his study of Pauline epistemology (2006) proposes, Paul grounds ethical knowledge in a theological story—"a grand narrative of humanity's relationship with its Creator" (p. 155). This framework invites hermeneutical engagement by locating "the mundane events of one's life properly into the context of the theological story" and points beyond conceptual knowledge to a relational *"knowledge of God and of Christ"* (p. 155; italics original). We might note here the focus on locating a particular narrative ("the mundane events of one's life") with as larger theological storyline ("a grand narrative"). Location matters in the pursuit of knowledge.

In theological reflection, human locatedness has a creational basis. The biblical narrative begins with the creation of the world and of humanity, with human beings being made in God's image (Gen 1:26–27). As Bauckham (2002) observes, "Creation in the image of God both assigns a certain likeness to God and at the same time makes clear that this is precisely a likeness in created form" (p. 174). This creature status implies that humans are finite, located, and dependent on their God. Even with humankind's lofty call to image God, there remains an "immeasurable gap that separates Creator and creature" (McClendon, 1994, p. 159).

Yet it is important to note the temporal or narrative placement of this affirmation of createdness. Human finitude and location are based "in God's intention at creation, rather than in the fall and its consequences" (Brown, Dahl, & Corbin Reuschling, 2011, p. 67). Since the Christian theological tradition has placed emphasis on the impact of the fall upon human knowing, it is important to affirm that finitude is not a result of sin but is a creational given. We do acknowledge, with the tradition, that sin has an impact on human knowing, often referred to as the noetic effect of sin. Sin can distort the lenses through which we see the world. And this distortion can be one of "both knowledge of fact and knowledge of value," that is, affecting what we know and what we love (Plantinga, 2000, p. 207). Yet, as we have suggested in our discussion of natural theology (chapter 4), people may still experience divine revelation—both general and special—in spite of potential blind spots and distortions arising from their finite locations or from the reality of sin. In fact, blind spots and distortions are best identified and addressed or corrected by a more communal approach to knowing.

Objectivity, Tradition, Location

The case on interfaith dialogue shows signs that its participants were assuming the objectivity of their work, something that would be expected at any scholarly conference. The apparent stance of both Carl and Khalid in their presentations fit what Hart calls "simple appeals" to what the text says—a way of coming to the text that tends to ignore the impact of tradition. For example, Carl argued that we should take the language of "God said" in the Pentateuch as proof for a "literal hermeneutic"—that is, for understanding all biblical language as non-symbolic. In a sense, this hermeneutic removes any need for tradition or for conceiving of revelation—including that found in the Bible—as mediated.

Ruth and Hamza gave expressed attention to particular interpretative traditions in their papers, so it is not surprising that Ruth thought Hamza's work was the most interesting for her own engagement. This avenue of dialogue between those of different faiths, like Hamza and Ruth, seems promising, especially as it presses each scholar to understand their own tradition well enough to be able to describe it to someone who adheres to another religion. This level of understanding invites both appropriation and critique of one's own tradition, making a dialogue between Ruth and Hamza even more potentially fruitful. It requires each conversation partner to be intersubjectively open to someone with a different horizon of understanding and a willingness to learn from and be influenced by the other person (Race, Kenney, & Rao, 2005). This can offer a relational experience of distanciation with respect to one's own tradition (or discipline). Unfortunately, a number of relational barriers inhibited any such dialogue (see p. 127).

We find it telling, if not surprising, that not one of the scholars explicitly addressed their own social location (something not typically done in these scholarly settings). Yet the differences of location among these scholars were visibly apparent throughout the conference—in the languages individual scholars spoke, the clothing they wore, and even the places where they sat in the room. The Islamic scholars who were the first invited guests to the conference sat in the front, with the exception of the female scholars who sat in a backrow. The Christian scholars, some of whom had been invited just the week before the conference, sat toward the back of the room. Most were male, so Ruth was very aware of her femaleness as she took a seat next to her colleague, John.

This leads us to inquire about the gender dynamics of the case. The disciplines represented at this conference are heavily male-dominated, especially in their more conservative wings. So, it's not surprising that Ruth's awareness of her gender was heightened; we suspect this was also the case for the women from the United Arab Emirates (U.A.E.), all of whom wore burqas. Each of these four women presented from their seats in the backrow using a microphone. The rest of the participants spoke via microphone from table at the front of the room. It was not clear to the participants from the U.S. whether this was their normal protocol for conferences that included both men and women, or if this was a result of being in a cross-cultural, co-ed setting. Whatever the specific purpose, the result was an apparent highlighting of their difference as women, while at the same time signaling their lesser power or status by eliminating their voice from the front of the room. Ruth found herself identifying with these dynamics of their participation and felt, as she was presenting, that she lacked a measure of authorization that seemed to attend her male counterparts, whether from Christian or Islamic context.

Our Own Locations

We have been advocating for the need to acknowledge the reality of interpretive and interdisciplinary location(s) on a theoretical level. While we could conclude the discussion at this point, it feels important to us to give some space to naming our own disciplinary and social locations and to note how these locations impact our scholarship. These brief remarks are not meant to be exhaustive but illustrative, so that our readers get a glimpse of our own processing of these issues and questions.

Jeannine: My Location

Although across our work, I have brought the voice of theologian to our conversations, my training is specifically in New Testament studies. So, while I readily consider my scholarly work as having theological import, it is likely the case that those trained in the specific discipline of theology will have already recognized in this book my location as biblical scholar. One deeply held value of my guild is to read any particular biblical author as much as possible on their own terms and in their original context, without recourse to other canonical authors except those on whom that author is dependent (e.g., Matthew's use of both various Old Testament texts and Mark in the crafting of his Gospel). This means that I will often be fairly hesitant moving to a theological synthesis across the canon (i.e., doing biblical or New Testament theology), even though I am part of an ecclesial tradition that is committed to such a canonical synthesis.

The values of my guild also lead me to grapple with any particular biblical author at a whole-book level. My training has taught me that reading of the Bible must press toward holistic rather than atomistic interpretation. A recent request for a theme Bible verse for an event I was helping to shape and lead caused me great consternation, since the isolation of a single verse to highlight what might truly be a biblical theme goes against all my training. It's as if a neon sign with the words "Proof-Texting!" flashes before me in these kinds of moments.

This scholarly location of the guild of biblical studies is paired in me and in my experience with the evangelical tradition within which I have been raised and in which I have spent my teaching career. This tradition affirms with ease the canonical synthesis I have just mentioned. In other words, my evangelical tradition is quite at home with biblical theology, even while my guild has a fairly ambivalent relationship with it. I straddle this tension, remaining committed to the distinctive voices of each New Testament author while also holding the conviction of an overarching unity across Scripture.

Another facet of my ecclesial and teaching context involves being a woman within evangelical traditions. Being female has made this an uneasy location for me, especially as a woman with a gift and passion for teaching the Bible growing up in a fairly fundamentalist church context. While approaching the text with a hermeneutic of trust (or a sympathetic hermeneutic; see Brown and Roberts, in press), I have learned to use judiciously a hermeneutic of suspicion vis à vis interpretations of certain biblical texts and themes from my own tradition, for example, ones that have reified exclusively male power across the social spectrum. As I have noted elsewhere (2013),

> my own experiences as a female biblical scholar in a church tradition and a guild that have been primarily shaped and almost exclusively led by men have caused me to be suspicious of various readings of the text offered from these contexts. The application of a hermeneutic of suspicion toward the reading traditions of which I am a part has shaped my own reading values and perspective.

Steve: My Location

I locate myself theologically within the Wesleyan tradition and continue to resonate with (a) the epistemological orientation of the Wesleyan quadrilateral drawing on scripture, reason, tradition, and experience (Brown, 2004); (b) Wesley's goal of developing a practical theology and using science to help alleviate human suffering; and (c) the Wesleyan emphasis on social justice as an essential part of holiness and spiritual formation. Wesley's general relational ministry strategy of using group dynamics (i.e., bands and class meetings) and confession of sins to facilitate authentic self-confrontation and spiritual transformation during the eighteenth century revival in England has also shaped my relational and systemic orientation toward psychotherapy and spiritual formation. I am not leading group confession of sin, but my focus on relational dynamics as the primary source of change fits the tradition. Certain strands of the Wesleyan tradition that have influenced relational and process theologies offer conceptual convergence with relational psychotherapies.

The Wesleyan tradition is also known for sometimes inculcating a compulsive quest for perfectionism, and extensive personal therapy has helped partially temper that tendency in me that is linked to this "shadow side" of Wesleyan holiness traditions. This shift developed for me during my doctoral training in psychology, more specifically the subfield of counseling psychology, which exposed me to relational psychoanalytic theories and the benefits of authentic, depth exploration of one's emotional and relational experiences. Actually, Wesley's emphasis on the affections and his pull toward contemplative Catholic streams of apophatic spirituality (including "dark nights of the soul") resonate with aspects of contemporary relational psychoanalysis, however Wesley may have been too quick in his attempts to resolve internal/unconscious tensions and return to a conscious pursuit of virtue. I have also come to identify strongly with existential and continental philosophy traditions, which reveal the poignant human dilemmas we face, such as anxieties about making commitments or the losses that are inevitable with personal growth or constructing new understandings. Existentialism contrasts the optimism of the Wesleyan traditions and reminds me that integration necessarily includes dealing with the tragic forces of non-being (e.g., death, guilt, loss, oppression).

My doctoral training in counseling psychology, postdoctoral work in marriage and family therapy, and subsequent teaching in those fields has grounded me in social science disciplines that (a) tend to be dialectical about objective and subjective poles of knowing, (b) value both empirical science and contextual-systemic awareness of human diversity, and (c) emphasize positive human strengths and values, allowing a deeper conceptual integration of science and ethics than in some other fields. Ironically, I now have a faculty appointment with the clinical psychology PhD program at Boston University in the Department of Psychological and Brain Sciences, and clinical psychology is a field that has been more closely aligned with medicine and the natural sciences. I appreciate the clinical psychology emphasis on rigorous science and the realism about struggles with severe psychopathology, which are sometimes downplayed in positive psychology literatures. I am encouraged by the emerging work on positive-clinical psychology as a dialectical orientation to these issues.

I am a highly privileged white (primarily Norwegian-Scottish-Irish-American), straight, Christian, cisgender male whose formal theological education vastly over-emphasized theologians in my same demographics. Therefore, it has been important and transformative for me to study various contextual and liberation theology traditions (including Black, Latinx, Asian, American Indian, Feminist, Womanist, Postcolonial, and Queer theologies), as well as other religious traditions. This has heightened my awareness of the locatedness and limitations of my own worldview and practices and has enabled me to hermeneutically encounter alternative horizons of understanding. The liberation traditions prophetically herald the spiritual and existential centrality of justice and community, and the role of power and oppression in shaping what gets counted as "knowledge." Insights from these traditions have lined up with certain branches of systemic approaches to psychotherapy in ways that have helped me view therapy as a prophetic practice of inviting, and sometimes perturbing, systems toward transformation and justice rather than rebalancing a status quo.

Hermeneutics as Formational and Relational

Our goal in this chapter has been to analyze how hermeneutics contributes to interdisciplinary integration between psychology and theology. We'd like to conclude by attending to the formational and relational dynamics of hermeneutics for integration. Our relational anthropology of personhood leads us to some differing emphases from Jones' (2010) more foundationalist approach to integration based on an anthropology of rationality; it places us closer to the formation-based approach of Coe and Hall (2010) and the communal hermeneutics of Wright et al. (2014).

Pressing toward greater hermeneutical awareness can be a significantly formative process, particularly when pursued relationally in conversation with diverse others. Caputo (1987) referred to "hermeneutics as a lesson in humility" (p. 258). In fact, the formation of humility is a theme among several authors advocating for relational psychoanalytic approaches to hermeneutics (e.g., Cushman, 2007; Mangis, 1999; Orange, 2011; Stern, 2003). At its best, hermeneutical reflection focuses needed attention on the self as interpreter, the numerous traditions and communities that have impacted one's hermeneutic, and one's concrete interpretive practices that are formed and reformed relationally over time. I (Jeannine) have found that, in teaching a first-semester seminary Hermeneutics course, students regularly move from equilibrium to disequilibrium and back again as they are faced, often for the first time, with the specter of their own *hermeneutic*. I share with them these words from Achtemeier (1969) as we begin the course:

> If theology is to make sense *now* about the meaning of Jesus Christ whose career took place *then*, it has in that moment engaged in a transfer of meaning. It has carried out a hermeneutic . . . the question is whether that hermeneutic . . . is to be the object of deliberate theological reflection, or whether it is to be assumed and allowed to operate without the benefit of theological clarification.
>
> *(p. 14)*

Making one's own hermeneutic "the object of deliberate theological reflection" is often a daunting and anxiety-provoking task. And in the anxiety and self-reflection, there comes the opportunity for change and for greater levels of differentiation.

We would suggest that grappling with the hermeneutical nature of integration can lead to a more differentiated stance toward one's own discipline, an important relational capacity. Recognizing that academic disciplines, like psychology and theology, are themselves *located* presses toward a thicker set of questions about their location. *What are the ultimate aims of my discipline as it has been constructed and conceived? Who have been the architects of my discipline, and how has their social location impacted its shape and direction? What are the core values of my discipline?* And, *how do my own values arise from and/or interact with those of my discipline?*

This greater level of differentiation in relation to our home discipline can help us move into interdisciplinary conversation more productively with people from other disciplines. Differentiation helps us to not only conceive of the role of the various "players" in interdisciplinary integration—the integrators and their specific disciplines—but also to the relationships among these players. We envision these relationships forming *the spaces* between integrators and between an integrator and their home discipline (see Figure 5.2).

Our discussion in Chapter 3 about third spaces is appropriate to bring to the fore here. We use the language of "third space" to refer to the relationship or conversation between integrators in interdisciplinary work. And we suggest that this relationship warrants attention on its own terms (Sandage & Brown, 2015). By attending to this third space, we are more likely to honor rather than dismiss situations of conflict and anxiety that are inevitably part of the integrative process.

Granting the importance of our hermeneutical locations in respect to our disciplines allows us to acknowledge the space between ourselves and our home discipline as well, recognizing that anxiety and conflict may also be functioning in these relationships as we turn to navigate interdisciplinary conversations. For example, in integrative conversations it is fairly common for what's called "overreach" to occur. As Moran (2002) defines it, overreach is the idea of "name-dropping concepts and theorists without really understanding them or the huge conceptual distinctions that exist between different specialisms" (p. 159). When overreach happens, it is very likely that the first person to recognize it is the person whose discipline has been transgressed. By holding a differentiated stance toward our own discipline and avoiding collapsing the difference between ourselves and our discipline, we may be better able to interact with a colleague who is unintentionally overreaching. We may be in a better position to stay relationally focused and dialogue about the parameters of our discipline without carrying the anxieties of others from our discipline over the disciplinary transgression.

Differentiation is also necessary in the relational hermeneutics of interdisciplinary work since losses of cherished ideas can arise. Ricoeur (2007) makes a parallel point about mourning in the process of translating a text, where idealized notions of the perfect translation are confronted by difficult choices and a more realistic, imperfect goal of translational "equivalence" (p. 114). I (Steve)

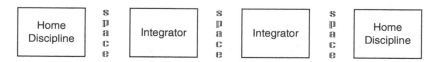

FIGURE 5.2 Relational Spaces in Integration

remember the feelings of anxiety and frustration in a conversation with Jeannine when I realized my rather simplistic understanding of a certain biblical theme was inaccurate. Jeannine had not challenged my ideas but was simply sharing some of her disciplinary expertise on the topic. Internally, I felt a temptation to withdraw from the conversation to try to preserve and protect my own prior understanding (or hermeneutic). The urge felt so defensive in the moment that I took time to reflect on it later and realized the biblical themes and my prior uncritical interpretation were unconsciously tied to certain relationships that had been hurtful to me. This realization about the relational hermeneutics involved eventually proved helpful, but in the moment I experienced grief.

In our view, these deconstructive and reconstructive dynamics of relational hermeneutics are ubiquitous in the conversational contexts of psychotherapy, education, and training; and differentiation is needed to make them formative and integrative (or re-integrative). This view of relational hermeneutics suggests practices like psychotherapy and education are potentially formative not through the transfer of information but through the back and forth of meaningful dialogue that inevitably involves questions, disputes, and the opening of new horizons while losing sight of old ones (Cushman, 2007). There is a certain level of personal and interpersonal security needed for this kind of relational hermeneutical process, but it is not anxiety-free.

So, hermeneutical losses can generate anxiety in the midst of the relational integration process, but risk of construction can also be anxiety-provoking. We have watched this repeatedly occur among students in integration courses and diagnosed it in ourselves. This constructive process can be particularly intense for our students when they prepare and deliver in-class presentations of their integrative work, which we consider incredibly valuable in the relational integration process. If stewarded well with a good balance of support and challenge, this group process of relational hermeneutics facilitates differentiation-based formation.

Throughout our work, we have conceived of and argued for integration between psychology and theology that, ideally, happens between psychologists and theologians rather than within a single disciplinarian. This coheres with the notion that hermeneutics is a communal activity—a peopled endeavor. As McClendon (1994) writes, "knowing is a social, not a solitary, accomplishment" (p. 244). Hermeneutical processes are relational; they are informed by relational development as well as "our participation in particular community contexts" (Sandage & Brown, 2015, p. 173). We resonate with Yong's (2002) affirmation that

> interpretation can be said to be an intentional, teleological and transformative activity. It can be said to aspire to engage an other while enabling the other to retain its integrity and autonomy. And, it can be said to be communally defining as well as communally engaging.
>
> (p. 163)

Relational Dynamics

The relational dynamics of this case are particularly intriguing, since there were significant relational barriers to interreligious dialogue. A central relational barrier we could identify is *anxiety around difference*. Morgan and Sandage (2016) have described the differentiation that is necessary for competence in this type of interreligious dialogue. This conference brought together people from significantly difference locations—social, religious, cultural, and linguistic. It seems that anxiety over difference made it difficult for any of the participants to take the risk that would be required to move from isolated papers followed by a few brief comments to true dialogue. This was apparent during breaks and lunch, where the conversations were segregated. We hear of an additional layer of anxiety in Ruth's concern that she might appear unknowledgeable about Islam.

This case highlights some of the risks involved in interreligious dialogue and even raises the question of the framing of this interreligious conference. It was clear to the participants that religious and language differences would be at the center of this conference and there was little to no preparation required of participants other than preparing their own papers. Yet interreligious dialogue requires time devoted to learning about differences and practicing dialoguing skills (Larson & Shady, 2017), and research summarized in Chapter 3 shows simple contact between groups does not necessarily produce cooperative or integrative relationships. What might have happened if the conference participants had been asked to do some learning across their religious traditions? Or if more space had been given to dialogue with additional translators on hand to foster informal conversations? What if the conference would have included not only linguistic translators but also some time for an interreligious expert to offer a kind of hermeneutical translation to help the participants better understand their differing hermeneutical approaches? It is possible these measures could have helped participants to see similarities and differences across both religious traditions and hermeneutical methodologies and led to more differentiated understanding. Our point here is that this kind of relational integration work takes time, intentionality, and language learning. In his aptly titled article "Can We Talk?" Dueck (2002) offered a similar appraisal about the importance of language learning for fruitful integrative dialogue between psychologists and theologians. While we are emphasizing relational dynamics in integration throughout this book, it is also true that there is a level of basic knowledge of another discipline or religion that is important for meaningful understanding across differences.

Conclusion

In this chapter, we began by noting tensions in the academy around objectivity and subjectivity in the quest for knowledge. We then focused the central part of the chapter on our construction of a *hermeneutical realism* for the integration of psychology and theology, drawn from theorists in our own disciplines and also from reliance upon the work of Paul Ricoeur. After exploring the reality of location in integration, including offering glimpses into our own self-defined locations, we have concluded the chapter by identifying some of the relational dynamics of a hermeneutical approach to interdisciplinarity. Across the chapter, we have consistently suggested that relational integration is *hermeneutical*—that it always includes acts of interpretation. Yet this hermeneutical given does not stifle the possibility of gaining knowledge. Instead, recognizing our own locations and interpretative stances opens up spaces for potentially richer forms of interdisciplinary knowledge.

Bibliography

Achtemeier, P. J. (1969). *An introduction to the new hermeneutic*. Philadelphia: Westminster Press.

Baird, J. A. (1976). Content analysis and the computer: A case-study in the application of the scientific method to biblical research. *Journal of Biblical Literature, 95*(2), 255–276.

Barbour, I. G. (1966). *Issues in science and religion*. Englewood Cliffs, NJ: Prentice-Hall.

Barbour, I. G. (1990). *Religion in an age of science*. San Francisco, CA: Harper & Row.

Bauckham, R. (2002). *God and the crisis of freedom: Biblical and contemporary perspectives*. Louisville: Westminster John Knox.

Benjamin, J. (2004). Beyond doer and done to: An intersubjective view of thirdness. *Psychoanalytic Quarterly, 73*, 5–46.

Bernstein, R. J. (1983). *Beyond objectivism and relativism: Science, hermeneutics, and praxis*. Philadelphia: University of Pennsylvania Press.

Brown, J. K. (2007). *Scripture as communication: Introducing Biblical hermeneutics*. Grand Rapids, MI: Baker Academic.

Brown, J. K. (2013). Matthew's "least of these" theology and subversion of "us/other" categories. In N. W. Duran & J. P. Grimshaw (Eds.), *Matthew: Texts @ contexts*. Minneapolis, MN: Fortress Press.

Brown, J. K., Dahl, C. M., & Corbin Reuschling, W. C. (2011). *Becoming whole and holy: An integrative conversation about Christian formation*. Grand Rapids, MI: Baker Academic.

Brown, J. K., & Roberts, K. A. (in press). *The Gospel of Matthew: Two horizons new testament commentary*. Grand Rapids, MI: Eerdmans.

Brown, W. S. (2004). Resonance: A model for relating science, psychology, and faith. *Journal of Psychology and Christianity, 23*, 110-120.

Browning, D. S. (2003). Feminism, family, and women's rights: A hermeneutic realist perspective. *Zygon, 38*, 317–332.

Browning, D. S., & Cooper, T. D. (2004). *Religious thought and the modern psychologies*. Minneapolis, MN: Fortress Press.

Bultmann, R., & Ogden, S. M. (1960). *Existence and faith: Shorter writings of Rudolf Bultmann*. New York, NY: Meridian Books.

Caputo, J. D. (1987). *Radical hermeneutics: Repetition, deconstruction, and the hermeneutic project.* Bloomington, IN: Indiana University Press.

Coe, J. H., & Hall, T. W. (2010). A transformational psychology view. In E. L. Johnson (Ed.), *Psychology & Christianity: Five views* (pp. 199–226). Downers Grove, IL: InterVarsity Press.

Coleman, R. J. (2014). *State of affairs: The science-theology controversy.* Eugene, OR: Cascade.

Cooper-White, P. (2004). *Shared wisdom: Use of the self in pastoral care and counseling.* Minneapolis, MN: Fortress Press.

Cushman, P. (1995). *Constructing the self, constructing America: A cultural history of psychotherapy.* Reading, MA: Addison Wesley.

Cushman, P. (2007). A burning world, an absent God: Midrash, hermeneutics, and relational psychoanalysis. *Contemporary Psychoanalysis, 43*(1), 47–88. doi:10.1080/001075 30.2007.10745896

Dueck, A. (2002). Babel. Esperanto, Shillobeths and Pentecost: Can we talk? *Journal of Psychology and Christianity, 21,* 72–86.

Dueck, A., & Reimer, K. (2009). *A peaceable psychology: Christian therapy in a world of many cultures.* Grand Rapids, MI: Brazos Press.

Fayek, A. (2004). Islam and its effect on my practice of psychoanalysis. *Psychoanalytic Psychology, 21*(3), 452–457. doi:10.1037/0736–9735.21.3.452

Gadamer, H. G. (1989). *Truth and method* (Rev. ed., J. Weinsheimer & D. G. Marshall, Trans.). London: Continuum. (Original work published 1975)

Grassie, W. J. (1994). *Reinventing nature: Science narratives as myths for an endangered planet.* Unpublished doctoral dissertation, Temple University, Philadelphia.

Gregersen, N. H. (2015). J. Wentzel van Huyssteen: Exploring venues for an interdisciplinary theology. *Theology Today, 72*(2), 141–159.

Hart, T. (1996). *Faith thinking: The dynamics of Christian theology.* Downers Grove: InterVarsity Press.

Hart, T. (2000) "Tradition, authority, and a Christian approach to the Bible as Scripture." In J. B. Green & M. Turner (Eds.), *Between two horizons: Spanning New Testament studies and systematic theology* (pp. 183–204). Grand Rapids, MI: Eerdmans.

Hoffman, I. Z. (2009). Doublethinking our way to "scientific" legitimacy: The desiccation of human experience. *Journal of the American Psychoanalytic Association, 57,* 1043–1069.

Johnson, E. L. (Ed.). (2010). *Psychology & Christianity: Five views* (2nd ed.). Downers Grove, IL: InterVarsity Press.

Jones, S. L. (1994). A constructive relationship for religion with the science and profession of psychology: Perhaps the boldest model yet. *American Psychologist, 49*(3), 184–199. doi:10.1037/0003-066X.49.3.184

Jones, S. L. (2010). An integration view. In E. L. Johnson (Ed.), *Psychology & Christianity: Five views* (pp. 101–128). Downers Grove, IL: InterVarsity Press.

Kegan, R. (1994). *In over our heads: The mental demands of modern life.* Cambridge, MA: Harvard University Press.

Kerr, M. E., & Bowen, M. (1988). *Family evaluation: The role of the family as an emotional unit that governs individual behavior and development.* New York, NY: W.W. Norton & Company, Inc.

Larson, M.H., & Shady, S.L.H. (2017). *From bubble to bridge: Educating Christians for a multifaith world.* Downers Grove, IL: InterVarsity Press.

Linehan, M. M. (2015). *DBT skills training manual* (2nd ed.). New York, NY: Guilford Press.

Lonergan, B. (1972). *Method in theology.* New York, NY: Herder and Herder.

MacIntyre, A. (1990). *Three rival versions of moral enquiry: Encyclopaedia, genealogy, and tradition.* Notre Dame, IN: University of Notre Dame Press.

Maddock, J. W., & Larson, N. L. (1995). *Incestuous families: An ecological approach to understanding and treatment.* New York, NY: Norton.

Malony, H. N. (1999). John Wesley and psychology. *Journal of Psychology and Christianity, 18*(1), 5–18.

Mangis, M. W. (1999). An alien horizon: The psychoanalytic contribution to a Christian hermeneutic of humility and confidence. *Christian Scholar's Review, 28,* 411–431.

McClendon, J. W. Jr. (1994). *Doctrine.* Systematic Theology 3. Nashville, TN: Abingdon.

Melchert, T. P. (2013). Beyond theoretical orientations: The emergence of a unified scientific framework in professional psychology. *Professional Psychology: Research and Practice, 44*(1), 11–19. doi:10.1037/a0028311

Meyer, B. F. (1989). *Critical realism and the New Testament.* Eugene, OR: Pickwick Publications.

Mitchell, S. A. (1988). *Relational concepts in psychoanalysis: An integration.* Cambridge, MA: Harvard University Press.

Moran, J. (2002). Interdisciplinarity: The new critical idiom. New York, NY: Routledge.

Morgan, J., & Sandage, S. J. (2016). A developmental model of interreligious competence. *Archive for the Psychology of Religion, 38,* 129–158.

Nygren, A. (1972). *Meaning and method: Prolegomena to a scientific philosophy of religion and a scientific theology.* Philadelphia: Fortress Press.

Orange, D. M. (2011). *The suffering stranger: Hermeneutics for everyday clinical practice.* New York, NY: Routledge.

Piedmont, R. L., Williams, J. G., & Ciarrocchi, J. W. (1997). Personality correlates of one's image of Jesus: Historiographic analysis using the Five-Factor Model of personality. *Journal of Psychology and Theology, 25*(3), 364–373.

Plantinga, A. (2000). *Warranted Christian belief.* New York: Oxford University Press.

Powlison, D. (2010). Biblical counseling response. In E. L. Johnson (Ed.), *Psychology & Christianity: Five views* (2nd ed., pp. 194–198). Downers Grove, IL: InterVarsity Press.

Race, A., Kenney, J., & Rao, S. (2005). The interreligious insight paradigm: An invitation. *Interreligious Insight: A Journal of Dialogue and Engagement, 3,* 8–19.

Rahner, K. (1968). *Spirit in the world.* New York, NY: Herder and Herder.

Reynhout, K. A. (2013). *Interdisciplinary interpretation: Paul Ricoeur and the hermeneutics of theology and science.* Plymouth, UK: Lexington Books.

Reynhout, K. A. (2016). Moving beyond epistemology: Exploring hermeneutics as an alternative framework for the religion and science dialogue. *Philosophy, Theology, and the Sciences 3*(1), 72–96.

Richardson, F. C. (2011). A hermeneutic perspective on dialogical psychology. *Culture & Psychology, 17*(4), 462–472. doi:10.1177/1354067X11418544

Richardson, F. C., & Bishop, R. C. (2015). Philosophical hermeneutics and the one and the many. In H. Pedersen, M. Altman, H. Pedersen, M. Altman (Eds.), *Horizons of authenticity in phenomenology, existentialism, and moral psychology: Essays in honor of Charles Guignon* (pp. 145–164). New York, NY: Springer Science + Business Media. doi:10.1007/978-94-017-9442-8_10

Richardson, F. C., Fowers, B. J., & Guignon, C. B. (1999). *Re-envisioning psychology: Moral dimensions of theory and practice.* San Francisco, CA: Jossey-Bass.

Ricoeur, P. (1970). *Freud & Philosophy: An essay on interpretation* (D. Savage, Trans.). New Haven and London: Yale University Press.

Ricoeur, P. (1978). The hermeneutical function of distanciation. In F. Bovon & G. Rouiller (Eds.), *Exegesis: Problems of method and exercises in reading (Genesis 22 and Luke 15)* (pp. 297–319). Pittsburgh: Pickwick Press.

Ricoeur, P. (1981). *Hermeneutics & the human sciences* (J. B. Thompson, Ed. & Trans.). Cambridge, UK: Cambridge University Press.

Ricoeur, P. (2007). *Reflections on the just* (D. Pellauer, Trans.). Chicago: University of Chicago Press.

Ricoeur, P., & Ihde, D. (1974). *The conflict of interpretations: Essays in hermeneutics* (D. Ihde, Ed.). Evanston, IL: Northwestern University Press.

Roberston, D. (2010). *The philosophy of cognitive behavioural therapy: Stoic philosophy as rational and cognitive therapy*. London: Karnac Books.

Safran, J. D., & Muran, J. C. (2000). *Negotiating the therapeutic alliance: A relational treatment guide*. New York, NY: The Guilford Press.

Saks, E. R. (1999). *Interpreting interpretation: The limits of hermeneutic psychoanalysis*. New Haven, CT: Yale University Press.

Sandage, S. J., & Brown, J. K. (2015). Relational integration, part 1: Differentiated relationality between psychology and theology. *Journal of Psychology and Theology, 43,* 165–178.

Sandage, S. J., Cook, K. V., Hill, P. C., Strawn, B. D., & Reimer, K. S. (2008). Hermeneutics and psychology: A review and dialectical model. *Review of General Psychology, 12,* 344–364.

Schneiders, S. M. (1982). The paschal imagination: Objectivity and subjectivity in New Testament interpretation. *Theological Studies, 43*(1), 52–68.

Schüssler Fiorenza, E. (1988). The ethics of biblical interpretation: Decentering biblical scholarship. *Journal of Biblical Literature* 107(1) 3-17.

Schweiker, W. (1995). *Responsibility and Christian ethics*. New York, NY: Cambridge University Press.

Scott, I. W. (2006). *Paul's way of knowing: Story, experience, and the Spirit*. Grand Rapids, MI: Baker Academic.

Shults, F. L., & Sandage, S. J. (2003). *The faces of forgiveness: Searching for wholeness and salvation*. Grand Rapids, MI: Baker Academic.

Slife, B. D., & Christensen, T. R. (2013). Hermeneutic realism: Toward a truly meaningful psychology. *Review of General Psychology, 17*(2), 230–236. doi:10.1037/a0032940

Stern, D. B. (2003). Psychoanalytic discourse at the turn of our century: A plea for a measure of humility: Commentary. *Journal of the American Psychoanalytic Association, 51*(Suppl), 98–108.

Stern, D. B. (2015). *Relational freedom: Emergent properties of the interpersonal field*. New York, NY: Routledge.

Strawn, B. D., & Alexander, M. (2008). Correlation of self-perception and image of Christ using the five-factor model of personality. *Pastoral Psychology, 56*(3), 341–353. doi:10.1007/s11089-007-0106-x

Strawn, B. D., Wright, R. W., & Jones, P. (2014). Tradition-based integration: Illuminating the stories and practices that shape our integrative imagination. *Journal of Psychology & Christianity, 33*(4), 37–54.

Taylor, C. (1985). Self-interpreting animals. In *Philosophical papers: Vol 1. Human agency and language* (pp. 45–76). Cambridge, UK: Cambridge University Press.

Turner, G. (1997). St Thomas Aquinas on the "Scientific" nature of theology. *New Blackfriars, 78*(921), 464–476.

Wampold, B. E., & Imel, Z. E. (2015). *The great psychotherapy debate: The evidence for what makes psychotherapy work* (2nd ed.). New York, NY: Routledge.

Watts, F. (2012). Doing theology in dialogue with psychology. *Journal of Psychology and Theology* 40(1), 45–50.

Wolters, A. (2007). No longer queen: The theological disciplines and their sisters. In D. L. Jeffrey & C. S. Evans (Eds.), *The Bible and the university* (pp. 59–79). Grand Rapids, MI: Zondervan.

Wright, N. T. (1992). *The New Testament and the people of God.* Minneapolis, MN: Fortress Press.

Wright, R., Jones, P., & Strawn, B. D. (2014). Tradition-based integration. In E. D. Bland & B. D. Strawn (Eds.), *Christianity and psychoanalysis: A new conversation* (pp. 37–54). Downers Grove, IL: InterVarsity Press.

Yong, A. (2002). *Spirit-word-community: Theological hermeneutics in trinitarian perspective.* Burlington, VT: Ashgate.

6

RELATIONAL INTEGRATION AS DEVELOPMENTAL

In previous chapters, we have defined relational integration as interdisciplinary collaboration based on differentiated relationality drawing upon the concept of differentiation of self. In Chapters 4 and 5 we explored relational integration as (a) embodied and (b) hermeneutical, and in the present chapter we extend our description of relational integration to include developmental dynamics. We begin with a call to heighten developmental considerations in the integration of psychology and theology. We then examine the developmental pathways of spiritual formation in theology and of human development in psychology. Two key resources for "thinking developmentally" are attachment and differentiation, and we consider how different forms of attachment impact relationality and spirituality. Since dis-integration (or non-integration) is an integral part of development and formation, we explore the concept of dis-integration from psychological and theological perspectives. We conclude the chapter with a look at human development viewed from a narrative lens.

As in these previous chapters, we offer a case dilemma to illustrate and broaden our discussion of relational integration as developmental.

Losing Home

Paula (age 19, Swedish-American) was wrapping up a very difficult freshman year at a large university in the Midwest United States. She had grown up in a small, rural farming community several hours away where she had been a strong student, a two-sport athlete, and the homecoming queen. Her family farmed (corn and soybeans) and were a tight-knit group heavily involved in an evangelical Christian church in the Covenant tradition. Paula and her five siblings had learned to work hard on the farm, although her siblings sometimes complained she, as the youngest, had been protected from the hardest labor.

She had been both excited and nervous to go off to college to double major in English and education with a goal of teaching. Her first semester started out well as she got involved with a campus ministry, joined a global literature reading group, and made many new friends from diverse backgrounds. However, as spring semester now came to a close, Paula found herself severely depressed (with some fleeting suicidal ideation), helpless in trying to stop a new bulimic coping strategy of bingeing and purging, struggling to even pass several of her courses, and feeling almost constant guilt and spiritual confusion. Her attendance at the campus ministry had been quite sporadic over the semester, but at a recent Bible study on the Book of Romans a friend, Rose, became concerned when Paula declared quite forcefully about herself that she was "nothing but pond scum compared to God." To Rose, this sounded like something different than humility and she wondered if she should follow up with Paula, who looked tired, pale, and unkempt. Paula's parents were getting frustrated with her and had recently argued with her by phone as they had been asking for weeks when exactly she would be arriving home for the summer. Paula was stalling to see if she could put together summer work at the college to somehow avoid going home and having her family recognize her current condition, and also because her boyfriend Mark (age 22, Italian-American) had been pressing her to stay in town for the summer.

There was probably no singular factor causing her difficulties, however certain changes were evident after she started dating Mark in the fall. He was from a large Midwestern city and studying finance. They had met at a party on campus in the fall and quickly started dating. Mark was a rather dominating presence, and Paula was attracted to his confidence, intelligence, and broader life experience. She commented to a friend, "He knows where he's going in life and he knows everybody on campus." Mark was a heavy drinker, and their rapid sexual involvement was new for Paula and an eventual source of internal conflict with her Christian values which Mark did not share. He teased her about "being a prude" and was dismissive when she attended campus ministry events, referring to it as "youth group." Samuel (age 41, Scandinavian-American), one of the leaders in the campus ministry who knew Paula, had learned secondhand about some of these tensions with Mark and met with her for coffee several months before to confront her and warn her from the Bible about the dangers of "being unequally yoked with non-believers" (from 2 Corinthians 6:14). Paula said she *could see his point and would think about it, but she started skipping the campus ministry large group meetings after that, in part to avoid follow-up from Samuel. This was around the time her relationship with Mark turned even more conflict-ual and damaging. Mark had been controlling and verbally abusive before, but one Friday afternoon when Paula was packing to go home for the weekend Mark demanded she stay in town to watch one of his intramural sports events saying, "If you really care about me, you won't disrespect me like this." When Paula scoffed at his statement, he grabbed her violently by both her arms and yelled into her face. She was extremely scared and kind of shut down inside before unpacking her bags. That week, Paula went to the student health service and made an appointment to meet with an intern therapist, Naomi (age 24, Jewish-American, Practicing of Reform Judaism), who was immediately concerned with Paula's safety in relation to Mark.*

There are many potential integrative starting points for interpreting and conceptualizing a case like this one. In a clinical context with Paula as a psychotherapy client, it would be important to start, as Naomi does, with prioritizing her safety and also trying to understand thoroughly how she is making sense of her situation and her suffering. In this case, Paula ini-tially told her therapist she felt "torn up inside," "depressed and tired," and "conflicted" about the relationships in her life. After several therapy sessions, she offered the poignant description of her sense of dis-integration, "It's like there are parts of me connected to my family and my faith and other parts of me here [at college] and with Mark, and I can't figure out how to fit them together . . . or if they even *should* fit together. Maybe God doesn't want them to fit together . . . but there are much bigger problems in the world and it feels selfish that I am getting so affected by all this."

From a clinical psychology perspective, our attention might begin to hone in on assessing Paula's symptoms which suggest she could potentially meet criteria for a depressive disorder, an eating disorder, and even a trauma disorder, the latter possibly related to Mark's abuse and violence. Pastoral and theological perspectives within Paula's particular evangelical faith tra-dition might share a concern for these issues but would likely start with a spiritual focus and interventions aimed at Paula's recent distancing from God and Christian community, her sporadic and declining spiritual practice (e.g., prayer and Bible reading), and some of her behavioral choices in dat-ing and sexuality that conflict with that tradition (Samuel's focus). Naomi embodied several of our relational integration commitments by seeking to understand and pace Paula's religious language, beliefs, and values with respect and curiosity, asking questions when necessary and gradually explor-ing connections between Paula's religiosity and her feelings, questions, and struggles. In supervision after the third session, Naomi also helpfully processed her own countertransference of some anxiety about whether Paula would ask about Naomi's religiosity and subsequently accept their religious differences. This kind of self-awareness and processing of countertransference is a crucial part of remaining differentiated and offering clients a secure attachment.

In addition to these important initial considerations, we also suggest "thinking developmentally" about the case, something we explore in depth in this chapter.

Thinking Developmentally

We suggest that human development can serve as a window into relational integration. Development does not need to be the first consideration in conceptualizing a case like the one we address across the chapter, but we believe development involves a key set of dynamics that prove crucial to our understanding of relational integration and the overall frame we employ for such cases. Some theoretical approaches and frameworks within both social science and theology lack a developmental perspective or mindset, and so our focus on development also helps us differentiate the conceptual, analytical, and practical tools that fit our relational integration approach. There are many different theories of human development that can be employed, and we describe in this chapter our preferences for certain relational, systemic, and contextual frameworks.

The phrase *thinking developmentally* might be somewhat misleading since we do not mean an excessive cognitive focus and are seeking a relational integration of knowing (epistemology), being (ontology), and doing (ethics). But it is a shorthand way of referencing the need to bring a developmental awareness or mindset to relational integration, particularly when considering case conceptualizations and practical applications. In our view, thinking developmentally starts by considering a series of developmental questions, each of which can engage social science and theology. We will introduce these questions here and expand on these considerations further throughout this chapter:

1. Contexts—What are the developmental tasks the person, family, or organization is dealing with at the present time in their various nested contexts and sociocultural ecologies (Bronfenbrenner, 1979; Rogoff, 2003) that might be shaping their struggles and dilemmas? Are there particular developmental virtues that are needed given the present challenges? Why are problems happening at this particular time?

2. Continuity versus Change—What are points of continuity (stability) and change (de-stabilization) in the situation? Are there personal or systemic

transitions unfolding? How is the anxiety of change being managed by the various persons involved?

3. Strengths/Virtues—What are the developmental strengths and virtues of the individuals and systems? How can those strengths and virtues be utilized to facilitate further developmental integration?

4. Teleology—What are the ultimate goals or strivings (the telos) the various people are pursuing? What are they longing for? Have they lost touch with goals that feel meaningful? Developmental theories posit differing ultimate goals and concerns (Browning & Cooper, 2004), so part of relational integration is considering how our own developmental or teleological assumptions fit with the goals of those we are working with.

5. Losses—Human finitude means that development involves an existential process of gains and losses, so we can also ask if there are important losses that have occurred in a particular situation. If so, were they traumatic losses and how might that have impacted development? And have the losses been personally and relationally processed in meaningful ways or are the losses encapsulated and not constructively integrated into present narratives?

6. Relational Scaffolding—The concept of scaffolding was introduced by Wood and colleagues (Wood, Bruner, & Ross, 1976; also see Balswick, King, & Reimer, 2016) based on Vygotsky's developmental theory and suggests development moves forward with relational supports or scaffolding from others who position themselves optimally to help children master tasks that are just beyond their individual reach; this relational scaffolding is then sensitively pulled back when independent performance emerges. Thus, wise approaches to scaffolding are empowering of development without cultivating long-term dependence. The concept of scaffolding has now been applied more broadly across the lifespan and associated with ideas of cooperative or guided learning. This invites certain questions such as, what relational supports and resources are available to provide effective scaffolding for necessary developmental change? Conversely, are certain relationships or systemic factors working to undermine the needed scaffolding?

7. Non-Linear Transformation—Various developmental frameworks in social science and theology suggest constructive transformations are often preceded by periods of destabilization, deconstruction, or darkness (Sandage & Moe, 2013; Shults & Sandage, 2006; Worthington & Sandage, 2016), so we might ask whether problems or symptoms in a given case might possibly indicate a transformative growth process is emerging. Certain psychological and theological perspectives tend to assume positive change typically unfolds in a linear fashion; in contrast, we embrace relational and systemic perspectives on human development and spiritual formation that assume (a) deconstruction typically precedes reconstruction and that (b) positive growth is often accompanied by some level of anxiety and loss in the early phases (see Brown, Dahl, & Corbin Reuschling, 2011).

Thinking Developmentally

From a relational development perspective, it is important to note that Paula's struggles occur during a common developmental transition in Western cultural contexts of an emerging adult seeking to launch from home. This transition tests capacities to balance autonomy and dependence, which can be framed in relation to attachment and differentiation (see pp. 143–144). Paula is being stretched by her greater autonomy and anxiety related to the multitude of personal choices she has to manage. Her prior spiritual development focused on the protective security provided by conformity to family and faith community, and she enjoyed considerable personal success in that small-town context. However, her move into a large, impersonal university environment has meant a certain loss of being known and feeling respected. She has shown a strength in exploring new and more diverse relationships, and her initial participation in the global literature group represented her motivation to gain a broader understanding of the world.

Paula is also the first female in her family to go to college, a sign of courage and progress in the intergenerational context. But the internal anxiety and tension that have arisen with these new explorations have now revealed internal splits where she internalizes almost constant shame and guilt and views others (including God) as deeply disappointed in her. Put differently, she cannot see how to integrate these differing parts of life, and the pain and shame of this dis-integration has led to self-injurious and avoidant coping strategies that are not proving helpful. Her bingeing and purging can be viewed as a way she may be playing out at an embodied level her larger developmental and cyclical struggle with taking in the new and then feeling intense shame and a need for repudiation of it. While not a healthy coping strategy in terms of actually facilitating her development and well-being, she has ritualized a kind of unconscious attempt at integrating her implicit theology and psychology through the self-atonement of purging. Her initial attraction to Mark may have represented her pull to seek guidance, authority, and agency from someone to fill the loss of family and community, but the traumatic nature of his coercion and abuse has shattered Paula's sense of self, leaving her feeling confused, overwhelmed, ashamed, and lost. Her decision to take the step of seeking out a university therapist is a hopeful sign of reclaiming her personal agency and a willingness to receive help from others with needed expertise.

Spiritual Formation Within Human Development

As we consider developmental perspectives for integration, we want to highlight two overlapping concepts drawn from psychology and theology, respectively: human development and spiritual formation. In our view, "capacities for constructive integration are shaped relationally through human development and spiritual formation and, in turn, efforts at integration can facilitate development and spiritual formation" (Brown & Sandage, 2015, p. 181). By attending to both these frames for "thinking developmentally," we are able to focus attention on relational integration of both the finite and the infinite (Kierkegaard, 1980). As Kierkegaard explained, "Personhood is a synthesis of possibility and necessity" (p. 40), referring to infinitude and finitude, respectively. Social science theories of human development tend to focus on *necessity*, or human needs and processes of adaptation. Theologically shaped models of spiritual formation focus on possibility, that is, ultimate concerns and values and the creative or formative work of the Divine in reshaping personhood. Like Kierkegaard, we view psychological development and spiritual development/formation as interactive processes that can be differentiated but cannot be neatly separated (Balswick et al., 2016; Groeschel, 1983; Kegan, 1980; Loder, 1989, 1998; Spero, 1992). An exclusive focus on either human development or spiritual formation might imply an imbalance toward the descriptive (necessity) or the prescriptive (possibility), and Kierkegaard warns that either type of imbalance can lead to despair. While, for convenience, we use the term "development" in our relational integration model, in its use we have in mind this relational synthesis of human development and spiritual formation.

Our understanding of relational integration as developmental also includes a dialectical understanding of adaptation and potential transformation *through negation and re-centering*. Loder's theologically integrative and existential model of development suggests the human ego seeks psychosocial adaptation to the lived world of experience, but the ego is also haunted by ontological anxiety and forces of non-being. Thus, Loder (1998) argues "the study of human development from a spiritual and theological perspective necessarily includes the negative side" (p. 73). His Christian theological frame leads to him to posit that humans also long for existential and spiritual grounding that runs deeper than mere adaptation and includes a relational desire for connection to Divine Presence that is more stable than human attachments. Certain existential experiences of "the void" or non-being, such as those involving death, loss, guilt, isolation, or other existential themes, can rupture our ego structures and lead to developmental transformations and spiritual re-centering of the personality. This attention to negation and re-centering also coheres with our point made in prior chapters that dilemmas of integration (such as Paula's case) reflect a potentially formative relational process, as persons and systems grapple with a complex web of finitude and infinitude.

Negation as an important experience for interdisciplinary engagement has been explored by Andrea Hollingsworth (2011) in her analysis of this theme in the writings of David Tracy (theologian) and James W. Jones (psychologist and philosopher). She notes that both writers identify a kind of negation that is necessary for interdisciplinary dialogue; for Tracy, such dialogue involves risk of "all one's present self-understanding by facing the claims to attention of the other" (Tracy, 1987, p 93; Hollingsworth, p. 463). Jones explores negation, which he understands as "experiential knowing [which] requires a certain kind of 'letting go'—that is, a relinquishment of the driving obsession for distanciation from and controlling knowledge over the other" (Hollingworth, p. 465). For both scholars, loss or letting go is coupled with a "finding-of-self" (p. 466). As Hollingsworth concludes,

> To know well, we must risk losing ourselves in meaningful interaction across boundaries—including . . . disciplinary boundaries. We must become vulnerable to real engagement, real experience, real unknowing, and real loss if we are ever to come to transformative interdisciplinary insight.
>
> *(p. 466)*

Relational Resources for Integration: Attachment and Differentiation

Having looked at resources across philosophy, psychology, and theology for understanding the interplay of spiritual formation and human development, we now turn to highlighting some discreet themes that have potential for our relational model of integration. Specifically, we are drawn toward constructs that account for relational dynamics in the development of capacities for integration. Christian theologians across numerous traditions have described the importance of healthy community for spiritual formation (e.g., Grenz, 2006; Hayes, 2012; Hyun Lee, 2010; Pohl, 2011), and some Christians in the social sciences have pointed to the communal influences on the relational scaffolding necessary for human development and spiritual formation (e.g., Balswick et al., 2016; Brown & Strawn, 2012; Hardy, 2000; Johnson, 2007). While there are many constructs within relational theories of development that could be employed to account for the formative role of relational influences on development in providing holding environments for growth, we focus here on two particularly fruitful constructs, especially as they have important areas of convergence; *attachment* and *differentiation of self*. Both of these concepts have been found to contribute to healthy relational development and to enhance capacities for neurobiological integration (Schnarch, 2009; Siegel, 2010). Additionally, both constructs reference abilities to (a) regulate emotions, and (b) balance connection and autonomy in relationships (Hainlen, Jankowski, Paine, & Sandage, 2016; Skowron & Dendy, 2004); attachment literature tends to focus more on bonding and supportive relational regulation, whereas the literature around differentiation of self focuses on self-regulation and capacities to appreciate and manage differences. Finally, both constructs have been empirically related to processes of spiritual formation (Shults & Sandage, 2006; Worthington & Sandage, 2016).

Attachment, Integration, and Relational Spirituality

The role of attachment in human development is significant. As we have pointed out in Chapter 4, relational experiences actually influence brain functioning and capacities for neurobiological integration through coordinating connections between the limbic system and capacities for regulating emotions and differentiating self and other. Siegel (2007) has described the role of attachment in promoting mental health and differentiation in this way: "mental well-being is created within the process of integration, the linkage of differentiated components of a system into a functional whole" (p. 288). Integration of a person's mental functioning involves the differentiated growth of the brain's prefrontal fibers, and this process develops early in life through securely attached relationships that provide experiences of interpersonal attunement. This attunement, in turn, cultivates physiological regulation, intersubjectivity and empathy, mental coherence, and feelings of being loved. Healthy attachment and attunement from caregivers can also contribute to bilateral coordination of the left and right hemispheres of the brain, which helps integrate logical and linguistic processing with symbolic and emotional processing to achieve what Siegel (2007) calls horizontal integration of the brain (also see Hall & Porter, 2004). Empirical studies show that secure attachment is typically associated with healthy and mature forms of relational spirituality which, among theists, includes a sense of being loved by God, trust in God's care, and an ability to work through disappointments with God (Granqvist & Kirkpatrick, 2013). For securely attached individuals who are spiritual or religious, cognitive beliefs, associated symbols or images, and feelings about God or the sacred tend to align or integrate in cohesive ways.

Insecure Attachment Styles and Relational Spirituality

Not everyone has experienced secure attachment in their relational history, and insecurely attached forms of relational spirituality have been associated with spiritual instability and dysregulation, fear and mistrust of God, and a sense of distance from God (Sandage, Jankowski, Crabtree, & Schweer, 2015). Two dimensions of insecure attachment are ambivalent and avoidant. Individuals with insecure styles of attachment will often show, particularly under stress, limited flexibility in their interpersonal styles and methods of coping. These relational and emotional patterns reflect poorly differentiated modes of neurobiological functioning of the brain and nervous system (Brown & Sandage, 2015; Mikulincer & Shaver, 2007; Siegel, 2007). Ambivalently attached individuals have a limbic system that becomes hyper-aroused during stress, generating elevated levels of anxiety and frustration about the availability or responsiveness of others. This preoccupation with others can be admixed with feelings of shame about themselves and needing help, and this negativity about self can lead them to anticipate rejection. In certain situations, those with an ambivalent attachment style may also defer their own ideas to try to appease others from a dependent, one-down position, and they can also become reactively anxious and angry about subtle points of interpersonal tension and frequently feel the need to process issues over and over. This form of relational pursuit can cause others to feel like pulling back from the person, which further reinforces concerns about rejection or abandonment. These ambivalently attached relational patterns of preoccupation with others and emotional flooding hinder collaboration and the self-reflection and taking in of new information necessary for integrative learning.

Avoidantly attached individuals tend to deactivate their limbic system during stress or conflict by distancing emotionally and interpersonally and hiding any sense of vulnerability, which leads to difficulties connecting or collaborating with others. They prefer self-reliance, particularly when conflict arises, and may be unaware they communicate a kind of critical, one-up stance toward others. They often repress feelings of hurt or sadness during a relational conflict, but often hold onto hostile attitudes of unforgiveness for a long time (Mikulincer & Shaver, 2007; Worthington & Sandage, 2016). Their primal fears focus around (a) becoming engulfed by others and losing their sense of self or (b) the shame of revealing their vulnerability only to be rejected for it (based on past attachment experiences). These dismissive interpersonal tendencies can cause others to feel ignored or rebuffed, and the lack of empathy and tendencies toward narcissism of the avoidantly attached person can generate guardedness in others. Collaboration with others often breaks down due to rigidity, which can cause frustration in others, and their unwillingness to "give ground" to others or admit mistakes and limitations. This reinforces their preference for autonomy over the kinds of relational integration we are describing, and the non-integrative cognitive processes of avoidant attachment restrict the kinds of self-reflection and emotional awareness that contribute to holistic learning of new perspectives.

Summary

As we have argued, attachment has significant impact on a variety of relational issues. This dynamic becomes especially important for our consideration of relational dynamics in interdisciplinary integration. Securely attached individuals will likely have more success navigating the conflict often inherent in interdisciplinary work. Securely attached individuals exhibit more confidence when in the midst of relational conflicts; and they view conflicts as less threatening than their insecurely attached counterparts. They are also generally able to empathize with another person's perspective. A body of empirical studies comparing conflict management styles of securely attached individuals with those with insecure styles of attachment has shown that the former individuals have more collaborative or "integrative" styles of conflict management (Mikulincer & Shaver, 2007). An integrative style of conflict management in this research was defined as one that values the perspectives and concerns of both self and other and aims at collaboration.

To sum up, the developmental processes of attachment impact capacities for conflict management, collaboration, and various types of integration, thus making integration a relational and a developmental process. It will not be sufficient to simply encourage people to work harder to collaborate or to put students, scholars, or professionals into "collaborative learning groups," if they hold insecure attachment templates and lack capacities for self-awareness and self-regulation. It will be necessary to foster developmental or formative growth in capacities to manage anxiety and to relate in more differentiated ways (see Chapter 8).

Attachment Issues

Paula shows interpersonal and relational spirituality symptoms of an ambivalent or preoccupied attachment style, which includes negativity about self and a tendency to idealize others and assume they will have the solutions that cannot be self-generated. Among theists like Paula, this style of attachment has been associated with excessive spiritual dependence and risks for spiritual dysregulation characterized by frequent feelings of shame, worthlessness, and fear of abandonment by God combined with an internal lack of stable attachment to God's loving presence (Granqvist & Kirkpatrick, 2013; Hall & Edwards, 2002; Worthington & Sandage, 2016). Put differently, it is hard for persons like Paula to feel securely connected to God when struggling with "negative" feelings such as sadness, shame, guilt, or anger. Her unconscious impulse is to try to gain attachment with God or others by negating herself, and tragically the lack of efficacy of this approach contributes to more insecurity. Some of her healthy impulses to explore a broader world have also caused anxiety and fear of losing her prior sources of stability. Like others with this attachment style, Paula has intense emotions but tries to escape those feelings rather than reflect on them, and this limits her own integration of thoughts and emotions. From a relational integrative perspective, clients like Paula do not need solutions provided by their therapists but rather connection that helps tolerate difficult feelings and to engage into self-reflection, processing of grief, and making personal choices and decisions. This kind of relational process may potentate or follow from developmental changes in Paula's theology as she may start to view God as more differentiated, that is caring but less reactive, authoritarian, and judgmental toward her every move.

Looking at other persons in the case, both Mark and Samuel show signs of avoidant attachment. Mark's signs are more obvious in his dominating, non-empathic, and dismissive style of relating that results in violence when he becomes anxious over potential limits to his control of Paula. Samuel does not exhibit behavioral violence to Paula and might have been sincerely concerned about her well-being, but his approach to their differences did not convey relational strengths of dialogue or empathy and communicated a judgmental stance that Paula experienced as shaming. He emphasized his own perspective (informed by his interpretation of the Bible) as correct with little integrative interest in Paula's experience or understanding, and this did not result in Paula seeking him out for help. Avoidantly attached individuals tend to under-estimate the importance of relational dynamics in counseling or other forms of helping and tend to rely on cognitive or behavioral strategies. Samuel did not seem to be able to think developmentally about Paula's struggles, and he did not offer relational scaffolding but quickly moved into a directive, rescue-type approach based on a uni-dimensional diagnosis of Paula's problems as spiritual and moral. Samuel's own theological perspective was quite crisis-oriented (he would often say "God saves us from ourselves") and viewed God as the ultimate rescuer, and his approach to counseling was consistent with his personal theology.

Dis-Integration Anxiety

As we have been suggesting, the relational integration of psychology and theology involves developmental processes, with the goal of moving toward an increasingly complex and differentiated perspective. This progression will include transitional periods of dis-integration involving the loss of prior developmental schemas and strategies and the eventual emergence of new relational patterns and understandings.

Dis-Integration in Psychological Perspective

Psychoanalyst Melanie Klein (1946) has suggested that a certain vulnerability to disintegration is a normal (albeit defensive) part of early infant development: "the early ego lacks cohesion, and a tendency toward integration alternates with a tendency toward disintegration, a falling into bits" (p. 100). Human experiences of "disintegration" can also have serious negative consequences, as in the cases of (a) social disintegration for non-dominant group members who suffer discrimination, marginalization, and oppression; and (b) psychotic disintegration which impairs reality testing and psychosocial functioning. Yet more mild to moderate levels of episodic dis-integration (indicated here by our use of a hyphenated word) are common within liminal processes of developmental change and transformation as the individual or relational system undergoes crucibles of destabilization (or to use spiritual formation language, "dark nights of the soul") prior to arriving at a more complex reorganization (Albright, 2006; Shults & Sandage, 2006; Worthington & Sandage, 2016). Thus, we can think of dis-integration and reintegration as an ongoing dialectical process (Stuthridge, 2017), and mindful forms of dis-integration can potentially lead to more differentiated development (Schoenberg & Barendregt, 2016).

Drawing on Augustine's *Confessions* and his own phenomenological research, William James (1958, p. 143) described the internal discord and "unhappiness" of the divided self that necessitates a transformation or rebirth into a re-ordered personality. It is natural for anxiety to rise over the experience of internal divisions and also as dissonance, ambiguity, and loss of prior understandings or attachments increase. Such anxiety may initially generate defensive responses but can eventually prompt seeking or questing for new meaning. However, when such anxiety is overwhelming it may lead to trauma-based fight, flight, or freeze responses and a more chronic dis-integrated state. These dynamics of dis-integration anxiety can often be seen in various contexts that hold transitional processes requiring developmental adaptations. Some examples include: students in educational contexts (e.g., seminaries, clinical training programs), clients in psychotherapy or other treatment programs, patients in medical and rehabilitation settings dealing with serious injuries or illnesses, children entering daycare or school settings, immigrants or cross-cultural workers entering new cultural contexts, inmates in new correctional institutions, or seniors moving into geriatric or assisted living settings.

Dis-Integration in Theological Perspective

An influential paradigm for understanding dis-integration in theological perspective has been offered by Walter Brueggemann in his work on the Psalms (1984). He works through the Psalter with the categories of psalms of orientation, psalms of disorientation, and psalms of new orientation (see also Brueggemann, 1980). From this rough typology, he suggests two movements that characterize the life of faith expressed in the Psalter: a movement from "*settled orientation into a season of disorientation*" and a movement "*from a context of disorientation to a new orientation*" (1984, p. 20). The first movement is particular relevant to our discussion of dis-integration in developmental perspective. As Brueggemann observes, moving into disorientation

> constitutes a dismantling of the old, known world and a relinquishing of safe, reliable confidence in God's good creation. The movement of dismantling

includes a rush of negativities, including rage, resentment, guilt, shame, isolation, despair, hatred, and hostility . . . That dismantling move is a charac-
teristically Jewish move, one that evokes robust resistance and one that does
not doubt that even the experience of disorientation has to do with God
and must be vigorously addressed to God.

(p. 20)

Brueggemann offers to our work a theological normalizing of disorientation as
part of a life of faith. It is telling that the largest category of psalms is the category
of lament. Disorientation, or dis-integration as we are calling it, is the stuff of
life and doesn't necessarily inhibit the spiritual journey. This vision of faith as
including disorientation is also portrayed in the Old Testament's reflective wisdom literature—in Job and Ecclesiastes. These books address how the life of faith
is lived when grief and loss are front and center (Job) or when the meaning of life
is elusive (Ecclesiastes). These particular wisdom books provide a snapshot of life
in the throws of disorientation and dis-integration.

While there is no corresponding genre to wisdom literature in the New Testament, we could locate disorientation and dis-integration within the motif of
the kingdom's "already and not yet," and specifically in the hiddenness of God's
reign. While the decided emphasis in the New Testament is on the already—the
kingdom's arrival in Jesus the Messiah, there is an important counter voice in the
"not yet" motif. Some aspects of God's reign are still to come (e.g., final reckoning
as emphasized in Matthew). In between the already and the not yet exists another
reality, which a number of New Testament authors identify by the language of
hiddenness (1 Cor 2:7; Col 3:1–4; Rev 2:17). Matthew, in his Gospel, gives the
most concerted attention to this language and motif (e.g., Matt 11:25–27; 13:33,
35, 44). This hiddenness connects, according to Morse, to the proclamation of
the kingdom as "near" (or "at hand;" Matt 4:17). Important to Morse is that the
kingdom isn't announced as "*in hand*," as if it were something we have obtained
(p. 23). Instead, "[t]he kingdom *is* present in Jesus and his work; and it is present in
sometimes hidden ways" (Brown & Roberts, in press). This ambiguity or hiddenness
helps for understanding present suffering and tragedy and the sense of meaning-
lessness often experienced in life. The journey of faith is not unrealistically rosy in
the face of these ambiguities of life. And "[n]on-integration might be understood,
in part, as an expression of this hiddenness of God's kingdom in the present of
human experience" (Brown & Sandage, 2015, p. 183).

Understandings of Dis-Integration for the Integration of Psychology and Theology

The literature on the integration of psychology and theology includes minimal
attention to the necessary and potentially constructive role of dis-integration
(Brown & Sandage, 2015; Boyd, 2000; Cooper-White, 2008). Johnson (2011)

associates anxiety with only one of his (models of) three kinds of integration ("dissociated integration—subnamed, "the face of anxiety"). In discussion of the two categories he endorses ("strategic" and "maximal"), Johnson does not mention the presence or role of anxiety in such integrative efforts. Yet anxiety is a regular part of the integrative process regardless of what kind of integration is pursued; and anxiety can contribute ultimately to either differentiation (which facilitates integration) or ongoing unreflective and potentially destructive dis-integration. An important assumption within integrative discussion seems to be that a lack of integration is highly problematic. I (Jeannine) once participated in a forum about integration across three disciplines: biblical studies, leadership, and spiritual formation. The scholar representing the area of formation proposed that non-integration (or dis-integration) is in every case a result of the fall—of human sin. We have proposed a more developmental view of relational integration, in which a lack of integration is not fundamentally problematic or necessarily derived from human fallenness. Instead, non-integration may arise from human finitude; it may simply reveal our human creatureliness and locatedness (see chapter 5). In fact, every integrative effort "will uncover areas of discontinuity between disciplines" (Brown, Dahl, & Corbin Reuschling, 2011, p. 13). In our view, the presence of non-integration or dis-integration points to the developmental nature of human formation and the search for knowledge.

Our view on dis-integration anxiety sits closer to that of Shults (2012) who has proposed normalizing developmental episodes of dis-integration in psychology and theology. He has noted that it is quite natural for human beings to try to hold onto prior worldview frameworks or coping strategies but that this attempt may sometimes represent idolatrous motivations and anxious resistance to growth (see also Schnarch, 1997). While it seems a common assumption in many psychological and theological theories that positive change is linear, certain relational and systemic frameworks now reveal non-linear patterns of change in both psychotherapy (Gelo & Salvatore, 2016; Hayes, Yasinski, Barnes, & Bockting, 2015) and spiritual formation and transformation (Brown, Dahl, & Corbin Reuschling, 2011; Miller & C' de Baca, 2001; Sandage & Moe, 2013). Similarly, the large body of literature on post-traumatic growth suggests the dis-integration of trauma can, in some cases, precede transformative growth (Calhoun & Tedeschi, 2013; Skalski & Hardy, 2013).

Kohut (1984) described the powerful disintegration anxiety that erupts within the self as an individual experiences the loss of *prior sources of self-cohesion* and fears of fragmentation ascend. These sources of self-cohesion might be core theological or cultural beliefs or symbols, or they might involve an internal relationship with a person who has been idealized (e.g., a parent or other central caregiver, spiritual leader, professor, or therapist). Kohut described narcissistic rage as a disintegration product, an anxiety-driven attempt to hold together a fragmenting self or what we might call a fragile state of personal integration. From a theological perspective, narcissistic rage suggests a lack of existential or spiritual grounding; Tillich

(1957, p. 47; also see Peters, 1994) considered the hubris related to this lack of grounding to be the essence of "spiritual sin," arising from the refusal to accept one's human limitations.

Kohut's relational theory of self-development also suggested human needs to idealize others and, over time, to recover from the inevitable process of disappointment and de-idealization when our idealized others "show their finitude." Kohut suggested that throughout life humans need to connect with positive sources of idealization (referred to as selfobjects) that can be admired and gradually transmuted or integrated into resources for self-cohesion and self-regulation of anxiety. These selfobjects include parents and other authority figures or role models; they may also include more abstract symbols or principles a child identifies with and admires. "From a theological perspective, God is the ultimate source of idealization and all others carry the risk of idolatry" (Brown & Sandage, 2015, p. 184). Yet Kohut suggests that the process of idealization is fluid and adaptable; most people experience periodic disappointment with something or someone they have idealized. Disappointments may be more turbulent or traumatic if an individual has a fragile sense of self or is facing overwhelming stress. Yet these movements toward de-idealization, which are accompanied by disappointment, can ultimately work toward rather than work against a developmental process of maturing relational selfhood. Whether such de-idealization and disappointment is constructive depends upon the personal and relational dynamics involved in processing the losses and arriving at new understandings (Jones, 2002; Paine et al., 2017).

The contemplative or apophatic traditions of Christian spirituality have promoted the normalization of "dark nights of the soul" as a way of framing and understanding various deconstructive processes that can eventually lead to greater spiritual maturity. This movement from deconstruction to more integrative maturity is facilitated by surrendering "the grandiose entitlement that can lurk behind archaic forms of idealization" (Brown & Sandage, 2015, p. 184), especially when combined with various stances or capacities that have been shown to foster relational maturity. These capacities include humility, a tolerance of ambiguity (Hollingsworth, 2011), and risk of personal commitment (Kegan, 1994). We could also highlight once again Ricoeur's construct of the second naïveté (see Chapter 5); he offered this construct, which suggests a post-critical way of relating to belief, as a way to re-idealize the other while retaining a critical awareness. Ricoeur's movement from initial (unreflective) naïveté to "distanciation" to second naïveté has some analogy to the process in romantic relationships which moves from significant idealization in courtship to eventual disappointments and de-idealization, with the possibility of a healthy turn toward a more realistic and integrative process of re-idealization that can deal with disappointments with selfobjects (Mitchell, 2003; Worthington & Sandage, 2016).

These various interdisciplinary threads related to dis-integration all suggest that we should consider a certain level of dis-integration anxiety to be a common experience in development, particularly at transitions that potentiate growth toward a more mature and differentiated integration. Normalizing dis-integration and its accompanying anxiety is helpful for conceiving interdisciplinary relational integration, since it can be easy to idealize interdisciplinary dialogue from the onset. This argues for addressing and discussing the relational dynamics of such conversations as they begin. We might note in such discussions our propensity to assume success without loss or disorientation. Brueggemann (1984), in his reflection on the Psalms, notes that movements to places of disorientation and new orientation disclose

> an understanding of life that is fundamentally alien to our culture. The dominant ideology of our culture is commitment to continuity and success and to the avoidance of pain, hurt, and loss. The dominant culture is also resistant to genuine newness and real surprise. It is curious but true, that *surprise* is as unwelcome as is *loss*. And our culture is organized to prevent the experience of both.
>
> *(p. 22)*

Authentic interdisciplinary dialogue will move us into places of disorientation or dis-integration and surprise. Understanding these important spaces as developmentally appropriate can provide courage to enter the conversation.

Idealization and Reorientation

Paula eventually came to realize during therapy that beneath her self-loathing and disappointment in herself was intense anxiety and simmering anger over ways her Christian ideals (and the family relationships associated with those ideas) had let her down over the past year. She was able to remember a moment of fleeting anger and cynicism she experienced in the fall when raising a question about global poverty and suffering in her campus ministry small group. The leader, Marie (age 22; German-American), responded with a platitude ("God loves everyone and has a plan to bring about his kingdom.") and re-directed the conversation. She also remembered a couple of occasions over the past year where she started to voice some of her struggles in phone calls to her parents, but their anxious and overly spiritualized responses led her to the conclusion they could not handle hearing such things. Whether or not she was correct in that assessment, she lost trust and felt disappointed in them. Attachment theorists would interpret this as Paula finding her parents were not a secure base for her explorations nor a safe haven for her to return to with complex struggles. These feelings of attachment injury and the potential loss of the associated ideals were so shaming to her that she mostly blamed herself.

We also wonder how Paula's faith communities, both at home and at school, might have engaged a thicker set of theological resources for their life together. Her inherited spirituality seems be inadequate for helping her navigate her developmental process of de-idealization, dis-integration, and shame. If churches and ministries helped to normalize movements of disorientation and reorientation (Brueggemann's language), young people like Paula might have more success navigating the feelings of loss and surprise upon entering new life stages. By embracing such biblical resources as the psalms of lament (not simply psalms of praise and thanksgiving), Christian communities would offer a richer and more realistic picture of discipleship and formation. Brueggemann (1984) suggests that the rather minimal use of laments psalms in the church arises from a belief that "faith does not mean to acknowledge and embrace negativity. We have thought that acknowledgement of negativity was somehow an act of unfaith" (p. 52). He goes on to suggest that the use of lament psalms for the church is instead *"an act of bold faith"* (p. 52).

In order to help Paula to understand and manage her disappointment associated with idealization, we also need to consider the relational resources that will help hold her current developmental conflicts and tensions and support her in constructing a new integrative approach to her life. The people involved (whether family, friends, a therapist, a spiritual counselor, etc.) will need sufficient personal differentiation to tolerate her dis-integration anxiety without *rescuing* or *running away*.

Based on the case study, we might also note Mark's developmental struggles, which he does not appear to own or even recognize. In contrast to Paula's internalizing of negativity, Mark's avoidantly attached strategy for his "leaving home" process is one of claiming superiority and mastery while externalizing inferiority or vulnerability onto others. We could interpret his narcissistic rage and abusive violence as possibly arising from his own disintegration anxiety as Paula's idealization of him wore off and he feared losing control over her. As is typically the case, his idolatrous grasp for control achieves the opposite effect and Paula begins to further disconnect and distance from him. There is currently no empirically supported treatment for the narcissism that characterizes Mark and limited efficacy for treatments of perpetrators of interpersonal violence, making someone like Mark a very difficult person to help. He is unlikely to seek psychological or spiritual change until some serious failure or other negative consequences disrupt his working strategy of seeking validation through dominance and control of others.

Human Development Viewed Narratively

A helpful lens for "thinking developmentally" is a narrative one. We experience our lives as narratively plotted; and we tell our "stories" as ways of expressing and making sense of our lived experience. The developmental dynamics we have been discussing—attachment, differentiation, and dis-integrative disappointments—eventually shape narrative templates and personal identity; constructive changes in self-narratives also represent an important dynamic in therapeutic change processes (Angus & Constantino, 2017).

A narrative framing of human development also has interdisciplinary potential, since narrative methods have emerged in various sub-disciplines of theology and in psychology and social science. In biblical studies, narrative critical approaches have encouraged holistic readings of biblical narrative texts and have attempted to provide a counterpoint to historical criticism's focus on the "world behind the text" (Brown, 2013). Narrative theology has suggested the "priority of story" (Lindbeck, 1997), and has emphasized that "[s]tories help us configure a coherent view of ourselves and our life experiences; they are integrally related to our worldview" (Brown, 2007, p. 44). As such, narrative precedes and provides a framework for religious (and other) beliefs.

Narrative in Psychology

In psychology, McAdams' (2013, 2016) program of research on a narrative approach to identity development has highlighted the role of relational dynamics in the integrative life narratives that shape worldview dimensions of personality. McAdams has identified various narrative themes that can inform a person's self-identity and ways they interpret meaning in life, and he suggests that a secure style of attachment increases the probability in adulthood of narrating one's life story *in hopeful and coherent ways.* His research builds on Loevinger's (1976) earlier model of ego development in which "integration" represents the most mature personality, capable of reconciling various conflicts in life within a broader sense of meaningful identity. McAdams suggests human development involves ongoing dynamics of differentiation and integration through social or relational processes. These processes involve the incorporation of narratives from cultural, religious, and other social sources as a person narrates their own life story. Moreover, similar to our relational integration model, McAdams suggests that relational dynamics of differentiation and integration not only reflect developmental processes but can also serve to catalyze continued development and richness of narrative meaning over the lifespan.

McAdams and his colleagues have developed empirical coding procedures for identifying integrative memories and integrative complexity in autobiographical narratives provided by students. Integrative memories go beyond facts and reflect "coming to a new or deeper understanding about the self or others" (Bauer,

McAdams, & Sakaeda, 2005, p. 207). Importantly for our integrative discussion, this coding scheme requires "showing" in addition to "telling" about integrative development. That is, simply saying "I was transformed" by an event is not coded as an integrative memory unless a research participant also showed specific examples of that transformation, which reflects a more differentiated understanding. Integrative memories have been positively associated with measures of both maturity and well-being. And those scoring high in both maturity and well-being tended to interpret memories by emphasizing a relationally integrative process of coming to greater conceptual understanding of themselves and their relationships.

Additionally, integrative complexity in autobiographical narratives involves codings for differentiation and integration of thought. This is reflected in the autobiographical writer incorporating multiple points of view, awareness of mixed motivations or complex emotions, and understanding contradictory aspects of the self. McAdams and colleagues (2006) have shown a general trend toward greater narrative complexity in longitudinal research with undergraduates. On average, emerging adults move toward greater differentiation and integration in how they narrate their lives.

Of course, not all individuals move toward greater narrative integration. Like Siegel, McAdams suggests an individual's attachment style and other relational factors will contribute to developmental trajectories that move toward well-being and maturity versus those that become unhealthy. Narrating one's life story relies upon the neurobiology of memory, and trauma appears to impair the integrative function of the hippocampus (Siegel, 2007). When relational development is healthy or healing, people tend to move toward life narratives that involve authentic concern for the well-being of others. McAdams draws on Erikson's notion of generativity—a concern to contribute to the well-being of the next generation—to help differentiate trajectories of relational development in adults. Those who develop high levels of generativity in adulthood tend to hold integrative life narratives, which include "redemption sequences" that involve overcoming some obstacles or forms of suffering in moving toward a good outcome. This emphasis on generativity in human development is similar to the model of the reciprocating self of Balswick et al. (2016), who emphasize healthy relational selfhood as characterized by *I-Thou* capacities to both give and receive.

Narrative in Theology

An important offering narrative has made to theology comes in movement away from or at least beyond propositional theology by offering story a coherent framework for theological formulation (Brown, 2015). It is telling that in the Old Testament, narrative is the leading category, with theological affirmations being "subordinate to the narrative;" it is the narrative itself that gives such affirmations their meaning (Goldingay, 2003, p. 17). We might argue the same for the New Testament, with its narrative witness to Jesus and the church (Matthew-Acts) making up the majority of that testament. In Scripture, narrative is "logically prior" to doctrine (Lindbeck, 1997, p. 42). Propositions of themselves are insufficient, as Fackre notes, going on to provide this colorful metaphor: "When the Epic of God is 'pinned and classified like a butterfly in a collector's case' (J. B. Metz), the narrative quality of faith is dissolved into propositionalism" (2001 p. 199).

This attention to a more narrative theology leads to a consideration of the narrative framework of the whole of Christian Scripture for theological reflection. A number of proposals might be offered for understanding that whole, and one analogy for doing so has been a play with a number of acts that include creation, fall, redemption/mission, and final restoration (Wright, 1992; Bartholomew & Goheen, 2004; Vanhoozer, 2005; Wu, 2103). These storied or dramatic categories fit well with the narrative resources from psychology that we have been highlighting. Telling the story of God and God's people across the biblical narrative has points of resonance with the ways people might tell their stories (e.g., redemptive sequences). It is also interesting to note that the biblical narratives tend much more toward showing rather than telling. Characters, for example, are developed narratively through what they do and say more than by the narrator's direct descriptive statements about them (Brown, 2002).

Storied proposals potentially enhance the work done in biblical theology by allowing the individual voices of the biblical authors to remain more clearly intact. A storied framework is able to maintain tensions among these authors without collapsing them into a single (unison) voice. This provides an interesting analogy to Adler's (2012) psychological insights about "too-coherent narratives" (p. 330). He notes that, when a person narrates their experience, both low levels of coherence and "a rigid adherence to a tight story line" (by omitting or glossing over details that don't 'fit') may be harmful to the narrator (p. 330). The ability to tell our story of or the biblical story without omitting potentially incongruous details seems an important capacity for development. A storied approach also suggests a more dynamic hermeneutic for interpreting the Bible (Brown, 2015; see 2007), cohering with our view of hermeneutics as a located activity (Chapter 5).

Narrative Resources for Interdisciplinarity

This narrative research (from both theology and psychology) suggests that humans are created with a need to narrate their life stories in ways that authentically acknowledge struggles and contradictions while moving toward a hopeful and redemptive process of transformation, ultimately benefiting both self and others (i.e., generativity). This coheres well with the storied shape of the Christian Scriptures, which invites readers to understand their story within that larger story (Green, 2007). This kind of engagement (with Scripture) does not happen by simply reading the Bible (as if reading did not include neurobiological and psychosocial processes). Instead, a particular way of reading is invited that shapes "our imaginations, our patterns of thinking . . . [and so] our commitments and practices" (Green, 2007, p. 19–20). This coheres with some social science research which suggests we cannot bypass the developmental process through non-descript spiritual clichés ("I've been transformed") or by borrowing the narratives of others. Integrative developmental processes must be played out in one's own life and relationships; and maturity requires a process of meaningful and integrative narration of one's own life that is deeply embedded in and influenced by relationships (divine and human).

These narrative contours of self-identity suggest it is important for us to have supportive and well-differentiated relational spaces for authentically telling our stories in all their complexity. This may be particularly true for those entering helping professions (e.g., psychology, psychotherapy, spiritual and religious leadership, etc.) and other vocations that involve the care and development of persons (e.g., education, nursing, etc.). We will consider experiential and relational training strategies that engage narrative processes in Chapter 8 (also see Sandage, Jensen, & Jass, 2008). A key concern is that those with poorly differentiated or dis-integrated personal narratives may be at risk for projecting their views onto others or simply not having an intuitive sense of the narrative construction process, and a training context will not be the appropriate place for working through clinical levels of personal dis-integration. A supportive process of helping trainees or staff members locate professional therapeutic help represents a way educators or professionals can offer healthy attachment within boundaries and contribute to the personal development and integration of those who are struggling.

In interdisciplinary dialogue specifically, we would propose creating relational spaces for paying attention to the layers of stories that disciplinarians bring to the table: their personal stories and the stories of their communities, including the stories of their disciplines. At the outset of interdisciplinary projects, it can be helpful to share stories about prior interdisciplinary experiences, such as narratives about positive experiences and appropriately masked narratives about negative experiences. This can avoid idealism about the process and surface both hopes and fears about the current interdisciplinary endeavor and help clarify assumptions and commitments related to collaboration. For example, in an initial meeting I (Steve) had with a theologian to explore collaboration on a project, he mentioned an experience of being severely critiqued by a leading scholar in his field during a public presentation for not adequately engaging science related to his topic. The particular context of this presentation contributed extra sensitivities and added to the injury. It was helpful for me to hear this story and understand the issues involved as I brought my own empirical research skills into our collaborative work.

Narrative Motifs and Interdisciplinary Collaboration

In Paula's case, we might wonder where she could find people who could help her access and interpret the complexities of her own psychological and theological narratives. For example, her personal story seems to have threads of a previously successful young woman and protected youngest child from a small town who has become confused and lost in a bigger city. But what are the discordant threads to that narrative or the episodes that reveal other sides and strengths of Paula? Theologically, we could note the important theological theme of redemption that we have identified as crucial for any telling of the biblical story seems fairly absent from Paula's personal narrative with its themes of success and protection. Her "almost constant shame" (noted on p. 138) indicates an opportunity for experiences of redemption and freedom, especially if she can find an authentic connection and a secure base for exploring her own views of God and self, whether with Naomi, Samuel, Rose, or someone else who might build a trusting relationship with Paula.

Paula is at a point in her development where certain relational experiences are breaking up or dis-integrating her personal narrative and she has an opportunity for a script change from a rather simple or rigid ("too-coherent;" Adler, 2012) narrative identity toward a more differentiated and cohesive narrative identity (Holmes, 2001; Stuthridge, 2017). If she is able to move toward a more flexible and integrated narrative script, it will be important for her to experience relationships with "witnesses" who notice and reflect back episodes where these changes appear (Angus & Constantino, 2017). For example, when Paula in therapy recalls moments of de-idealization with her small group leader and her parents, she might be empowered to see these as places for her own theological and spiritual development—for finding a more adequate and robust spirituality that is able to grapple with the reality of evil and the inadequacy of spiritual platitudes for making sense of the disorientation she is experiencing.

We also wonder what an interdisciplinary consultation might look like between Naomi and Samuel, assuming Paula consented and wanted to pursue that form of integration. Would Samuel acknowledge and become curious about Naomi's psychological expertise and professional opinions to gain a more integrative perspective himself about how to be helpful to Paula? Would disclosure about Mark's violence and Paula's suffering generate in him a more compassionate and less directive pastoral stance, or would it generate more anxiety leading him to become even more dogmatic? Would Naomi be sufficiently differentiated to be respectful and curious about Paula's religious background and theology even if she has concerns about how it might be currently impacting her emotions and self-identity? Will she look for potential strengths and resources in Paula's religious community and faith tradition, or would anxiety about Paula's vulnerability lead her toward a rescuing stance that overrides Paula's sense of agency? Could Naomi reflect on both similarities and differences between her own religious background and that of Paula? Interestingly, Naomi and Samuel might share a similar desire to excise Mark from Paula's life, which is understandable in light of safety and other concerns, but beyond the crisis management they may also share the challenge of finding a patient and healthy developmental stance that aligns with Paula's formative need to grow in differentiation of self.

Conclusion

In this chapter, we have been considering relational integration with a developmental lens. A developmental perspective offers insights into the balance between the finite and the infinite for considering formation and development, as well as the importance of attachment for human growth and maturation. Thinking developmentally also normalizes the seasons of dis-integration, allowing both integration and dis-integration to be incorporated into a holistic model for integration. Finally, narrative resources can expand our ways of thinking about spiritual formation and human development. Viewed developmentally, relational integration invites capacities for understanding one's own story and the story of others.

Viewing relational integration from a developmental perspective also accents some dispositions that are conducive for interdisciplinary integration between psychology and theology. We draw upon Carla Dahl's framing of these dispositions as we conclude the chapter: (1) "The willingness to hear God's invitations in the voices of others;" (2) "A tolerance for ambiguity;" (3) "A spirit of exploration;" (4) "The capacity to live in the moment;" and (5) "The ability to manage anxiety" (Brown, Dahl, & Corbin Rueschling, 2011, pp. 21–22).

Bibliography

Adler, J. (2012). Sitting at the nexus of epistemological traditions: Narrative psychological perspectives on self-knowledge. In S. Vazire & T. D. Wilson (Eds.), *Handbook of self-knowledge* (pp. 327–347). New York, NY: The Guilford Press.

Albright, C. R. (2006). Spiritual growth, cognition, and complexity: Faith as a dynamic process. In J. D. Koss-Chioino & P. Hefner (Eds.), *Spiritual transformation and healing: Anthropological, theological, neuroscientific, and clinical perspectives* (pp. 168–186). Walnut Creek, CA: AltaMira Press.

Angus, L., & Constantino, M. J. (2017). Client accounts of corrective experiences in psychotherapy: Implications for clinical practice. *Journal of Clinical Psychology, 73*(2), 192–195. doi:10.1002/jclp.22432

Balswick, J. O., King, P. E., & Reimer, K. S. (2016). *The reciprocating self: Human development in theological perspective* (2nd ed.). Downers Grove, IL: InterVarsity Press.

Bartholomew, C. G., & Goheen, M. W. (2004) *The drama of Scripture: Finding our place in the Biblical story*. Grand Rapids, MI: Baker Academic.

Bauer, J. J., McAdams, D. P., & Sakaeda, A. R. (2005). Interpreting the good life: Growth memories in the lives of mature, happy people. *Journal of Personality and Social Psychology, 88*(1), 203–217. doi:10.1037/0022-3514.88.1.203

Boyd, J. H. (2000). The "soul" of the Psalms compared to the "self" of Kohut. *Journal of Psychology and Christianity, 19*(3), 219–231.

Bronfenbrenner, U. (1979). *The ecology of human development: Experiments by nature and design.* Cambridge, MA: Harvard University Press.

Brown, J. K. (2002). *The disciples in narrative perspective: The portrayal and function of the Matthean disciples,* SBLAB 9. Atlanta: Society of Biblical Literature.

Brown, J. K. (2007). *Scripture as communication: Introducing Biblical hermeneutics.* Grand Rapids, MI: Baker Academic.

Brown, J. K. (2013). Narrative criticism. In J. B. Green, J. K. Brown, & N. Perrin (Eds.), *Dictionary of Jesus and the Gospels* (pp. 619–624). Downers Grove, IL: InterVarsity Press.

Brown, J. K. (2015). Is the future of Biblical theology story-shaped? *Horizons in Biblical Theology, 37,* 13–31.

Brown, J. K., Dahl, C. M., & Corbin Reuschling, W. (2011). *Becoming whole and holy: An integrative conversation about Christian formation.* Grand Rapids, MI: Brazos.

Brown, J. K., & Roberts, K. A. (in press). *The Gospel of Matthew. Two horizons new testament commentary.* Grand Rapids, MI: Eerdmans.

Brown, J. K., & Sandage, S. J. (2015). Relational integration, part II: Relational integration as developmental and intercultural. *Journal of Psychology & Theology, 43,* 179–191.

Brown, W. S., & Strawn, B. D. (2012). *The physical nature of Christian life: Neuroscience, psychology, and the church.* New York, NY: Cambridge University Press.

Browning, D. S., & Cooper, T. D. (2004). *Religious thought and the modern psychologies* (Vol. 174). Minneapolis, MN: Fortress Press.

Brueggemann, W. (1980). Psalms and the life of faith: A suggested typology of function. *Journal for the Study of the Old Testament, 5*(17), 3–32.

Brueggemann, W. (1984). *The message of the Psalms: A theological commentary.* Minneapolis: Augsburg Pub. House.

Calhoun, L. G., & Tedeschi, R. G. (2013). *Posttraumatic growth in clinical practice.* New York, NY: Routledge/Taylor & Francis Group.

Cooper-White, P. (2008). Interrogating integration, dissenting dis-integration: Multiplicity as a positive metaphor in therapy and theology. *Pastoral Psychology, 57*(1–2), 3–15. doi:10.1007/s11089-008-0135-0

Fackre, G. (2001). Narrative theology from an evangelical perspective. In K. E. Yandell (Ed.), *Faith and narrative* (pp. 188–201). New York, NY: Oxford University Press.

Gelo, O. G., & Salvatore, S. (2016). A dynamic systems approach to psychotherapy: A meta-theoretical framework for explaining psychotherapy change processes. *Journal of Counseling Psychology, 63*(4), 379–395. doi:10.1037/cou0000150

Goldingay, J. (2003). *Old testament theology: Israel's gospel.* Downers Grove, IL: InterVarsity.

Granqvist, P., & Kirkpatrick, L. A. (2013). Religion, spirituality, and attachment. In K. I. Pargament, J. J. Exline, & J. W. Jones (Eds.), *APA handbook of psychology, religion, and spirituality (Vol. 1): Context, theory, and research* (pp. 139–155). Washington: American Psychological Association.

Green, J. B. (2007). *Seized by truth: Reading the Bible as scripture.* Nashville, TN: Abingdon Press.

Grenz, S. (2006). The social God and the relational self: Toward a theology of the *Imago Dei* in the postmodern context. In R. Lints, M. S. Horton, & M. R. Talbot (Eds.), *Personal identity in theological perspective* (pp. 70–92). Grand Rapids, MI: Eerdmans.

Groeschel, B. J. (1983). *Spiritual passages: The psychology of spiritual development.* New York, NY: The Crossroad Publishing Company.

Hainlen, R., Jankowski, P. J., Paine, D. R., & Sandage, S. J. (2016). Attachment predicting forgiveness, well-being, and social justice commitment: Mediator effects for differentiation of self. *Contemporary Family Therapy, 38,* 172–183. doi:10.1007/s10591-015-9359-1

Hall, T. W., & Edwards, K. J. (2002). The Spiritual Assessment Inventory: A theistic model and measure for assessing spiritual development. *Journal for the Scientific Study of Religion, 41*(2), 341–357.

Hall, T. W., & Porter, S. L. (2004). Referential integration: An emotional information processing perspective on the process of integration. *Journal of Psychology and Theology, 32*, 167–180.

Hardy, D. S. (2000). A Winnicottian redescription of Christian spiritual direction relationships: Illustrating the potential contribution of psychology of religion to Christian spiritual practice. *Journal of Psychology and Theology, 28*(4), 263–275.

Hayes, A. M., Yasinski, C., Barnes, J. B., & Bockting, C. H. (2015). Network destabilization and transition in depression: New methods for studying the dynamics of therapeutic change. *Clinical Psychology Review, 41*, 27–39. doi:10.1016/j.cpr.2015.06.007

Hayes, D. L. (2012). *Forged in the fiery furnace: African American spirituality*. Maryknoll, NY: Orbis Books.

Hollingsworth, A. (2011). The ambiguity of interdisciplinarity. *Zygon, 46*(2), 461–470.

Holmes, J. (2001). *The search for the secure base: Attachment theory and psychotherapy*. Philadelphia, PA: Brunner-Routledge.

Hyun Lee, S. (2010). *From a liminal place: An Asian American theology*. Minneapolis, MN: Fortress Press.

James, W. (1958). *Varieties of religious experience: A study in human nature*. New York, NY: Modern Library.

Johnson, E. L. (2007). Towards a philosophy of science for Christian psychology. *Edification: Journal of the Society of Christian Psychology, 1*, 5–20.

Johnson, E. L. (2011). The three faces of integration. *Journal of Psychology and Christianity, 30*(4), 339–355.

Jones, J. W. (2002). *Terror and transformation: The ambiguity of religion in psychoanalytic perspective*. New York, NY: Brunner-Routledge.

Kegan, R. (1980). There the dance is: Religious dimensions of a developmental framework. In J. W. Fowler & A. Vergote (Eds.), *Toward moral and religious maturity* (pp. 403–440). Morristown, NJ: Silver Burdette.

Kegan, R. (1994). *In over our heads: The mental demands of modern life*. Cambridge, MA: Harvard University Press.

Kierkegaard, S. (1980). *The sickness unto death: A Christian psychological exploration for upbuilding and awakening* (H. V. Hong & E. H. Hong, Eds. & Trans.). Princeton, NJ: Princeton University Press. (Original work 1849)

Klein, M. (1946). Notes on some schizoid mechanisms. *The International Journal of Psychoanalysis, 27*, 99–110.

Kohut, H. (1984). *How does analysis cure?* (A. Goldberg & P. E. Stepansky, Eds.). Chicago: University of Chicago Press.

Lindbeck, G. (1997). The story-shaped church: Critical exegesis and theological interpretation. In S. E. Fowl (Ed.). *The theological interpretation of Scripture: Classic and contemporary readings* (pp. 39–52). Malden, MA: Blackwell.

Loder, J. E. (1989). *The transforming moment*. Colorado Springs: Helmers & Howard.

Loder, J. E. (1998). *The logic of the spirit: Human development in theological perspective*. San Francisco, CA: Jossey-Bass.

Loevinger, J. (1976). *Ego development: Conceptions and theories*. San Francisco, CA: Jossey-Bass.

McAdams, D. P. (2013). *The redemptive self: Stories Americans live by* (rev. & expanded, ed.). New York, NY: Oxford University Press.

McAdams, D. P. (2016). *The art and science of personality development*. New York, NY: Guilford Press.

McAdams, D. P., Bauer, J. J., Sakaeda, A. R., Anyidoho, N. A., Machado, M. A., Magrino-Failla, K., . . . Pals, J. L. (2006). Continuity and change in the life story: A longitudinal study of autobiographical memories in emerging adulthood. *Journal of Personality*, *74*(5), 1371–1400. doi:10.1111/j.1467–6494.2006.00412.x

Mikulincer, M., & Shaver, P. R. (2007). *Attachment in adulthood: Structure, dynamics, and change*. New York, NY: Guilford Press.

Miller, W. R., & C' de Baca, J. (2001). *Quantum change: When epiphanies and sudden insights transform ordinary lives*. New York, NY: Guilford Press.

Mitchell, S. A. (2003). *Can love last? The fate of romance over time*. New York, NY: W.W. Norton.

Morse, C. (2010). *The difference heaven makes: Rehearing the gospel as news*. New York, NY: T & T Clark.

Paine, D. R., Moon, S. H., Sandage, S. J., Langford, R., Patel, S., Hollingsworth, A., Bronstein, M., & Salimi, B. (2017). Group therapy for loss: Intersubjectivity and attachment in healing. *International Journal of Group Therapy*, *67*, 565–589.

Peters, T. (1994). *Sin: Radical evil in soul and society*. Grand Rapids, MI: Eerdmans Publishing Company.

Pohl, C. D. (2011). *Living into community: Cultivating practices that sustain us*. Grand Rapids, MI: Eerdmans.

Rogoff, B. (2003). *The cultural nature of human development*. New York, NY: Oxford University Press.

Sandage, S. J., & Brown, J. K. (2012). Converging horizons for relational integration: Differentiation-based collaboration. *Journal of Psychology and Theology*, *40*, 72–76.

Sandage, S. J., & Brown, J. K. (2015). Relational integration, part I: Differentiated relationality between psychology and theology. *Journal of Psychology & Theology*, *43*(3).

Sandage, S. J., Jankowski, P. J., Crabtree, S., & Schweer, M. (2015). Attachment, spirituality pathology, and God images: Mediator and moderator effects. *Mental Health, Religion, and Culture*, *18*, 795–808.

Sandage, S. J., Jensen, M. L., & Jass, D. (2008). Relational spirituality and transformation: Risking intimacy and alterity. *Journal of Spiritual Formation and Soul Care*, *1*(2), 182–206.

Sandage, S. J., & Moe, S. (2013). Spiritual experience: Conversion and transformation. In K. I. Pargament, J. J. Exline, & J. W. Jones (Eds.), *APA handbook of psychology, religion, and spirituality (Vol. 1): Context, theory, and research* (pp. 407–422). Washington, DC: American Psychological Association.

Schnarch, D. (1997). *Passionate marriage: Keeping love and intimacy alive in committed relationships*. New York, NY: Henry Holt and Company.

Schnarch, D. M. (2009). *Intimacy and desire: Awaken the passion in your relationship*. New York, NY: Beaufort Books.

Schoenberg, P. A., & Barendregt, H. P. (2016). Mindful disintegration and the decomposition of self in healthy populations: Conception and preliminary study. *Psychological Studies*, *61*(4), 307–320. doi:10.1007/s12646-016-0374-6

Shults, F. L. (2012). Dis-integrating psychology and theology. *Journal of Psychology and Theology*, *40*(1), 21–25.

Shults, F. L., & Sandage, S. J. (2006). *Transforming spirituality: Integrating theology and psychology*. Grand Rapids, MI: Baker Academic.

Siegel, D. (2007). *The mindful brain: Reflections on attunement in the cultivation of well-being*. New York, NY: W.W. Norton & Co.

Siegel, D. (2010). *Mindsight: The new science of personal transformation*. New York, NY: Bantam Books.

Skalski, J. E., & Hardy, S. A. (2013). Disintegration, new consciousness, and discontinuous transformation: A qualitative investigation of quantum change. *The Humanistic Psychologist, 41*(2), 159–177. doi:10.1080/08873267.2012.724271

Skowron, E. A., & Dendy, A. K. (2004). Differentiation of self and attachment in adulthood: Relational correlates of effortful control. *Contemporary Family Therapy: An International Journal, 26,* 337–357.

Spero, M. H. (1992). *Religious objects as psychological structures*. Chicago: University of Chicago Press.

Stuthridge, J. (2017). Falling apart and getting it together: The dialectics of disintegration and integration in script change and self-development. *Transactional Analysis Journal, 47*(1), 19–31. doi:10.1177/0362153716681029

Tillich, P. (1957). *Systematic theology* (Vol. 2). Chicago: University of Chicago Press.

Tracy, D. (1987). *Plurality and ambiguity: Hermeneutics, religion, hope*. San Francisco, CA: Harper and Row.

Vanhoozer, K. J. (2005). *The drama of doctrine: A canonical linguistic approach to Christian theology*. Louisville: Westminster John Knox.

Wood, D., Bruner, J., & Ross, G. (1976). The role of tutoring in problem solving. *Journal of Child Psychology and Child Psychiatry, 17,* 89–100.

Worthington E. L., Jr., & Sandage, S. J. (2016). *Forgiveness and spirituality in psychotherapy: A relational approach*. Washington, DC: American Psychological Association.

Wright, N. T. (1992). *The new testament and the people of God*. Minneapolis, MN: Fortress Press.

Wu, J. (2013). Biblical theology from a Chinese perspective: Interpreting Scripture through the lens of honor and shame." *Global Missiology 4*(10), 1–31.

7

RELATIONAL INTEGRATION AS INTERCULTURAL

In this chapter, we focus our attention on relational integration as intercultural. By "intercultural," we mean to highlight the specific importance of cultural differences, but the thematic use of "intercultural" in our relational integration model can also prompt awareness of a broad constellation of diversity, justice, alterity, and intersectionality considerations which are crucial to relationally integrative practice as we understand it. As we have argued throughout this book, differentiation is essential to our relational integration model. As such, we believe that what counts as integration can and should take differing forms based on unique contextual considerations and a plurality of differing combinations of psychological and theological traditions. We want to underscore the differentiated relational processes we have found to be helpful for integration rather than specifying a singular description of what integration should "look like" for any particular situation.

We begin the chapter by addressing the minimal engagement with diversity considerations in the theology/psychology integration literature. We then explore the concept of alterity for orienting well toward difference, addressing in turn ethnocentrism and intercultural competence as two distinct stances toward difference. We highlight our relational integration model more particularly in a third section that attends to the acculturation challenges of integration. We conclude by exploring what a mature alterity offers to a spirituality that thematizes relationality. As we have in Chapters 4–6, we engage a case across the chapter to explore some of the intercultural possibilities for relational integration.

Diversity and Justice in the Healing Process

Keisha (age 35, female, African-American) and Mike (age 39, male, American-Indian, Lakota name—Mika) agreed to see a couple therapist after a three-year downward spiral in their eight-year marriage. They had met while both were working in state government in a Midwestern city in the U.S. Mike had held a position in water conservation which he loved, and Keisha had worked as an administrative assistant in the division of social services in a job she found rote and bureaucratic. Four years ago, they had moved to another city for Keisha to complete a master's degree in mental health counseling. The first year of the transition seemed to be going relatively well. Mike was able to piece together several consulting jobs which meant travel but ongoing income. Keisha enjoyed her graduate studies in counseling which validated her vocational shift and her sense of "God's calling" on her life to "help those who are hurting." But Keisha's mom died from an aggressive form of cancer during her second year in training, and this prompted struggles in her faith as her mom had been her key spiritual mentor. She continued to regularly attend services at an African Methodist Episcopal church but she could not emotionally enter into worship or prayer and was disturbed by jarring feelings of anger and mistrust at God.

Keisha also felt Mike was starting to become distant or even pulling away around the time of her mom's death. For example, she thought he seemed to be extending his travel beyond the necessary work days and showed little interest in meeting her graduate school friends or talking about her new experiences and insights. She told a friend she felt she was "losing him," and this abandonment felt deeply unfair to her at a time she felt so vulnerable. Mike complained to his cousin (his key confidante) that Keisha was "absorbed in her new world," was "always trying to analyze" him with her new psychological theories, and had become "constantly angry and demanding." Mike also had trouble understanding Keisha's "dramatic fight with God" (as he put it). His own orientation toward Lakota spirituality was less verbal and more private and reflective, explaining to his cousin, "I feel spiritual . . . I mean in touch with the Great Spirit . . . when I am out in nature and sense how the rhythms and processes of life are beyond me. I feel re-grounded. I can't understand Keisha's spirituality and how she gets so disappointed at not getting what she expects, as though God is like a parent. I don't want to judge her . . . but it kind of repels me because I think she has the same unfair expectations and disappointments in me." While drifting apart emotionally, Mike and Keisha shared a sense of unfairness in their marriage.

Mike had been resisting Keisha's request to go to couple therapy for several months, saying he was too busy and not interested, but the tipping point came one Friday night when they met up for a late dinner. As they left the restaurant, a group of white males were across the street, and one yelled a sexually harassing statement at Keisha punctuated by a racial slur. Keisha was enraged and yelled back at the guy, which prompted mocking laughter and more insults from the whole group. Mike pulled her away, and after they got home they went in separate rooms and avoided each other for the rest of the weekend. Keisha had been actively working on her racial and overall diversity consciousness since taking a multicultural course her first semester of graduate school, and she had been repeatedly trying to process social issues related to sexism, racism, and homophobia with Mike. He acknowledged such issues to some extent based on his experience growing up on a reservation in the rural Midwest, but he tended to minimize previous experiences that Keisha had been complaining about—for example, servers ignoring them in restaurants, a landlord who wouldn't rent to them for mysterious reasons, a white client in her practicum who questioned her educational credentials and asked for another therapist after one session, two psychology professors who seemed dismissive of diversity issues in their courses, and a friend of Mike's who frequently made stereotyping comments and jokes about "what women are like." Mike said he didn't see the benefit of "ruminating on that shit" (his words). However, this latest incident was unambiguous to him and traumatic for both of them, and Mike now realized they were not able to handle the multiple stressors and challenges they were facing without some help.

Keisha got a referral from their pastor for couple therapy with Ed (age 41; biracial, Irish-American and Korean-American), a marriage and family therapist practicing with a large group practice which listed "Christian counseling" and "spiritual integration" as areas of specialization on their website. This raised anxiety for Mike, as he entered the first session wondering if he would be in a one-down position with a therapist who might be biased toward Christianity. Keisha had her own anxieties, namely wondering if Ed could understand and "handle" the rawness of her experiences of racism and her recent spiritual struggles or if he might side with Mike in a minimizing stance due to gender.

Diversity in the Integration of Psychology and Theology

Before offering some key concepts and central considerations for *relational integration as intercultural*, we first want to give our assessment of the ways diversity is attended to or minimized in integration as it is currently practiced. This analysis of the current landscape focuses on omissions around diversity from the integration literature, the gender dynamics around these omissions, and the problematizing of "integration" by postcolonial scholars.

The Dearth of Diversity in Integration Literature

Over the years, numerous authors have voiced concern about the need for greater attention to diversity in evangelical discourse on psychology and theology (Dueck & Reimer, 2009; Eriksson & Abernethy, 2014; Hook & Davis, 2012; Yangarber-Hicks et al., 2006). As early as 1981, H. Newton Malony issued a call for greater awareness of cultural differences in the integration of psychology and theology. Nearly three decades later in a postscript to their review of seminal works in the history of integration, Stevenson, Eck, and Hill (2007) reveal how little had changed with their suggestion, "[t]he future of integration ought to give voice to include a greater range of voices from women, cultural minorities, non-clinicians, and international perspectives to avoid the irony of tolerating separate silos of thought in literature labeled integrative" (p. 376). In their article reflecting on "forty years of integration," Hook and Davis (2012) note that the very limited engagement of multicultural and social justice concerns in integration literature might reflect (a) differences among Christians as to whether diversity and justice are important spiritual concerns and (b) the religiously privileged status of Christians in the North American context despite claims of marginalized status among many Evangelicals (Schlosser, 2003). McNeil (2005) has articulated this concern in personal terms by describing his experience as an African-American navigating the psychology-theology integration dialogue. He observes that his "identity as an evangelical Christian was affirmed, but other identities (ethnic and cultural) and loyalties . . . were dismissed or ignored." He goes on to identify and critique Euro-American privilege underlying the "tacit assumption that an evangelical Christian identity freed from any particularity was the exclusive lens with which to interpret the world" (p. 141).

Sadly, despite these repeated calls for greater attention to diversity and more diverse voices in the integration of psychology and theology, progress in this area appears minimal at best. McMinn and colleagues (2015) found doctoral students in Christian clinical psychology programs reported receiving more training in spiritual and religious diversity than doctoral students at other APA-accredited programs but less training in ethnic, racial, or socioeconomic diversity. The literature on integration also remains largely minimizing of diversity and justice concerns. If the five views book on psychology and Christianity (Johnson, 2010) is examined from a diversity perspective, we notice the authors are eight white males. Similarly, the volume *Counseling and Christianity: Five Approaches* (Greggo & Sisemore, 2012) includes seven white authors, six male and one female.

This state of affairs is especially perplexing given the ready examples of diversity engagement in psychology and psychotherapy literatures (e.g., Sue & Sue, 2015) and in biblical studies and theology (e.g., Mbuvi, 2017; De La Torre, 2013). Progressive, diversity-sensitive resources are available within both theology and psychology, although it must be acknowledged that in each guild historically marginalized voices still find themselves sometimes kept at the margins (e.g., Schüssler

Fiorenza, 2000). The reality that few such resources are available in literature on the interface or integration of theology and psychology calls for attention and redress, though we would be remiss if we failed to mention a resource that stands out for its attention to diversity. The editors of a volume on practical theology (Cahalan & Mikoski, 2014) include diverse cultural, social, and gender perspectives; the book also includes a chapter specifically on "White Practical Theology" (Beaudoin & Turpin, 2014) to avoid universalizing white racial perspectives and to engage explicitly historical realities of white supremacy.

Gender and Integrative Dialogue

As we noted above, two fairly recent volumes dedicated to the integration of psychology/counseling and Christianity (Johnson, 2010; Greggo & Sisemore, 2012) include exclusively Caucasian contributors and only surface one woman among their fifteen authors. This latter dynamic also deserves attention in the category of diversity issues. While we have already reflected on the role gender and gender views have on preferred modes of integrative dialogue (hierarchical or egalitarian; Chapter 3), here we would highlight how gender considerations impact who is at the table for integrative conversation.

An important gender dynamic arising from integration between psychology and theology is the constitutions of both fields, especially in evangelical contexts. In general, theology and biblical studies have both been heavily male-dominated fields until quite recently. And even with more women entering these guilds, experiences of sexism and some amount of marginalization continue to be all too common for women in these disciplines. Even at present, statistics from the Association of Theological Schools indicate that women make up only about 25% of full-time faculty in all ATS member schools (with little change between 2012–2016). A U.K. study indicates that women make up 29% of academic staff in theology and religious studies, with the greater percentage for early career academics/lecturers (37%) and many fewer at the professor level (16%) (Guest, Sharma, & Song, 2013). In evangelical institutions and arenas, the disparity is often greater, with some higher educational institutions refusing on theological grounds to hire women to teach in theology or biblical studies. Creegan and Pohl (2005) in their study of evangelical women in theological disciplines of the academy have chronicled a variety of exclusionary challenges as women have sought to find a place of belonging in evangelical institutions within theological education. In their study, they describe the liminality experienced by many as they find themselves *Living on the Boundaries* (the title of their book) in spaces outside of and between Evangelicalism and the academy. And Elouise Renich Fraser (1998), in *Confessions of a Beginning Theologian*, writes of her own experience of liminality as a theologian in the academy: "I developed the fine art of belonging on the outside" (p. 41). Turning to psychology, in North America women seem to have a much higher representation among psychologists than among women in theological disciplines (APA, 2016; see also APA, 2017).[1] It may be that some women experiencing and expressing a divine calling to ministry and who were barred from pursuing theological education in their own ecclesial contexts found psychology and therapy to be places to live out their callings in spite of stricter gender parameters.

Into this dynamic, the disposition at least in some contexts to prioritize and privilege theology over psychology for interdisciplinary conversations can result all too frequently in men having the upper hand in conversations with women. In this context, we suggest that the ongoing assertion of theology as "queen of the sciences" in some circles results in an ironic hierarchical arrangement of men over women (Sandage & Brown, 2010). We raise the irony because, regardless of intention, there can be harmful effects to those in interdisciplinary conversations with less power and access. As we have noted,

> for our particular egalitarian and relational approach, important dimensions of integration involve (a) the ability to take the perspective of the other in considering the impact of our language, and (b) the willingness to consider the actual social justice implications of theoretical positions.
>
> *(Sandage & Brown, 2010, p. 24)*

We recognize we bring our own social locations and experiences to these gender considerations. After I (Steve) recently gave a lecture on relational integration as intercultural based on ideas explored in this chapter, a white male audience member complained with significant levels of affect that I had denigrated white males. He went on to voice a feeling that white males are "under attack" in U.S. society. The latter part of his complaint seemed to invoke his sense of a sacred past in U.S. society that was being lost or stolen. As a white male myself, I (Steve) am not seeking to disparage the contributions of whites or males, but I am inviting awareness of the demographics of those involved in conversations about integration and other issues while also arguing for the benefits of diversity. The fact that certain dominant group members can feel emotionally and socially threatened or even victimized by affirming diversity and calling for inclusion highlights the need for a nuanced, integrative approach to these issues that seeks to understand the complex interplay of emotions, sacred values, and sociocultural contexts.

As a white female in a theological discipline in a seminary, I (Jeannine) sometimes find myself in the disconcerting position of being granted privilege in integrative conversations by virtue of my identity as a biblical scholar, while sensing how my voice as a woman sometimes carries less weight or is more easily discounted (Brescoll, 2011). From another angle, I am grateful when other biblical scholars show appreciation for my voice and my publications and provide them for students not simply because I offer a (or, worse *the*) "female" point of view but because they value my contribution specifically and, more generally, greater diversity at the table. And yet I do consider my passion for integrative conversation and collaboration to emerge potentially from my gender, at least the ways I have been socialized as a female in my cultural context, with high value placed on collaboration and relationality.

There has been a small body of literature over the past twenty-five years on ways gender and other forms of diversity might shape differential preferences for integration in graduate training in psychology (e.g., McNeil, 2005; Ripley, Garzon, Hall, Mangis, & Murphy, 2009; Watson, Prevost, Faries, & Para-Mallam, 2001). In short, women and cultural minorities often report preferences for approaches to integration that emphasize experiential, relational, justice, and environmental considerations as compared with approaches that convey an overriding emphasis on abstract philosophical or conceptual issues. As argued throughout this book, we resonate with these stated preferences as important parts of a relational integration process. In our view, universities, training programs, clinics, religious communities, and other systems that want to effectively promote the relational integration of theology and psychology will need to cultivate (a) diversity competence and commitments to social justice, (b) healthy relational dynamics within their institution, and (c) opportunities for experiential education and growth in self-awareness.

Postcolonial "Integration"

An important resource for gaining insight into diverse perspectives for the integration of psychology and theology comes from postcolonial perspectives. There is a growing postcolonial literature in both psychology (e.g., Fanon, 1963; Comas-Diaz, 2000) and theology (e.g., Choi, 2015; Crowell, 2009; Dube, 2012; Haker et al., 2013) that expands and challenges mainstream and majority views from each field. Our emphasis on intercultural dynamics finds great value in reflection on postcolonial studies, since they highlight the distortions that can come from normalizing privileged voices. Arukwe (2014), for example, voices the prophetic postcolonial critique that challenges the Eurocentric narrative that European cultural groups are superior to other cultures and have typically brought benevolent, civilizing influences to other cultures.

In terms of interdisciplinarity, postcolonial scholars would tend to problematize a word like "integration" and investigate the ways the term might (a) imply assimilation of minorities into dominant power structures; (b) connote smooth harmony of perspectives that masks important realities of differences in social power; and (c) dissociate traumatic experiences of suffering within larger social systems of oppression. From a postcolonial perspective, our attempts at relational integration must attend to and include dealing with ruptures, many textured differences, and broken narratives and symbols that are not easily repaired. We are drawn to the work of scholars like Comas-Diaz (2000) in psychology, who emphasizes the etiological influence of racism, discrimination, and other colonizing aspects of sociopolitical oppression on mental health problems, which can generate a range of trauma symptoms including shame, rage, hopelessness, identity confusion, and spiritual demoralization. We also appreciate the theological and ethical perspectives of Miguel De La Torre in *Embracing Hopelessness* (2017), who offers a particular vision of hopelessness that eschews Christian triumphalist perspectives in the pursuit of justice.

Sharp (2013) has articulated a postcolonial pastoral theology which suggests the need to move past a prior focus in pastoral theology and pastoral psychology on the intrapsychic and interpersonal to include more attention to communal, contextual, and intercultural dynamics. Choi (2015) has offered a postcolonial theological and interdisciplinary perspective on Korean immigration experiences and the challenges of selfhood in contexts of oppression. In application to case situations like the one above, these works by Choi, Sharp, and other postcolonial authors invite important questions such as:

1. Who is seen and who is invisible?
2. Who feels constantly under a magnifying glass?
3. What cultural narratives subtly inform interpretations and potential misunderstanding of stories?
4. Who is empowered with agency to interpret their own experience and who is not?
5. How do dynamics of social privilege impact what is happening and how that is understood?
6. How do systemic factors contribute to suffering for some persons while simultaneously generating justifications for that suffering?
7. What would help with intercultural empathy and mutual intercultural learning in a certain set of contexts?

In this first section of the chapter, we have illuminated the difficulties of attending to significant difference in the integrative process. Stances toward such difference range from minimization (which we seem to see in the integration literature overall), to power stances over (in areas of gender difference), to careful attention to how even the language of "integration" might support hegemony if care is not taken to recognize, value, and actualize difference in integrative spaces.

Ed's Role of Differentiation and Cultural Humility

Keisha and Mike bring to couple therapy several intersections of identity (e.g., ethnicity and religion) as individuals, as well as intercultural and intersectional differences as a couple. We would actually suggest all couples are intercultural to some extent. And as Waldman and Rubalcava (2005) note, intercultural couples often experience "conflicting unconscious cultural presumptions" (p. 228) that contribute to deep conflicts. It is important to surface those cultural presumptions, and a therapist can help this process through empathy, curiosity, lack of judgment, and an operative belief that cultural differences are ultimately beneficial. As an example in this case, Keisha operated from a cultural conflict style of *engagement* and assumed it was loving to share intense emotions in relationships and to communicate directly about conflicts (Hammer, 2005). In contrast, Mike had internalized an *accommodation* style of conflict management which utilizes a more emotionally restrained and indirect style of communication. Some parts of the marital estrangement Mike and Keisha were experiencing could be reduced by helping them get attuned to their differing cultural assumptions about conflict and loving ways of relating during conflict. This is part of the differentiation work with couples—helping them understand cultural differences in less judgmental and polarizing ways.

This begs questions about Ed and his level of training and effectiveness in working with diversity. Ed has trained in a program with strong multicultural and diversity emphases throughout the curriculum, which included cognitive, experiential, and clinical skill components. He had also engaged in personal therapy with considerable attention to his own biracial and bicultural experiences and identity, his parents' struggles with intercultural issues in their own marriage, and his struggles encountering racism which is sometimes overlooked among Asian-Americans. The clinic where Ed practiced did not have a strong commitment to diversity training, but Ed joined a monthly consultation group outside his clinic with three other therapists who valued attending to issues of diversity and justice in their own clinical practice. This personal work connects to a crucial awareness of and appreciation for difference that we have been highlighting in this chapter. Ed's personal work also represented a strong level of the kind of "expanded self-examination" that Tummala-Narra (2015) recommends for clinicians pursuing cultural competence, which needs to be practiced in ongoing ways beyond formal training and throughout one's career.

These efforts led Ed to empathize with Keisha in her growing racial and diversity consciousness and her anger about racism; yet he could also understand Mike's reluctance to engage those issues and remembered feeling that way himself in the past. By asking questions of Mike and Keisha about their cultural values and perspectives rather than presuming he knew what and how they thought, Ed also showed cultural humility and modeled a less reactive relational stance. Hook and Watkins (2015, p. 661) have defined cultural humility as a willingness to reflect on one's own cultural position, an awareness of limitations in comprehending the culture and worldview of others, and openness to the culture and identity of others. There is growing empirical support for cultural humility as a therapist characteristic that contributes to effective outcomes in psychotherapy (Hook, Davis, Owen, & DeBlaere, 2017).

Although a Christian himself, Ed was also skilled at taking a differentiated stance on religion and spirituality and communicated an interest in understanding Mike's Lakota spirituality rather than privileging Keisha's faith, something that would have been easy to do based on his own self-identity and the privilege that Christianity continues to hold in the U.S. context (Schlosser, 2003). This differentiated stance coheres with the fifth question we offer from a post-colonial perspective (distilling Choi and Sharp's works): How do dynamics of social privilege impact what is happening and how that is understood? Ed's relationally integrative stance avoided unhelpful triangulation and eventually served to metabolize the intense anxiety and hurt that Mike and Keisha had about their religious differences. Ed's respectful and curious way of relating to each about their spiritualities, such as Mike's reverence for the sacredness of water and Keisha's belief that if you care about someone (including God) you will fight with them, helped this couple begin to relate more openly and effectively amidst their differences (i.e., growth in differentiation). Mike and Keisha each began to learn new information about one another's relational spirituality while listening to Ed dialogue with their partner. This could be likened to a form of "witness" which couple therapy affords—the therapist communicates with one partner while the other can listen without the emotional intensity of direct communication or feeling the need to defend one's own perspective. Frequently, new relational insights emerge when this kind of space for witness is provided.

Alterity and Orienting Well Toward Difference

Having introduced some current gaps as well as potential resources for interdisciplinarity between psychology and theology, we turn to the construct of alterity and its importance for understanding *relational integration as intercultural*. Alterity or "otherness" poses some complicated dynamics for integration. We define alterity as "developmental forms of relating to the *differentness* of others" (Sandage, Jensen, & Jass, 2008, p. 183). Alterity ("otherness") poses some complicated dynamics for integration. On the one hand, "othering" can be oppressive when prejudice and stereotypes are used to perpetuate social exclusion or domination of certain groups (i.e., "others") who are deemed unlike one's own group. On the other hand, social and cultural differences are a given and so experiences of alterity are unavoidable and can even be potentially constructive for spiritual and relational development (Sandage et al., 2008). Numerous continental philosophers and social scientists have explored the relational and intersubjective dynamics of alterity and the importance of orienting to difference in ways that do not diminish the humanity of self or other (Sandage, Paine, & Morgan, in press). A central example is Levinas' ethical philosophy of alterity, which heralded the ethical importance of facing and caring for the *Other* in their full humanity and also described the initial, potentially traumatizing impact of encountering the radical difference of others we can never really know. Benjamin (1998, 2004) takes a more descriptive and nuanced developmental approach to alterity as a social scientist and psychoanalyst (for a fuller discussion of her work, see Chapter 3). She describes a developmental capacity for mutual recognition in relation to alterity—a capacity that balances appreciation for the complexity of actually knowing other human subjects while remaining hopeful that some degree of knowing is possible with appropriate capacities for differentiation and humility.

We find a fruitful biblical analogy to alterity in Paul's stance toward otherness in Romans. In a letter devoted to the relationship of Jew and Gentile (1:16–17; 1:18–4:25; 9:1–11:36), it is not surprising that Paul addresses conflicts over specific differences between these groups in 14:1–15:13. An important overriding theme in this section of text is Paul's exhortation to extend welcome (*proslambanō*) across difference (14:1; 15:7). He addresses two groups in this passage: the weak, who abstain from meat and observe sacred days (14:1–2; 15:1), and the strong, who don't share the stricter convictions of the weak (14:3; 15:1). Paul anticipates the tendencies of each group when he forbids the weak from judging the strong for their freedoms and the strong from despising the weak for their narrower set of convictions (14:3). Some interpreters of Romans understand the division between weak and strong to be, in part, an ethnic one (Shogren, 2000), and this makes sense given immediate contextual factors (15:8–13) and the setting of Romans, in which Jewish believers in Rome, recently returned from an exile under Emperor Claudius, find themselves in a more marginalized position in the faith community (Wright, 1995).

What is important for our discussion here is that Paul doesn't call the weak (likely many of whom are Jews or Jewish converts) to conform to the strong (many or most of whom are Gentiles) and vice versa. Instead, he takes what we might call a *differentiated stance* toward the two groups. And while not asking either group to assimilate to the other, Paul does require a change of attitude and action. He especially requires those with greater privilege—those identified as "strong" (15:1)—to act out love to their fellow believers ("the weak") by refraining from leading them away from their convictions ("causing them to stumble;" 14:13–15). "For Paul, unity in the body of Christ does not mean the sameness of all the members; it means the solidarity which can endure the strain of the differences" (Käsemann, 1971, p. 3).

The Problem of Ethnocentrism

As we have noted, experiences of alterity are inevitable and can work for good or ill. *Ethnocentrism* presents a problematic way to encounter and process alterity. Ethnocentrism involves the belief and perception that one's own ethnic or cultural perspective is the standard of goodness for all cultures. This framework typically operates at an implicit or unconscious level and impedes the ability to empathize or engage with other cultural perspectives. Those operating from ethnocentrism rely upon poorly differentiated templates for perceiving and understanding cultural differences, using prejudice and stereotyping to interpret intercultural experiences. Ethnocentrism can be the natural result of certain homogeneous socialization experiences and a human propensity for in-group bias, although colonizing systems reinforce and may even reify or mandate ethnocentric attitudes. But in healthy developmental processes, exposure to cultural differences combined with relational resources of intercultural education and formation can help individuals move beyond ethnocentrism as an interpretive orientation in life.

It is helpful here to note the biblical vision for something beyond ethnocentrism, and we appreciate Eric Barreto's work on Luke-Acts and offer his summary of the role of difference in Acts:

> At core, the author of Luke-Acts views our differences as a gift from God to be treasured, not a difficulty to be overcome. Ethnic and racial differences are not the problem. Prejudice and racism inject our differences with the sinful notion that our difference leads to superiority and inferiority or the distorted belief that our differences are merely cultural cues for determining who is in and who is out, rather than emblems of God's gift of diversity.
> *(Barreto, 2011, p. 131)*

The Developmental Model of Intercultural Sensitivity (DMIS; Bennett, 2004) identifies four developmental orientations toward cultural differences that are ethnocentric: (a) denial, (b) defensiveness, (c) reversal, and (d) minimization. While none of these ethnocentric orientations fit Barreto's interpretation from Acts of human "differences as a gift from God," they deviate from this biblical vision in differing ways. Individuals operating from *intercultural denial* tend to be disinterested in and avoid awareness of cultural differences; they typically do not have strong conscious opinions about and deny the relevance of cultural differences. This posture is difficult to maintain with any level of exposure to cultural diversity. Those operating from *intercultural defensiveness* tend to believe their own culture is superior to other cultures and feel threatened by those they perceive to be from other cultural groups. *Intercultural reversal* essentially reverses defensiveness and generates perceptions that one's own culture is shameful or inferior to others; this stance often involves idealizing other cultures in ways that do not reflect accurate and authentic understanding of those cultures. Both intercultural defensiveness and reversal involve polarized mindsets about cultural differences and heightened levels of affect about intercultural issues (Hammer, 2011).

Minimization is probably the most common ethnocentric orientation among adults in the U.S., based on research to date; it involves a superficial acknowledgement of cultural differences combined with an emphasis on similarities across cultures. In the U.S., minimization involves privileging European-American cultural norms and values ("Eurocentrism") and typically involves a belief that the policies and practices of social institutions are generally fair and just. From a racial perspective, this results in difficulty understanding or questioning the operative dynamics of white supremacy and white privilege and the oppressive capacities of social institutions. For cultural minorities in the U.S., minimization can be viewed as the resilient achievement of assimilation despite cultural forces of discrimination, all the while requiring the sacrifice of a minority person's cultural identity and often activating fear of differentiated stances such as speaking out against prejudice and bigotry. For Euro-Americans in the U.S., minimization involves participation and implicit endorsement of the colonizing systemic dynamics of white supremacy and xenophobia and impedes the capacity to relate effectively across cultural differences.

The Relational Capacities of Intercultural Competence

In contrast to ethnocentrism, *intercultural competence* is "the ability to think and act in interculturally appropriate ways" and with sensitivity to "relevant cultural differences" (Hammer, Bennett, & Wiseman, 2003, p. 422) and is conceptually similar to multicultural competence (Sue & Sue, 2015). Intercultural competence involves effective relating across cultural differences, which requires developmental capacities that move beyond ethnocentrism to more flexible intercultural mindsets and a differentiated capacity for cultural intersubjectivity (i.e., "understanding of the interaction of one's own cultural perspective in relation to the cultural perspective of others;" Brown & Sandage, 2015). Intercultural competence exists along a continuum, and the most extensively validated assessment tool for intercultural competence, the Intercultural Development Inventory (IDI; Hammer, 2011), is based on the DMIS. This developmental approach to intercultural competence fits with our relational integration emphases on developmental processes and on the important roles of relational experiences and affect in shaping templates about self and other. *We consider intercultural competence to be a core capacity necessary to effectively engage in relational integration.*

In Hammer's (2011) model, intercultural competence involves capacities for cultural frame-shifting and behavioral code-switching. Intercultural *frame-shifting* is the ability to empathize or take the perspective of others who are culturally different. Frame-shifting does not necessarily entail endorsing another cultural perspective as optimal or "good;" rather, it involves the ability to understand how another cultural perspective can make sense within that cultural context or plausibility structure. This requires self-awareness of one's own worldview lens and the ability to differentiate the perspectives of self and other. Behavioral *code-switching* is the capacity to adjust one's behavior to fit other cultural styles. This may include behaviors such as the level of affect or directness expressed in communication, the amount of eye contact offered, and the management of physical closeness or distance during interactions.

Based on the DMIS, there are three intercultural orientations that fit within the range understood as intercultural competence: (a) acceptance, (b) adaptation, and (c) integration. Individuals operating from *intercultural acceptance* accept the notion that cultural diversity is generally beneficial and are open, curious, and actively engaged in seeking to understand cultural differences, even if they are not sure how to navigate cultural differences in their behavior. *Intercultural adaptation* combines strong capacities for cognitive frame-shifting and behavioral code-switching to enable persons to generally function effectively within intercultural encounters; this stance is developed through considerable intercultural experience. Since most individuals and systems in the U.S. are ethnocentric, the development of capacities for intercultural competence mean an individual with this stance may be at risk of feeling estranged or dislocated. The intercultural awareness attending adaptation involves empathic attunement to human suffering and seemingly intractable systemic dynamics of oppression, so there is a risk for vicarious trauma and depression. In the DMIS, *integration* involves the formative ability to holistically manage intercultural competence as a lifestyle in light of these risks, which will require wisdom in building social support and self-regulatory practices for dealing with intercultural stress and anxiety.

Systemic and Theological Lenses

Discussion of clinical case studies like that of Mike and Keisha often pulls for a strong focus on the clients. But from postcolonial and intercultural influences on our relational integration model, we want to reverse figure and ground and draw attention to the historical and systemic forces surrounding this couple. This could involve many different questions and points of reflection.

1. We could note, for example, that Keisha and Mike are each from communities that historically have suffered from attempted genocide by whites in the U.S., leaving legacies of intergenerational trauma and loss. A therapist might assess how each client understands those legacies and ongoing sources of struggle, and the extent to which they can support each other as they grapple with these trauma effects. The recent shared episode with sexism and racism is an opportunity for them to cultivate more secure attachment dynamics (i.e., supportive connection) in their marriage for coping with these painful realities.

2. We could also note the intercultural minimization in many of the systems that have surrounded Mike and Keisha, including their workplaces, the schools they have attended, and, to a large extent, their spiritual communities. Mike and Keisha have successfully assimilated into the middle class of a white dominant society, which is to their credit. However, those surrounding systems often demanded they each deny or feel shame about their cultural heritage (i.e., an experience of reversal). Moreover, these systems have not cultivated the advanced skills in intercultural competence necessary to develop an intimate intercultural marriage. It is noteworthy in this context that Keisha's training in multiculturalism in her graduate program seemed to initiate a rupture in their marriage by causing minimization to no longer work as a shared perspective. And while spirituality had been a source of strength for both at certain points, neither had found resources within their traditions to relate to one another in hospitable ways across religious differences. Ed's relational integration strategy in this regard was not to gloss over their actual differences but to encourage each to explore their own traditions and their personal integrity for ways they could relate respectfully toward the other in the midst of their pain and their differences. Mike reflected on the traditional Lakota value of humility (*Unsiiciyapi*), which increased his desire to be more open to understanding Keisha's perspective on various issues, including spirituality. Keisha began to meditate on sources within the biblical tradition for questioning God and what she perceived to be God's direct actions in taking her mother from her: Old Testament narratives like Jacob's struggle with God (Gen 32:22–32) and Hannah's lament for a son (1 Sam 1:1–20), as well as the significant number of laments in the Psalter (e.g., Pss. 10, 13, 22, 31). These texts that give voice to struggling with God had already resonated with Keisha's belief that if you care about someone (including God) you will fight with them. Keisha came to see that her relational spiritual orientation toward wrestling or struggling with both God and Mike was well-intentioned but was dissonant for Mike and miscommunicated her real desire to connect with him. Mike came to understand that his more introverted spiritual style and values of quiet personal reflection were fine but that he had failed to attach with Keisha in her pain over the loss of her mother and her experiences of racism and injustice. This process moved Mike and Keisha toward greater capacities for emotional solidarity and connecting amidst pain and anxiety. In light of the systemic discrimination they faced, they also realized they needed to develop some shared community support beyond what had started with Ed in therapy.

An interesting point of theological and relational tension in the case involves the respective images of God and the sacred held by Mike and Keisha. Mike identifies this difference as Keisha's view that "God is like a parent," while his own image of the sacred has to do with "the rhythms and processes of life [that] are beyond me." While we might be tempted (at least from a Christian viewpoint) to identify Mike's understanding of the sacred as less personal than Keisha's, it would be important to ask each client how they see the sacred in relation to themselves (in line with the question, *Who is empowered with agency to interpret their own experience and who is not?*). This relational spirituality (Worthington & Sandage, 2016) conversation surfaced the fact that Mike *did* view the Great Spirit as God the Creator, which surprised Keisha; however, consistent with Lakota traditions he believed the Great Spirit was comprised of a combination of male and female traits. He also believed the appropriate attitude before the Great Spirit was one of humility, and for him this did not include making requests or complaints as much as trying to be reverent, reflective, and grateful.

During this relational spirituality dialogue, which lasted for several therapy sessions, Mike became more open and vulnerable in sharing some of his deep resentment about ways Christians had historically colonized American Indians in an attempt to destroy their religions and cultures. Keisha found this painful though helpful to hear, and her recent multicultural training offered her tools in cultural humility to take this in and empathize with Mike's feelings. She could see that her past judgmental stance toward Mike's seemingly ambiguous spiritual beliefs, which arose partly out of her desire to connect with him, had actually exacerbated some of these historical wounds. These were challenging conversations, but they were helpful to Keisha and Mike to further differentiate by developing the ability to continue to communicate amidst differences and high levels of emotion.

To add more complex layering to the theological question of God as personal or impersonal, we would note that Mike's spirituality seems to foster deep relationship (one that is highly "personal"?) with the world around him as well as with "the Great Spirit." Keisha's understanding of God as parent involves fairly direct access to the divine, which can be seen in her reference to "God's calling" on her life to "help those who are hurting." This sense of direct access and relationship might contribute to her assumption that God is somehow directly responsible for her mother's death (seen in her anger and mistrust of God immediately after that loss). What is interesting theologically is that various Christian traditions navigate differently questions of God's agency in suffering and evil; not all of them see in the ubiquitous calamity and suffering of life the direct hand of God. It might be helpful in analyzing this case (and walking alongside Keisha) to consider whether there are metaphors for understanding God as personal beyond that of parent, as when Jesus identifies himself as friend to his followers (John 15:14–15). It might also be productive to explore with Keisha if biblical metaphors of God as mother (e.g., Deut 32:18b; Ps 131; Isa 49:14–16; 66:12–13) might cast a different light on her disappointment with God. Exploring Keisha's and Mike's images of the divine in thoughtful and theologically informed ways could help foster mutual understanding and potentially mutual influence.

The Acculturation Challenges of Integration

This DMIS intercultural framework for understanding psychosocial challenges of integration provides insights for our model of relational integration. We would note that such insights find some correspondence in Dueck (1995), who highlights the systemic acculturation challenges of integrating psychology and theology in *Between Jerusalem and Athens: Ethical Perspectives on Culture, Religion, and Psychotherapy*. Writing as an intercultural psychologist rooted in the Mennonite Christian tradition, Dueck uses the term "Jerusalem" as a metaphor for his sense of religious and cultural community (a home base, of sorts) and "Athens" as a metaphor for the more diverse, cosmopolitan contexts of mainstream psychology. He describes his own personal journey of moving back and forth between Jerusalem and Athens, so to speak, and the combination of both stimulation and loss he came to experience in both contexts. The analogy seems a helpful one, since religious conservatives might be skeptical of psychotherapy and might perceive dangers from mainstream psychology (i.e., Athens) as leading to compromises of faith. Alternatively, occupants of Athens may be wary of those who maintain identity commitments and involvements within religious communities (Jerusalem). For those traveling between Jerusalem and Athens, it may be necessary to tolerate the ambiguity of never feeling perfectly at home in either while still relating effectively in both (cf. the liminality discussed above in relation to gender). This is essentially a challenge of differentiation and intercultural competence. Our experience with clinical trainees who are religious is that they often resonate with the kinds of intercultural challenges of integration that Dueck is describing and find it beneficial discussing these issues in group settings once they are into their second year or beyond of clinical training. Trainees, and even mature clinicians, will often describe experiences of loss and invalidation, identity confusion, conflicting values, and points of ambiguity. Healthy relational supports during this process are crucial for constructing a sense of personal and professional integration and a cohesive sense of identity.

Berry (2013) has been a leading intercultural scholar in the psychology of acculturation, describing *integration* as one of four acculturation strategies used by immigrants or cultural minorities. In Berry's model, integration is a strategy of holding onto one's cultural heritage while also seeking to engage in regular interactions with other cultural groups. Some will pursue interactions with other cultural groups while minimizing their own cultural identity (assimilation). Others will engage in acts of separation to maintain their cultural heritage while avoiding other cultural groups. Marginalization may emerge when it proves difficult to maintain one's cultural identity and difficult to integrate into larger social networks. Research has shown integration is the acculturation strategy that is commonly associated with the best psychosocial adjustment and essentially involves the ability to negotiate (or integrate) at the same time differing cultural perspectives (Berry, 2013). Berry's overall model of acculturation rightly identifies that these are not simply personal choices by members of non-dominant groups but are influenced by the policies, attitudes, and relational dynamics of the dominant host society. For example, there is empirical evidence that multicultural ideology among host society members predicts greater tolerance and personal contact with immigrants (Hui, Chen, Leung, & Berry, 2015), whereas racism is negatively related to integration efforts (Kunst, Thomsen, Sam, & Berry, 2015). Thus, we would highlight that acculturation and intercultural integration involve crucial relational or systemic dynamics and the overall intercultural sensitivity and competence of host systems, which may range from highly oppressive to radically hospitable (Choi, 2015).

We find these insights and research findings on intercultural forms of integration to be highly relevant to the *intercultural nature of the relational integration of psychology and theology*. Disciplines like psychology and theology can each be likened to cultures, or, perhaps more accurately, constellations of cultures since neither discipline is monolithic. While interdisciplinary work among scholars and professionals is not nearly as challenging as immigration, there are intercultural dynamics in interdisciplinarity that require navigating important differences in disciplinary languages, customs or practices, epistemological assumptions, and social networks. We are curious that the need for intercultural or multicultural competence has hardly been discussed in the literature on the integration of psychology and theology. For example, in the five views book for relating psychology and Christianity (Johnson, 2010), none of the authors emphasizes the importance of intercultural competence or the positive value of diversity, although Collins (2000) did so in an earlier "four views" edition of that volume. Dueck and Reimer (2009) offer a rare exception in their book on Christian therapy in a multicultural world.

Based on our historical overview (Chapter 2) on the emergence of the concept of integration (and using Berry's model), it seems fair to suggest that efforts at integrating psychology and theology may have initially developed, in part, as an acculturation strategy to help Evangelicals to engage psychology and the wider social networks associated with the fields of psychology and mental healthcare. However, as we have suggested, the abstract literatures on the integration of psychology and theology tended to frame the problems as primarily epistemological rather than relational, ethical, and intercultural. These literatures on intercultural development and acculturation can further illuminate some of the complex and stressful dynamics that emerge in moving through the relational spaces "between"—in this case, between religious communities and more secular academic and professional contexts.

The Contribution of Mature Alterity to Relational Spirituality

While we could attend to many connective points between a mature alterity and significant facets of a relational spirituality, we highlight at the conclusion of this chapter two qualities that have emerged as integral to a relationally integrative spirituality that thematizes a healthy perspective on alterity arising from intercultural competence: *social justice commitment* and *hope*.

The Importance of Social Justice Commitment

One reason for the lack of intercultural engagement in integration literature could be that constructs like intercultural competence and social justice are often controversial among Christians and are believed by some to be more about "political correctness" than spiritual formation (Bell, Sandage, Morgan, & Hauge, in press; Labberton, 2010). This is ironic given the strong themes of social justice that resound across the Old Testament Torah (e.g., Exod 23:6–9; Deut 16:18–20; 27:19) and prophets (e.g., Isa 42:1–4; 61:1–3; Hos 12:6; Mic 6:6–8). According to the Gospel writers, Jesus stands fully in this tradition of enacting justice for the poor and downtrodden (e.g., Matt 12:18–21; Luke 4:16–21; 6:20–22; Brown, 2013b). Matthew in his Gospel particularly highlights the motif of "little ones" and "the least of these" to identify those who desperately need justice (10:40–42; 18:6–14; 25:31–46). And Matthew calls disciples of Jesus to be like their master in enacting justice and standing in solidarity with those in destitute circumstances (5:10; 23:23; 25:40, 45; Brown, 2013a). Given the wealth of biblical material pointed toward a commitment to justice as integral to the life of Jesus' followers, an affirmation of social justice engagement among Christians should be the norm.

john powell (2012) in his insightful interdisciplinary book, *Racing to Justice: Transforming our Conceptions of Self and Other to Build an Inclusive Society*, argues that "social justice and spirituality are . . . in a recursive relationship" (p. 197) and that relational forms of spirituality must address social suffering and injustice in addition to ontological suffering. He explains, "Spirituality and justice call us to move beyond the egoistic self to something deeper, more intimate and authentic, but less private. This move requires recognition of our interconnectedness and our interbeing" (p. 227). To explore some similar connections between justice, alterity, and spirituality, Sandage et al. (2008) have described a relational spirituality model drawing on an integration of theology and psychology and have suggested intercultural competence and social justice commitment are related-yet-distinct dimensions of mature forms of alterity. That is, mature alterity would be characterized by high levels of intercultural competence and a commitment to social justice. Based on the relational spirituality model, experiences of alterity are understood to potentially generate anxiety that might catalyze spiritual growth or transformation depending on the relational spirituality dynamics that get mobilized. Clearly, the anxiety of alterity does not automatically lead to growth and sometimes reinforces stereotypes, prejudices, and defensive alterity processes. Therefore, individual differences in forms of alterity (e.g., relatively open versus defensive) appear to interact with individual differences in relational spirituality variables (e.g., humility versus grandiosity).

A program of empirical research on intercultural competence (measured by the IDI), social justice commitment, and relational spirituality among graduate students in an evangelical context has offered some initial validation of the thesis linking mature alterity to Christian spiritual formation. Intercultural competence has been positively associated with spiritual well-being, meditative prayer, gratitude, humility, differentiation of self, quest religiosity (i.e., a "seeking" orientation of valuing religious questions), and negatively associated with spiritual grandiosity and spiritual instability/dysregulation (Jankowski & Sandage, 2014; Paine, Jankowski, & Sandage, 2016; Sandage & Harden, 2011; Sandage & Jankowski, 2013; Sandage, Li, Jankowski, Frank, & Beilby, 2015). Thus, intercultural competence is related to many core features of Christian spiritual maturity. In fact, the IDI, while not an instrument intended to measure relational integration, offers some interesting conceptual and empirical associations to many of the key relational dynamics we have been exploring throughout this book—humility versus grandiosity, differentiation of self versus insecure attachment, and spiritual orientations that are grounding, grateful, and curious versus ones that are dysregulating, polarizing, and insecure. We have also found the IDI to be an immensely valuable practical tool in training efforts to enhance intercultural competence with indirect benefits in fostering awareness of the relational integration capacities necessary for interdisciplinary collaboration.

Empirical studies with graduate students in the same evangelical context have also found social justice commitment to be positively associated with faith maturity, humility, differentiation of self, hope, positive religious coping, and forgiveness (Bell et al., in press; Jankowski, Sandage, & Hill, 2013; Sandage, Crabtree, & Schweer, 2014; Sandage & Morgan, 2014). These results connecting social justice commitment and healthy spiritual formation are particularly striking, given the contested nature of social justice in some evangelical contexts.

The Virtue of Hope

Hope is another quality that is integral to relationally integrative spirituality arising from intercultural competence. We would also emphasize that hope has been positively correlated with social justice commitment (Sandage et al., 2014; Sandage & Morgan, 2014). Numerous social philosophers, theologians, and educational theorists have described the unique role of complex and mature forms of hope in promoting and sustaining a commitment to social justice. The forms of hope that promote social justice must be distinguished from naïve optimism or more superficial forms of optimism that use defense mechanisms to deny or repress the systemic realities of evil or gloss over the long, painful struggle and sacrifice that are often needed to make social progress. Martin Luther King, Jr. (1986) pointed to the pivotal role of hope in the civil rights movement:

> Then something caused me to see at that moment the real meaning of the movement. That students had faith in the future. That the movement was based on hope, that this movement had something within it that says somehow even though the arc of the moral universe is long, it bends toward justice.
>
> *(p. 52)*

King noted the "long" kind of hope needed for social justice, whereas educational theorist Paulo Freire (1998) wrote of "critical hope" that integrates capacities to be "upset about injustice" without falling into the kinds of "cynical and immobilizing fatalism" that diminish motivation (p. 70). Freire's form of critical hope indirectly highlights the capacities for emotion regulation necessary for social justice commitment, more specifically the capacity to be angry and avoid falling into despair. Cornell West (2004) prophetically advocates for a "hard-won tragicomic hope" or "mature hope" which is both clear and honest about injustice and tragedy in social systems while also cultivating "courage to hope for betterment against the odds without a sense of revenge or resentment" (p. 216). King, Freire, and West and numerous other theologians (e.g., Boff & Boff, 1987; Brown Crawford, 2002; Cone, 1999) have each articulated integrative forms of mature hope as subversive to unjust systems in the pursuit of liberation and also speak to ways complex or post-critical hope contributes to the integrative resilience necessary to sustain social justice activism while simultaneously encountering the powerful systemic forces of oppression.

It is important to distinguish these types of mature or critical hope offered by theorists of color from more simplistic and defensive forms of positive thinking (e.g., "But things are getting better, right?") expressed by some whites and other dominant group members when discussing issues of racism, injustice, and oppression. When this defensive type of hope is expressed, it is likely an expression of "white fragility" and the expectation by some whites to be "constantly protected from racial distress" (Liu, 2017, p. 354) combined with a limited development of resilience for emotionally dealing with realities of social oppression. Similar fragile and defensive reactions can be found across other aspects of dominant group status. Defensive hope is unable to integrate painful emotions or difficult realities, so those relying on defensive hope tend to be unsuccessful in building relationships with those who have suffered from oppression.

Mature and complex forms of hope are relevant to our relational integration model in several ways. First, relational integration as we understand it requires similar capacities to hold and face painful and anxiety-provoking realities of human suffering, including injustice and oppression, with a hopeful, resilient motivation and activism to pursue a better, more just reality. Second, our experience has been that relational integration is most effectively developed by dealing with real world problems, and pedagogically this can include use of case studies (which we describe further in Chapter 8). By using case studies describing complex problems and experiences of suffering, we often see trainees vacillate between idealism and excessive optimism, on the one hand, and helpless despair on the other. Interestingly, we find that in dealing with difficult case studies, trainees too often either assume nothing can be done or presume that change will be immediate with a simple intervention. Relational integration requires mature hope that can lead to the capacity to envision or construct new ways of responding to seemingly intractable problems. Third, the mature and complex forms of hope described above in relation to difficult social justice issues pull for highly nuanced theological and psychological integrations, revealing ways some of the richest dialectical forms of relational integration can emerge from relating a prescriptive ideal or virtue (hope) to difficult descriptive realities (injustice). Too often, integration has been pursued for only one side of the dialectic, and typically the ideal side.

Hope, Resilience, and Healing

Our relational integration model suggests the personhood and relational capacities of therapists, including capacities for mature alterity, are more important than technical expertise. This is consistent with self of the therapist emphases in the couple and family therapy field and psychoanalytic traditions that focus on self-awareness and personal development among clinicians. The crucial contribution Ed made to this case was to relate to Keisha and Mike out of mature alterity and complex hope, which contributed to his capacity to offer into the situation differentiation of self and humility. From a relational psychotherapy perspective, clients often need new relational experiences, such as encountering humble and differentiated others, that can revise the limbic templates that shape their own relational styles more than they need didactic teaching or directive solutions (Lewis, Amini, & Lannon, 2000).

In this case, Ed's embodiment of complex hope meant he had the resilience to enter deeply into Keisha's feelings of pain, fear, and rage related to both racism and the difficult loss of her mother, while also empathizing with Mike's ambivalence about entering into those dark places. Systems therapists describe this as a relational ethic of multi-directed partiality or engaging in empathy for the differing members of a relational system rather than siding for one member or against another. This can be identified as a relational practice of justice, which serves to cultivate similar capacities in the couple's relationship.

Keisha's experience of Ed's empathy and intersubjectivity began to soothe some of her resentment at Mike for "not understanding." Over several months, Ed effectively paced his invitations to Mike to try to connect more fully to Keisha in her vulnerability and outrage. As is often the case, this prompted a memory in Mike. Around the age of eight, he witnessed his favorite uncle being assaulted by a group of white police officers who were arresting him after a conflict with the manager of a restaurant over the bill. This terrifying early trauma was also intensely shaming to Mike at the time, as he saw the humiliation on his grandmother's face in the restaurant while the manager yelled at his family to leave and "go back to your reservation." Mike's dissociative strategy for coping with racism probably kicked in at that time, as he recalled an internal resolve to contain his feelings and "not be a problem" for his family.

This therapy process also helped Keisha understand Mike's narrative and begin to see him in a more differentiated way, as more than "just not caring" about her struggles. With Ed's help and modeling and his own personal risk-taking, Mike eventually developed the ability to attach with Keisha in her vulnerability, and this began to reverse the effects of the earlier attachment injuries when she felt abandoned by him in her trauma and loss. The therapy process served to relationally integrate mutual trust and a more differentiated form of couple spirituality between Keisha and Mike that allowed them to connect and process social *and* existential suffering, as powell (2012) advocates. In this way, therapy proved to be healing and developmentally formative of new levels of strength, resilience, and a shared social justice commitment of "standing together."

Conclusion

In this chapter, we have taken on the challenge of locating intercultural interests and competencies at the heart of a model for the integration of psychology and theology. We have noted that intercultural awareness and mature forms of alterity have often been sidelined or ignored in such integrative conversations. And we have suggested that there is solid empirical evidence for taking a more differentiated and intercultural perspective in understanding relational integration and relational spirituality. Our work in this chapter's case study has illustrated a key relational integration thesis, namely, that diversity and justice are not auxiliary concerns in psychotherapy and community life. Rather, diversity and justice are dynamics within relational processes that are constitutive of healing.

Note

1 This publication acknowledges numerous contributors on p. vi and references many excellent studies at the end, however we want to note the irony that the American Psychological Association (APA) organization is listed as the official author of this penetrating analysis which traces patterns of inequity for women in the field of psychology. We cannot acknowledge all the contributors to this document but at least want to mention the names of the real people from the APA Center for Workplace Studies credited for this project: Peggy Christidis, PhD; Auntre Hamp, MEd, MPH; Luona Lin, MPP; Andrew Nigrinis, PhD; Karen Stamm, PhD; and Marlene Wicherski.

Bibliography

American Psychological Association. (2016). *2015 survey of psychology health service providers.* Washington, DC: Author.

American Psychological Association, Committee on Women in Psychology. (2017). *The changing gender composition of psychology: Update and expansion of the 1995 task force report.* Retrieved from www.apa.org/women/programs/gender-composition/index.aspx

Arukwe, N. O. (2014). Teaching emancipatory postcolonial knowledge: An African university teacher's experience. *Journal of Black Studies, 45*, 180–204.

ATS data tables 2016–2017. Composition of faculty and compensation of personnel. Retrieved August 30, 2017, from www.ats.edu/uploads/resources/institutional-data/annual-data-tables/2016-2017-annual-data-tables.pdf

Barreto, E. D. (2011). Negotiating difference: Theology and ethnicity in the Acts of the Apostles. *Word & World, 31*, 129–137.

Barrett, S. E., Lau Chin, J., Comas-Diaz, L., Espin, O., Greene, B., & McGoldrick, M. (2005). Multicultural feminist therapy: Theory in context. *Women & Therapy, 28*(3/4), 27–61. doi:10.1300/J015v28n03_03

Beaudoin, T., & Turpin, K. (2014). White practical theology. In K. A. Cahalan & G. S. Mikoski (Eds.), *Opening the field of practical theology: An introduction* (pp. 251–270). Lanham, MD: Rowman & Littlefield.

Bell, C. A., Sandage, S. J., Morgan, T. D., & Hague, D. J. (in press). Relational spirituality, humility, and commitments to social justice and intercultural competence. *Journal of Psychology and Christianity.*

Benjamin, J. (1998). *Shadow of the other: Intersubjectivity and gender in psychoanalysis.* New York, NY: Routledge, Inc.

Benjamin, J. (2004). Beyond doer and done to: An intersubjective view of thirdness. *Psychoanalytic Quarterly, 73*, 5–46.

Bennett, M. J. (2004). Becoming interculturally competent. In J. Wurzel (Ed.), *Toward multiculturalism: A reader in multicultural education* (2nd ed., pp. 62–77). Newton, MA: Intercultural Resource Corporation.

Berry, J. W. (2013). Integration as a mode of immigrant acculturation. In E. L. Grigorenko, E. L. Grigorenko (Eds.), *U.S. immigration and education: Cultural and policy issues across the lifespan* (pp. 41–57). New York, NY: Springer Publishing Co.

Boff, L., & Boff, C. (1987). *Introducing liberation theology.* Maryknoll, NY: Orbis Books.

Brescoll, V. L. (2011). Who takes the floor and why: Gender, power, and volubility in organizations. *Administrative Science Quarterly, 56*(4), 622–641.

Brown Crawford, A. E. (2002). *Hope in the holler: A womanist theology.* Louisville, KY: Westminster John Knox Press.

Brown, J. K. (2013a). Matthew's "least of these" theology and subversion of "us/other" categories. In N. W. Duran & J. P. Grimshaw (Eds.), *Matthew: Texts @ contexts.* Minneapolis, MN: Fortress Press.

Brown, J. K. (2013b). Narrative criticism. In J. B. Green, J. K. Brown, & N. Perrin (Eds.), *Dictionary of Jesus and the Gospels* (pp. 619–624). Downers Grove, IL: InterVarsity Press.

Brown, J. K., & Sandage, S. J. (2015). Relational integration, Part II: Relational integration as developmental and intercultural. *Journal of Psychology & Theology, 43,* 179–191.

Cahalan, K. A. & Mikoski, G. S. (2014). *Opening the field of practical theology: An introduction.* Lanham, MD: Rowman & Littlefield.

Choi, H. A. (2015). *A postcolonial self: Korean immigrant theology and church.* Albany, NY: State University of New York Press.

Collins, G. R. (2000). An integration view. In E. L. Johnson & S. L. Jones (Eds.), *Psychology & Christianity: Four views* (pp. 102–129). Downers Grove, IL: InterVarsity Press.

Comas-Díaz, L. (2000). An ethnopolitical approach to working with people of color. *American Psychologist, 55*(11), 1319–1325. doi:10.1037/0003–066X.55.11.1319

Cone, J. H. (1999). Calling the oppressors to account: Justice, love, and hope in Black religion. In Q. H. Dixie & C. West (Eds.), *Courage to hope: From Black suffering to human redemption* (pp. 74–85). Boston: Beacon Press.

Creegan, N. H., & Pohl, C. D. (2005). *Living on the boundaries: Evangelical women, feminism and the theological academy.* Downers Grove, IL: InterVarsity Press.

Crowell, B. L. (2009). Postcolonial studies and the Hebrew Bible. *Currents in Biblical Research, 7*(2), 217–244.

De La Torre, M. A. (2013). Doing Latina/o ethics from the margins of empire: Liberating the colonized mind. *Journal of the Society of Christian Ethics, 33*(2), 3–20.

De La Torre, M. A. (2017). *Embracing hopelessness.* Minneapolis, MN: Fortress Press.

Dube, M. (2012). *Postcolonial feminist interpretation of the Bible.* St. Louis: Chalice Press.

Dueck, A. C. (1995). *Between Jerusalem and Athens: Ethical perspectives on culture, religion, and psychotherapy.* Eugene, OR: Wipf & Stock.

Dueck, A. C. (2002). Babel, Esperanto, Shibboleths, and Pentecost: Can we talk? *Journal of Psychology and Christianity, 21*(1), 72–80.

Dueck, A., & Reimer, K. (2009). *A peaceable psychology: Christian therapy in a world of many cultures.* Grand Rapids, MI: Brazos Press.

Eriksson, C. B., & Abernethy, A. D. (2014). Integration in multicultural competence and diversity training: Engaging difference and grace. *Journal of Psychology and Theology, 42*(2), 174–187.

Fanon, F. (1963). *The wretched of the earth.* New York, NY: Grove Press.

Fraser, E. (1998). *Confessions of a beginning theologian.* Downers Grove, IL: InterVarsity Press.

Freire, P. (1998). Pedagogy of freedom: Ethics, democracy, and civic courage (P. Clarke, Trans.). Lanham, MD: Rowman & Littlefield Publishers, Inc.

Greggo, S. P., & Sisemore, T. A. (2012). *Counseling and Christianity: Five approaches.* Downers Grove, IL: InterVarsity Press.

Guest, M., Sharma, S., & Song, R. (2013). *Gender and career progression in theology and religious studies: Project Report.* Durham, UK: Durham University.

Haker, H., Susin, L. C., & Metogo, E. M. (2013). *Postcolonial theology.* London: SCM Press.

Hammer, M. (2011). Additional cross-cultural validity testing of the Intercultural Development Inventory. *International Journal of Intercultural Relations, 35,* 474–487.

Hammer, M. R. (2005). The Intercultural Conflict Style Inventory: A conceptual framework and measure of intercultural conflict approaches. *International Journal of Intercultural Research, 29,* 675–695.

Hammer, M. R., Bennett, M. J., & Wiseman, R. (2003). Measuring intercultural sensitivity: The intercultural development inventory. *International Journal of Intercultural Relations, 27,* 421–443.

Helms, J. E., Nicholas, G., & Green, C. E. (2012). Racism and ethnoviolence as trauma: Enhancing professional and research training. *Traumatology, 18,* 65–74.

Hook, J., Davis, D., Owen, J., & DeBlaere, C. (2017). *Cultural humility: Engaging diverse identities in therapy.* Washington, DC: American Psychological Association.

Hook, J. N., & Davis, D. E. (2012). Integration, multicultural counseling, and social justice. *Journal of Psychology and Theology, 40*(2), 102–106.

Hook, J. N., & Watkins, C. J. (2015). Cultural humility: The cornerstone of positive contact with culturally different individuals and groups? *American Psychologist, 70*(7), 661–662. doi:10.1037/a0038965

Hui, B. H., Chen, S. X., Leung, C. M., & Berry, J. W. (2015). Facilitating adaptation and intercultural contact: The role of integration and multicultural ideology in dominant and non-dominant groups. *International Journal of Intercultural Relations, 45*70–84. doi:10.1016/j.ijintrel.2015.01.002

Jankowski, P. J., & Sandage, S. J. (2014). Meditative prayer and intercultural competence: Empirical test of a differentiation-based model. *Mindfulness, 5*(4), 360–372. doi:10.1007/s12671–012–0189-z

Jankowski, P. J., Sandage, S. J., & Hill, P. C. (2013). Differentiation-based models of forgivingness, mental health and social justice commitment: Mediator effects for differentiation of self and humility. *The Journal of Positive Psychology, 8*(5), 412–424. doi:10.1080/17439760.2013.820337

Johnson, E. L. (Ed.). (2010). *Psychology & Christianity: Five views* (2nd ed.). Downers Grove, IL: InterVarsity Press.

Käsemann, E. (1971). *Perspectives on Paul.* Philadelphia, PA: Fortress Press.

King, M. L., Jr. (1986). Love, law, and civil disobedience. In J. M. Washington (Ed.), *A testament of hope: The essential writings and speeches of Martin Luther King, Jr.* (pp. 43–53). New York, NY: HarperOne. (Reprinted from The New South, December 12, 1961, pp. 3–11)

Kunst, J. R., Thomsen, L., Sam, D. L., & Berry, J. W. (2015). 'We are in this together': Common group identity predicts majority members' active acculturation efforts to integrate immigrants. *Personality and Social Psychology Bulletin, 41*(10), 1438–1453. doi:10.1177/0146167215599349

Labberton, M. (2010). A mighty river or a slippery slope?: Examining the cultural and theological forces behind the new interest in justice. *Leadership, 31*(3), 20–24.

Lewis, T., Amini, F., & Lannon, R. (2000). *A general theory of love.* New York, NY: Vintage.

Liu, W. M. (2017). White male power and privilege: The relationship between white supremacy and social class. *Journal of Counseling Psychology, 64,* 349–358.

Malony, H. N. (1981). Integration: The adjoiners. In G. R. Collins & H. N. Malony (Eds.), *Psychology & theology: Prospects for integration* (pp. 85–123). Nashville, TN: Abingdon.

Mbuvi, A. M. (2017). African Biblical studies: An introduction to an emerging discipline. *Currents in Biblical Research, 15*(2), 149–178.

McMinn, M. R., Vogel, M. J., Lewis Hall, M. E., Abernethy, A. D., Birch, R., Galuza, T., . . . Putman, K. (2015). Religious and spiritual diversity training in clinical psychology doctoral programs: Do explicitly Christian programs differ from other programs? *Journal of Psychology and Theology, 43*(3), 155–164.

McNeil, J. D. (2005). Unequally yoked? The role of culture in the relationship between theology and psychology. In A. Dueck & C. Lee (Eds.), *Why psychology needs theology: A radical reformation perspective* (pp. 140–162). Grand Rapids, MI: Eerdmans.

Morgan, J., & Sandage, S. J. (2016). A developmental model of interreligious competence: A conceptual framework. *Archive for the Psychology of Religion, 38*, 129–158.

Paine, D. R., Jankowski, P. J., & Sandage, S. J. (2016). Humility as a predictor of intercultural competence: Mediator effects for differentiation of self. *The Family Journal, 24*, 15–22.

powell, j. a. (2012). *Racing to justice: Transforming our conceptions of self and other to build an inclusive society*. Bloomington, IN: Indiana University Press.

Race, A., Kenney, J., & Rao, S. (2005). The interreligious insight paradigm: An invitation. *Interreligious Insight: A Journal of Dialogue and Engagement 3*, 8–19.

Ripley, J. S., Garzon, F. L., Hall, M. L., Mangis, M. W., & Murphy, C. J. (2009). Pilgrims' progress: Faculty and university factors in graduate student integration of faith and profession. *Journal of Psychology and Theology, 37*(1), 5–14.

Sandage, S. J. & Brown, J. K. (2010). Monarchy or democracy in relation integration? A reply to Porter. *Journal of Psychology and Christianity 29*(1), 20–26.

Sandage, S. J., Crabtree, S., & Schweer, M. (2014). Differentiation of self and social justice commitment mediated by hope. *Journal of Counseling and Development, 92*, 67–74.

Sandage, S. J., Dahl, C. M., & Harden, M. G. (2012). Psychology of religion, spirituality, and diversity. In P. C. Hill & B. Dik (Eds.), *Psychology of religion and workplace spirituality* (pp. 43–62). Charlotte, NC: Information Age Publishing.

Sandage, S. J., & Harden, M. G. (2011). Relational spirituality, differentiation of self, and virtue as predictors of intercultural development. *Mental Health, Religion, & Culture, 14*, 819–838. doi:10.1080/13674676.2010.527932

Sandage, S. J., & Jankowski, P. J. (2012). Spirituality, social justice, and intercultural competence: Mediator effects for differentiation of self. *International Journal of Intercultural Relations 37*, 366–374. doi:10.1016/j.ijintrel.2012.11.003

Sandage, S. J., Jensen, M., & Jass, D. (2008). Relational spirituality and transformation: Risking intimacy and alterity. *Journal of Spiritual Formation and Soul Care, 1*, 182–206.

Sandage, S. J., Li, J., Jankowski, P. J., Frank, C., & Beilby, M. (2015). Spiritual predictors of change in intercultural competence in a multicultural counseling course. *Journal of Psychology and Christianity, 34*, 168–178.

Sandage, S. J., & Morgan, J. (2014). Hope and positive religious coping as predictors of social justice commitment. *Mental Health, Religion, and Culture, 17*, 557–567. http://dx.doi.org/10.1080/13674676.2013.864266

Sandage, S. J., Paine, D. R., & Morgan, J. (in press). Relational spirituality, differentiation, and mature alterity. In T. M. Crisp, S. L. Porter, & G. A. Van Tenselhof (Eds.), *Psychology and spiritual formation: A psychologically and theologically informed spirituality*. Downers Grove, IL: InterVarsity Press Academic.

Schlosser, L. Z. (2003). Christian privilege: Breaking a sacred taboo. *Journal of Multicultural Counseling and Development, 31*(1), 44–51.

Schüssler Fiorenza, E. (2000). Defending the center, trivializing the margins. In H. Räisänen (Ed.), *Reading the Bible in the global village: Helsinki*. Atlanta: Society of Biblical Literature.

Sharp, M. A. M. (2013). *Misunderstanding stories: Toward a postcolonial pastoral theology*. Eugene, OR: Pickwick Publications.

Shogren, G. S. (2000). Is the kingdom of God about eating and drinking or isn't it? (Romans 14:17). *Novum Testamentum 42*(3), 238–56.

Sorenson, R. L. (2004). *Minding spirituality*. Hillsdale, NJ: The Analytic Press.

Stevenson, D. H., Eck, B. E., & Hill, P. C. (Eds.). (2007). *Psychology & Christianity integration: Seminal works that shaped the movement*. Batavia, IL: Christian Association for Psychological Studies.

Sue, D. W., & Sue, D. (2015). *Counseling the culturally diverse: Theory and practice* (7th ed.). New York, NY: Wiley & Sons.

Tummala-Narra, P. (2015). Cultural competence as a core emphasis of psychoanalytic psychotherapy. *Psychoanalytic Psychotherapy, 32*, 275–292.

Waldman, K., & Rubalcava, L. (2005). Working with intercultural couples: A contemporary psychodynamic approach. *American Journal of Psychotherapy, 59*, 227–245.

Watson, T. S., Prevost, S. B., Faries, S., & Para-Mallam, F. (2001). Gender differences in the integration literature: A content analysis of JPT and JPC by gender and integration type. *Journal of Psychology and Theology, 29*(1), 52–61.

Wengst, K. (1988). *Humility: Solidarity of the humiliated*. Minneapolis, MN: Fortress Press.

West, C. (2004). *Democracy matters: Winning the fight against imperialism*. New York, NY: Penguin Group.

Worthington Jr, E. L., & Sandage, S. J. (2016). *Forgiveness and spirituality in psychotherapy: A relational approach*. Washington, DC: American Psychological Association.

Wright, N. T. (1995). Romans and the theology of Paul. In D. M. Hay & E. E. Johnson (Eds.), *Pauline theology* (Vol. 3, pp. 30–67). Minneapolis, MN: Fortress Press.

Yangarber-Hicks, N., Behensky, C., Canning, S. S., Flanagan, K. S., Gibson, N. S., Hicks, M. W., . . . Porter, S. L. (2006). Invitation to the table conversation: A few diverse perspectives on integration. *Journal of Psychology and Christianity, 25*(4), 338–353.

8

RELATIONAL INTEGRATION IN FORMATION-BASED PRACTICE

Our strategy throughout the book has been to bring together theory, research, and practice, as we define and explore our model of relational integration. A primary way we have kept our eye on application is through the case studies and vignettes we have offered in most chapters. In this final chapter, we offer focused attention on praxis as the outworking of our theoretical framework. We begin by working out what relational integration for psychology and theology might look like "on the ground," as psychologists and theologians take the interdisciplinary turn. This first section concludes with more focused applications to theologians (from Jeannine) and psychologists (from Steve). In the latter half of the chapter, we turn to the outworking of relational integration in education and training, in clinical practice, and in congregations.

Relational Integration in Psychology-Theology Dialogue

In an effort to provide summative reflections on the kind of interdisciplinary integration we have been commending in this book, we offer here a brief sketch of what our model of relational integration might look like in practice.

First of all, we have been commending across the book a way of pursuing integration that involves two or more disciplinarians. While single-integrators are quite able to work at the intersection of disciplines, we have found that significant and successful integration among people of different disciplines is still fairly uncommon, even with more frequent calls for interdisciplinarity in the academy and among practitioners. A relational approach encourages people of different disciplines to come together for authentic conversation around areas of resonance and distinctiveness in their respective fields. Relational integration allows that anxiety and conflict are part and parcel with interdisciplinary work, and, in fact, can often be conduits for integrative insights.

As multiple integrators come together, we suggest that it can be helpful for interdisciplinary conversation to focus on each person offering potentially integrative insights from their own discipline and research; i.e., offering from places of strength. What can seem like an intuitive route to integration—a disciplinarian studying in a field outside their "home territory"—may actually be less fruitful than having conversations where scholars or practitioners share their expertise, with no particular agenda for how that expertise might prove to be integrative. This act of "offering" to those from other disciplines provides an opportunity for someone in another discipline to hear potential points of resonance in their own field—in their "home territory." In this configuration of *offering* and *reception* (Brown, Dahl, & Corbin Reuschling, 2011), strength meets strength (ideally), and some key dilemmas of interdisciplinary work, such as overreach and cherry-picking, can be avoided. This way of conceiving the integrative process does not bypass the possibility of conflict and the reality of relational anxiety. Yet it provides a way forward for participants to offer their best and strongest work into integrative conversation.

Second, a relational model of integration presses those involved to address issues of privilege and power. While in the abstract it may be possible to rank the priority of certain disciplines over others for integration focused on certain domains of knowledge, when two or more disciplinarians work together integratively it is much more difficult to sustain such prioritization and the privileging of one person's voice over another that accompanies it. A relational model accents the embodied nature of integration and how one discipline's priority over another amounts to differentials of power on the level of personal interaction and relational dynamics. If theology is really "queen of the sciences," then in relational terms theologians hold sway over psychologists in the integration of these two disciplines. Or, if psychology is the more scientific of the two disciplines and so has epistemological priority over theology, then the reality relationally is that psychologists will likely exert power over theologians in integrative conversations. And neither scenario tends to foster the relational capital necessary for sustained, productive interdisciplinary work. In fact, such hierarchical stances tend to alienate the disciplinarian with less privilege, cutting off possibilities of productive dialogue (for some positive and negative examples of this kind of process, see Sandage, Paine, & Devor, 2014).

As a result, crucial to relational integration is the identification of fears about loss of power and autonomy that can easily happen when moving into interdisciplinary spaces. It is important not to idealize interdisciplinarity in ways that foster surprise or dismay when integrative conversations don't proceed smoothly and when the participants experience anxiety and fear of loss of disciplinary autonomy or identity. Normalizing anxiety around these issues can be a helpful first step toward increasing interest and participation in interdisciplinary conversation.

One way to address one's own anxiety and fear around these issues is to cultivate curiosity as an interdisciplinary virtue. Increased curiosity seems to diminish anxiety. Conversely, "[a]s the need to defend against anxiety increases, the need to know diminishes, and one's mind becomes incrementally closed to different views." (Johnson, 2009, p. 121). As I (Jeannine) exhort my students, *When you're feeling anxious, get curious.* And I have commended, in concert with Carla Dahl and Wyndy Corbin Reuschling (2011), an interdisciplinary process in which "we have attempted to *offer* with humility, *receive* with curiosity, and *integrate* with creativity" (p. 11).

As we have discussed in a thematic way in this volume, humility is a virtue related to how one manages power and orients to self and other. Humility and the closely associated capacity to tolerate ambiguity were mentioned as important traits necessary for integration nearly forty years ago in Carter and Narramore's (1979) influential book. Recent definitions of humility highlight multiple dimensions that are supportive of relational integration, including (a) self-recognition of strengths and limitations, (b) low self-focus oriented toward others' wellbeing, (c) openness to diverse others and ideas, and (d) emotional self-regulation, particularly of pride and shame (Davis et al., 2016; Jankowski et al., 2013; Owens, Johnson, & Mitchell, 2013; Paine, Jankowski, & Sandage, 2016). And as we have seen in Chapter 7, humility is consistent with intercultural competence by promoting realistic self-awareness (including cultural self-awareness) combined with openness to other perspectives and an ongoing process of intercultural learning (Paine, Jankowski, & Sandage, 2016). Humility also supports social justice commitment by relativizing the importance of social status and facilitating concern for the well-being of others, including others who experience marginalization and injustice (Bell et al., in press). Wengst (1988) has argued that positive construals of humility in both the Hebrew Bible and the New Testament emphasized humility as (a) deemphasizing social status and (b) positively committing to communal solidarity with the socially marginalized, countering the highly stratified Graeco-Roman social structure and the corresponding pejorative attitude toward humility more generally. All of these aspects of humility make it a crucial virtue for relational integration.

Third, relational integration requires a differentiated stance toward one's own discipline and toward one's interdisciplinary colleagues. As we have suggested throughout this book, *differentiation is part of the process of relational integration.* Differentiation means a dialectical or "both/and" perspective about differences between disciplines. This involves accepting that different disciplines will have unique languages, methodologies, assumptions, and goals, while also assuming there will be some underlying points of mutual interest and convergence to be discovered. We have framed differentiation in Chapter 7 as consistent with intercultural competence and as an intersubjective, nonjudgmental stance of holding in mind one's own disciplinary perspective while seeking to understand another. In addition to humility and tolerance for ambiguity, Carter and Narramore (1979) also have noted the need among integrators for "a balanced expression of one's intellect and emotions" (p. 119), a key dimension of differentiation.

Fourth, within the academic guilds there are also disciplinary differences that we would describe as sociological practices. By "sociological practices," we mean things like (a) whether papers are read formally or power point is used at conference presentations; (b) whether single-author or multi-authored publications are normative; (c) whether books that get widely reviewed or peer-reviewed articles with high citation counts are the most valued academic achievements; or (d) whether or not one needs to join an organization to attend their conference. These, along with concrete things like differences in reference styles in publications, are some of the "everyday hassles" of relational integration. Flexibility and commitment are necessary to stretch beyond one's disciplinary norms to embody and learn from other practices.

Finally, we want to offer a realistic vision for relational integration. Part of that realism is the acknowledgement that sometimes interdisciplinary integration cannot or will not happen. Given a host of variables, some scholars or practitioners who commit themselves to an integrative project may find the anxieties surrounding real conversations of integration too daunting or not worth the investment of time and energy that they require. Others may not find the safe places needed for interdisciplinary collaboration, even as they are intent on pursuing integration. It is also possible that two scholars or practitioners may be operating from such diverging paradigms that it is hard to find integrative traction. In such cases, it will be important to not over-generalize about a discipline and to explore other conversation partners from a particular discipline who might offer a better fit for one's approach to relational integration.

Implications for Theologians (Jeannine)

As I (Jeannine) attempt to anticipate some responses from theologians to our integration model of relational integration, I think back to my early experiences of integration with colleagues in the social sciences and in psychology specifically, I remember the feeling (and I still feel it often enough) of being out of my element, being sure that my inadequate knowledge of these areas would be revealed in interdisciplinary conversation. This sense of being found out for not having sufficient knowledge is a frequent anxiety in interdisciplinary discourse, so that entering this discourse takes a measure of courage and risk. In my reflections on the work of integration of my discipline with social science and ethics in *Becoming Whole and Holy* (2011), I reflect that

> Integration is an adventure, but it is not for the faint of heart. It involves self-disclosure, trial and error, and the risk of feeling incompetent as you venture outside your area of expertise. So it is an adventure best experienced with friends who are both honest and trustworthy.
>
> *(pp. 172–73)*

Engaging in relational integration between psychology and theology as a theologian allows me to *not be any kind of expert in psychology*, since Steve brings that expertise in spades. And the relational model we propose requires me to trust that expertise, even while holding in differentiated fashion my own contributions from biblical studies and theology. Yet an ongoing commitment to interdisciplinary dialogue doesn't allow me to simply remain a novice in psychology. While I lean on Steve's expertise and guidance to point me toward important psychological resources, it is incumbent upon me to take initiative to learn more about the field of psychology—its methods, assumptions, and conclusions. Much as a commitment to a learning posture is essential as one moves across cultural boundaries and toward intercultural competence (Safir, 2017), a learning stance contributes to interdisciplinary conversation. This involves listening well to others in the conversation but also beginning to do our homework in the secondary discipline to become more conversant with its ways and insights—yet without having to attain a level of mastery.

For example, a key construct to our relational model is differentiation of self. My early learning about this concept occurred in conversations with colleagues, at times in team teaching contexts. The value of the concept drew me into further reading about it, with the guidance of colleagues who had a much better grasp on the scholarship around it. As I began to assign my students readings on this topic (e.g., Majerus & Sandage, 2010) even when not in a team-teaching context, I needed to be even more conversant about differentiation of self so that I could lead class dialogue around this concept.

This kind of secondary engagement with psychology is complemented by the primary relational engagement with our colleagues who are experts in that field. The beauty of relational integration among multiple disciplinarians is that the development of a healthy secondary knowledge of another field of study is always connected to our primary engagement with actual disciplinarians in that field who can guide, correct, and resource their fellow integrators along the way. The truth of the matter is that I am frequently in danger of overreaching in psychology because I am not an expert in the field and so will not always know when I overstep disciplinary boundaries. Steve will recognize immediately these moments of overreach and, in healthy dialogue, has the opportunity to address them so that I gain greater insight into the parameters of his discipline. Another unhealthy tendency that is curbed in relational integration is a fairly monolithic view of the alternate discipline. While I have a clear perspective on the variegated nature of biblical studies and theology, with their multiple voices and perspectives, I have a more monolithic perspective on psychology that derives from my more limited knowledge of the field. Yet collaborating with a psychologist gives me insight into the wide range of psychologies that are part of that discipline.

A final consideration for theologians or biblical scholars entering interdisciplinary conversation with psychologists relates to power differentials inherent in the various institutions and systems we inhabit. In some of these spaces, psychology and so psychologists are given the upper hand due to the identification of their work as scientific (over against theology viewed as hermeneutical). In others, as in some seminaries, theology and so theologians and biblical scholars will be given privilege and preference. It is important in either situation to think clearly about the rationales for privileging one set of voices or the other. For my part, I would remind theologians of the hermeneutical nature of all knowledge (see Chapter 5) in order to clearly distinguish theology or biblical studies from the Bible, especially as its viewed as revelatory and so as having unique authority. A discipline is not its source material, any more than a disciplinarian can be simply equated with their discipline (Sandage & Brown, 2010). Interspaces exist between the Bible, the discipline of biblical studies or theology, and the theologian as practitioner of the discipline. To grant theologians privilege over psychologists because they study the Bible involves a disregard, whether explicitly or implicitly, of the reality of hermeneutical location.

Implications for Psychologists (Steve)

I (Steve) have some theological training and enjoy theology, nevertheless the vast terrain of theology, religion, and biblical studies can feel daunting to me at times as a psychologist. The formal discipline of psychology has had just over a century to generate literature, whereas people have been doing theological and exegetical work for millennia. For those who are overwhelmed, I suggest starting small by finding a book or two in theology or biblical studies that seem relevant to something you are trying to understand. Popular level books might be helpful to get oriented, but eventually I suggest challenging yourself with some theological or religious works that are scholarly. (Note: I have known professional psychologists who complain about people reading superficial self-help books while basically doing the same in the religious or theological sphere.) If possible, I suggest then trying to find someone with theological or religious training to converse with about what you have been reading and questions that arise.

The diversity of religious and theological perspectives and traditions can be dizzying, but this diversity should not be minimized. There is a tendency among some psychologists and psychotherapists to try to boil theology or religion down to some singular feature translated into a psychological category (e.g., coping), but this flattens the contributions of those disciplines. We have suggested valuing and exploring diverse traditions and accepting that this is work that will take some time. A good starting point might be to explore religious traditions in one's family of origin history; to do so, there are resources available for constructing a spiritual and religious genogram (or family tree) (Hodge, 2001, 2005). While some therapists may do a family genogram as part of their clinical training to identify emotional and relational patterns, spiritual and religious dynamics are not always part of that assignment. This could lead to reading and learning more deeply about traditions in one's own family background.

Integration can also be pursued by partially resisting the powerful pragmatic, medicalized, and functionalist pulls from psychology and psychotherapy fields and, in contrast, exploring one's own understanding of topics like wholeness, well-being, happiness, or ideal human functioning (Sandage, 2012). Virtue topics (e.g., hope, gratitude, humility, compassion, forgiveness) within psychology are also ripe for this kind of reflection and analysis. We have suggested these are areas within psychological/psychotherapeutic literatures that often have embedded values, ethical stances, or assumptions about ultimate concerns that can be related back to spiritual, religious, theological, or cultural traditions (Browning & Cooper, 2004; Sandage et al., 2008). One strategy trainees have found helpful is to pick a virtue topic of interest they believe to be important for mental health and human development and then study both social science and theological or religious resources related to that virtue to work toward an integrative understanding.

I also want to restate that relational integration work is best sustained *relationally*, so I recommend psychologists and psychotherapists interested in this relational integration approach try to develop an ongoing consultation or conversation group. This might be a group with other psychologists or clinicians that meets monthly or with some regular rhythm, or it could be an interdisciplinary group. I would recommend starting by sharing about one's own spiritual or religious background and current questions and interests. There could be some common readings or a focus on case study applications of integration (more on this below) to pursue integration. At the Danielsen Institute where I teach and practice, we have groups like this (of 4–6 staff or trainees) meeting weekly for seventy-five minutes during the academic year, and the groups are intentionally organized on an annual basis to be diverse in order to foster our awareness of other traditions. I have also seen students and practitioners in other settings who have organized their own peer consultation groups to explore integration over many years together. The keys seem to be choosing group members who are curious about interdisciplinary questions and open to other perspectives and then continuing to cultivate differentiated relational dynamics in the group.

Standard case consultation practices in many clinical settings may not typically offer much intentional space to explore this kind of relational integration, as we have described it. However, some clinicians might find it interesting (and differentiating) to raise questions about theological or religious integration in those settings if such concerns are being overlooked in case consultations. One argument for such angles of exploration could be related to the ethics of culturally competent practice. Even if the norms of the group do not shift to regular attention to theological or religious issues, this intervention might surface some clinicians who are motivated for further integrative conversations or meetings.

Relational Integration in Education and Training

Some of our most rewarding experiences in pursuing interdisciplinary integration together have occurred in the seminary classroom. In 2009, we had the opportunity to team teach a new course in the master's degree curriculum at the institution where we both taught at that time. The course is a senior seminar that focuses on integration among the various areas of the curriculum, including biblical, theological, and historical theology, transformational and pastoral leadership, and personal and spiritual formation. The institutional commitment to fostering interdisciplinary integration in the classroom allowed for faculty from two different disciplines to be with the students each week in a seminar-styled learning environment.

Our focus in that first team-taught course was on topics of hermeneutics and human development, and we brought together topics and themes from these disciplines that we anticipated would have integrative potential for our class discussions. Our topics included the following:

- Story, coherence, and attachment
- Relational hermeneutics
- General and special revelation
- Icons and idolatry
- Hermeneutics of suspicion and hermeneutics of trust
- Gender competence and intercultural competence
- Honor/shame and status
- Wholeness and holiness

The conversations in that course were rich and often brought us to unanticipated places, even though the two of us had initial conversations on each set of themes prior to leading the students in discussion. As professors, the unplanned conversations have been places of reward as well as risk and have called for a greater level of differentiation in our teaching. It is also the case that the themes we introduced in this course have provided places for ongoing reflection and exploration—they are ones that we continue to explore and draw upon in our work.

A core learning component in this course even to the present has been the use of case study methodology (Sandage & Brown, 2012). Each student writes a case based on a real-life dilemma in ministry or counseling that the student has observed or experienced (appropriately masked for confidentiality). The student integratively analyzes the case and suggests strategies for it, first in a class presentation, which includes peer and faculty feedback, and then in a final paper. Students are asked to analyze the case from a number of perspectives, including from biblical/theological, social science, and ethical angles, with the latter including intercultural and social justice dynamics. They are also asked to attend to their own countertransference or subjective reactions in relation to the case (see Chapter 7). They do not need to "over-share" highly personal information with the instructors or the class but are asked to tune into their personal reactions in order to maintain a differentiated stance by noting points of sympathy or bias that may come up for them. The practice of attending to countertransference can be initially challenging for some students who are not used to tuning into personal subjectivity and so may offer cognitive or conceptual abstractions even when asked to consider countertransference.

Overall, the process of this assignment moves toward addressing the case from these angles with the goal of providing integrative applications among them, although we try to resist the quick urge to offer solutions before adequately conceptualizing the problems in the case from integrative perspectives. When students present in class and discussion unfolds, it is useful to note aspects of integration that are left out or under-developed (e.g., biblical/theological, social science, diversity and justice, etc.). At a final stage of reflection and writing, they are asked to address points where integration did not happen for them; i.e., points of non-integration (or "not yet" integration), including their reflections on the "countertransference" they brought to the case.

Using case study methodology contributes to integrative learning for a variety of reasons and in a number of ways. Cases are multifaceted and so provide opportunity for thick analysis. And as they often require the convergence of multiple perspectives for adequate understanding, they pull for integration. "A well-written case that problematizes a certain ministry [or therapeutic] dilemma with real human characters can invite integrative applications as an exercise in practical wisdom" (Sandage & Brown, 2012, p. 75). Cases facilitate agile movements between theory and praxis and can helpfully turn abstractions and platitudes toward more reflective applications. Yet a case dilemma, because of its complexity, is open-ended and does not require a singular solution. As such, case discussions often move down unexpected and fresh paths.

Cases also press toward systemic analysis and solutions. In class presentations around cases, students often begin by attending to individual characters in the case, critiquing or extolling any particular character's actions and qualities. Almost inevitably in the class discussion, however, the context that informs and helps to explain these characters begins to surface in the class's collective imagination. Questions begin to circulate around these contexts and systems: *What systemic realities have been active that help us understand why a character does what they do and how characters interact with one another?* Often, attention begins to form around people and situations not explicitly addressed in the case—a sign that the realities of systems are coming into view.

In our experience, we have found there is value in having students write from real experiences, even if they mask certain features and fictionalize the details to some extent. By returning to a past experience rather than hypothesizing a totally fictional one, more of the person is engaged, including autobiographical memory regions of the brain. The process of drawing on personal experiences while working toward differentiated cognitive reflection can serve what Siegel (2010) calls "memory integration" (p. 73). Feedback from students has affirmed that student-written cases based on real life experiences are often deeply formative, especially when the student has been a part of the scenario that is reflected in the case. Their reflection on their past involvement and experience often requires them to differentiate themselves from the situation as they remember it, providing opportunity for new realizations and, sometimes, personal resolution. In some cases, students may struggle with shame or regret for not handling a situation differently at the time. This should, of course, be met with relational sensitivity and empathy, but the overall process can serve to mitigate shame and cultivate a humble rather than perfectionistic professional template for ongoing learning.

Relational Integration in Clinical Practice

While we have offered applications of our relational integration model at various points in this book, we thought it would be helpful here to summarize a few of the main counseling and psychotherapeutic strategies that fit our understanding of relational integration in clinical practice. (Note: we will use the term psychotherapy broadly for convenience but mean to encompass various forms of counseling, psychotherapy, and clinical practice, despite the fact there can be meaningful differences in these vocational roles and practices.)

First, we want to affirm our belief that counselors and therapists could work in relationally integrative ways from various theoretical orientations; nevertheless, our approach is most consistent with a strong emphasis on the working therapeutic alliance as a key source of gain in positive changes. Our model puts relational dynamics in the foreground of integration, and this would also apply to psychotherapy. This is consistent with a very large body of empirical evidence supporting connections between the development of a collaborative client-therapist alliance and treatment outcomes (Wampold & Imel, 2015). The most widely researched three-dimensional model of the collaborative working alliance initially developed by Bordin (1979) involves (a) agreement about *tasks*, (b) agreement about *goals*, and (c) quality of the relational *bond* between client and therapist. We would highlight that we find this model not only helpful clinically but equally appropriate for the working alliance in interdisciplinary relationships. We also agree with Doran and colleagues (Doran, 2016; Doran, Safran, & Muran, 2016, 2017) about the need to complement the focus on collaborative dynamics with attention to differences and rupture-repair dynamics as a key aspect of the therapeutic alliance in clinical work and the overall facilitation of differentiation. So, we expect that the therapeutic alliance in relationally integrative clinical work needs to ultimately move toward collaboration. Yet collaboration is not always immediate, and differentiation can be fostered by the repair of ruptures and renegotiation of the working alliance.

Second, our relational integration model suggests it is important to start by working from clients' spiritual, religious, theological, and cultural traditions and values. This is an exercise in pacing (see Chapter 4) by engaging the languages they use, seeking to understand their beliefs, values, and practices, and considering ways these may be relevant to the process of psychotherapy. This can be assessed through some preliminary questions asking clients whether they (1) have spiritual or religious commitments or practices we should know about as their therapist, and (2) whether they see ways those commitments or practices are relevant to our work in psychotherapy (Tan, 1996). Some clients will answer no to the first question initially, but more may develop or come to the surface later. Other clients may answer yes to the first and no to second question, again at least initially. There is some empirical evidence that many clients wish to discuss spiritual, religious, or existential concerns in their treatment (Ganje-Fling, Veach, Kuang, & Houg, 2000; Martinez, Smith, & Barlow, 2007; Rose, Westefeld, & Ansley, 2008) and that highly religious or spiritually committed clients tend to show better outcomes when treatment integrates their religion or spirituality (Worthington, Hook, Davis, & McDaniel, 2011). The point of these questions and this approach is to be relationally responsive to understanding clients' perspectives and preferences, while neither neglecting this area nor forcing it. Throughout the therapy process, it is also important to attend to opportunities where clients introduce something related to their spiritual, religious, theological, or cultural perspectives and to show respectful curiosity and interest (Sorenson, 2004); this stance counters tendencies among some therapists to minimize or show negative bias toward these concerns (Cragun & Friedlander, 2012; Cornish, Wade, Tucker, & Post, 2014).

The question of working across differences in religious or theological traditions between therapists and clients is largely overlooked in the five views books on Psychology and Christianity (Johnson, 2010) and Christianity and Counseling (Greggo & Sisemore, 2012) and other literature on the integration of psychology and theology. Our perspective, similar to Dueck and Reimer (2009), is to start with clients' traditions or worldviews while maintaining an internal differentiated or intercultural awareness of how our own theological and cultural lens may interact with the clients' lenses and with the clinical process. As we have noted earlier, this becomes even more complex in relational modalities (couple, family, group therapy) where there are three or more worldviews in the room. Some of the more nuanced challenges of differentiation can come when clinicians are working with clients who are actually from their own general religious tradition but embody it in very contrasting ways. This can be particularly triggering of countertransference and the felt need to argue with or "correct" a client's perspective or to feel an urge to "save" them from certain problems arising from one's own experience. Regaining a differentiated relational stance allows clients to struggle developmentally with their own process of integration and allows a third space for clients to encounter God or the sacred in transformative ways we cannot predict as clinicians (Salimi, Sandage, & Stavros, 2016).

As we have suggested in an earlier article (Brown & Sandage, 2015), this relationally integrative approach to pacing means that for some clients we may start with a stronger focus on scripture (like Biblical counselors; Powlison, 2010), while for others our starting point may be theological and philosophical aspects of Christian traditions (like Christian psychologists; Roberts & Watson, 2010), while for some we might bring to the fore other perspectives that fit the clients' worldviews. In some cases, clients who have experienced religious abuse may need tight boundaries respected about *not* venturing into sacred terrain for a period of time until trust develops and some level of trauma symptoms are reduced. This willingness to flexibly and respectfully enter into a client's "world" has analogy to an incarnational theology, which affirms that God has come to be with God's creation in Jesus the Messiah (e.g., John 1:14–18).

Over time, differences in theological perspectives between therapists and clients will likely emerge, and these differences can be constructively engaged to foster differentiation and intersubjectivity. The key ethical principle of respecting client autonomy fits our developmental and spiritual emphasis on differentiation, so there are numerous relational, spiritual, and moral reasons that clients should not be overpowered by the counselor or therapist's theological perspective. When the relationship unfolds in healthy, differentiated ways, it is possible that clients may integrate or appropriate parts of the counselor/therapist's horizon of understanding into their own (cf. Gadamer's fusion of horizons; see Cushman, 1995, 2007).

Pacing clients' spiritual, religious, and theological traditions is also consistent with the cultural humility we discussed in Chapter 7; i.e., the "ability to maintain an interpersonal stance that is other-oriented (or open to the other) in relation to aspects of cultural identity that are most important to the [person]" (Hook et al., 2013, p. 2). Client perceptions of cultural humility on the part of their therapist have been positively associated with therapeutic alliance and also have positively predicted clinical outcomes (Hook, Davis, Owen, & DeBlaere, 2017; Hook, Davis, Owen, Worthington, & Utsey, 2013; Owen, Tao, Drinane, Hook, Davis, & Kune, 2016). This is consistent with interculturally competent practice and suggests that clinicians need to resist either denigrating or idealizing clients' traditions or practices. This does not mean clinicians need to personally endorse those beliefs, values, or practices as ideal, good, or even ultimately beneficial. But it is important for therapists to develop intersubjective understanding to appreciate the function and plausibility of those beliefs, values, and practices from the client's contextual horizon and prior relational experience. Systemically, it is also important to understand that there are key dilemmas or conflicts for each client within their own set of traditions or values, and so it is important to explore those dilemmas and conflicts (i.e., their own integrative challenges) before recommending our own solutions (which is a lead move; see Chapter 4).

Our understanding of relational integration processes in psychotherapy is also tied to the relational spirituality model articulated by Worthington and Sandage (2016). A key clinical strategy, which we have illustrated in cases in this book, is to try to understand the client's relational dynamics with God or the sacred and how these relational dynamics may correspond to or compensate for attachment experiences with parents or other key relational figures (see also Granqvist & Kirkpatrick, 2013; Hall & Fujikama, 2013). Duvall (2000) described assessing client's "unconscious theologies," which are not their expressly stated beliefs but their more implicit theologies and God-images that often emerge during stress or vulnerability. For example, a client may admit feeling they are profoundly disappointing to God (the Father) in ways that parallel their experience of being a disappointment to one or both parents, perhaps particularly their father. Like many relational depth therapy approaches, we think it is important to surface and consider these relational spirituality connections and to provide corrective relational experiences that can help shift attachment templates about self and other in ways that foster a sense of love, acceptance, intimacy, and forgiveness (see Lewis, Amini, & Lannon, 2000).

The relational dynamics that promote differentiated integration involve a balancing of challenge and support or pacing and leading (also see Maddock & Larson, 2004; Shults & Sandage, 2006; Worthington & Sandage, 2016). This means there needs to be empathy, validation, mirroring, and expressed concern for the client (support/pacing) along with questions that explore dilemmas and conflicts the client is experiencing (challenge/leading). From a systemic perspective, questions are often the best intervention to invite exploration and self-confrontation, although it is important that these are honest and sincere questions. It is intriguing to us that the Jewish and Christian Scriptures often highlight the use of questions for relational and religious exploration—from the divine question to Adam after he has disobeyed God ("Where are you?" Gen 3:9) to Jesus' many questions to those who approached him (with the following being a small sampling):

- "Do you believe I am able to do this?" to two individuals who are blind coming to Jesus for healing (Matt 9:28)
- "You of little faith . . . why did you doubt?" to Peter when he falters on the sea (Matt 14:31)
- "Who do you say I am?" to his disciples (Matt 16:15)
- "What do you want?" to two of John's disciples as they turn to follow after Jesus (John 1:38)
- "Do you want to get well?" to a man who had been unable to walk for 38 years (John 5:6)

One of my (Steve) favorite questions (drawing from Schnarch, 1997) is to ask clients if a certain behavior or decision reflects their "anxiety or integrity." If paced well, this question invites self-reflexive personal confrontation about motives, values, defensive processes, and growth—all key issues from a relational integration perspective. It is also true that, as human beings, we often struggle with ambivalence between competing values, including a desire to grow and change and anxiety about the same. Schnarch's (1997) idea that sin includes a lack of courage and a "refusal to desire and grow" (p. 400) is helpful in this regard. But sometimes we may also hold two positive values that are in conflict without realizing it, and losses will be involved in making a choice (Kegan & Lahey, 2009).

As we have suggested at several points in this book, relational integration often emerges from places of dis-integration, including losses, traumas, or transitions *when healthy relationships become part of the processing of those experiences.* So clinically, it is helpful to listen for experiences of loss, disappointment, or transitions and the meanings attached both relationally and spiritually or theologically. Throughout the book, we have also considered some of the specific issues or emotions that may be especially challenging to integrate for some conservative religious clients, such as grief, sexuality, embodiment, anxiety, shame, or anger, among others. Sometimes a concrete question, such as "How do you experience connections between your faith and your sexuality?" might be met with an immediate response, "They aren't." But such a question might also open integrative dialogue and exploration. This can also be a valuable space for considering or revisiting the client's spiritual practices to help them find ways of seeking spiritual grounding and emotion regulation, while also tolerating the ambiguity of discovering and constructing new integrative understandings.

The collaborative emphasis of our relational integration model means that we also value consideration of whether it may be beneficial to collaborate with clergy, chaplains, or other spiritual or cultural/community leaders in a given case. Some clients will appreciate this kind of opportunity for more input on their situation and sign a release, whereas other clients will not want or feel a need for this. Relational sensitivity requires finding out the information clients do and do not want shared. But when clients affirm this move, there is often an opportunity to have two-way dialogue with leaders who are in the clients' community or natural ecology and to work out ways those leaders might support or enhance the work the clients are doing in therapy. These community leaders can also offer insights and translations of the traditions that may inform the therapists involved. In a minority of cases, it may also become apparent that there are dis-integrative tensions between the leader's input and that of the therapist, which can also be important to understand in order to prevent barriers to change.

Finally, and probably most importantly, we want to return to our emphasis on the formation of the self of the therapist and their own relational community. From our relational integration model, psychotherapists need technical skills and expertise, but personal integration, well-being, and maturity are more important. Therapists need the differentiated capacity and resilience to stay in spiritual and existential crucibles with clients without rescuing or running away (Sandage & Shults, 2007; Shults & Sandage, 2006; Worthington & Sandage, 2016). This kind of committed relational presence by therapists can roughly image God for clients. Given the clinical risks of vicarious trauma and burnout through chronic exposure to suffering, it is also vital that therapists cultivate the kinds of spiritual practice, relational support (personally and professionally), and ongoing existential and theological development that we have considered throughout the book.

Relational Integration in Congregational Practice

Relational integration in congregational practice starts with considering multiple ways of enhancing the relational development of congregants. This might seem to be an obvious goal for congregations, however our experience is that it often doesn't happen without intentionality. Additionally, relational development is best pursued within an integrative framework drawing on psychology and theology and woven into various aspects of educational and spiritual formative programming (Sandage, Jensen, & Jass, 2008). We find it helpful to ask the question, "Where, within congregational life, would people get constructive and formative feedback on their relational style?" Attachment and differentiation are key constructs that can be helpful integrative starting points considered in parenting classes, couples enrichment interventions, groups for singles or seniors, and many other kinds of ministry programs.

In a similar fashion, we suggest that efforts to enhance the intercultural competence of all congregants should be a standard part of ministry. This is not only crucial for outreach efforts and forming a system that is hospitable to new people but will also help make use of internal differences for navigating conflicts within the congregation. There should be experiential components to this, but it will be helpful for relational integration to provide teaching and discussion of the psychological and theological aspects of intercultural competence that we have described in Chapter 7. Since intercultural competence can be validly measured with the Intercultural Development Inventory (Hammer, 2011), use of that tool could be particularly important for congregants who want to get involved in missions or outreach efforts that will move them across cultural contexts.

As with clinical practice, relational integration in congregational life involves systems drawing on psychology and theology to engage topics that are sometimes non-integrated in religious life. These topics could include loss, sexuality, divorce, mental health struggles, and various forms of recovery. Congregations that offer recovery programming and support groups have the potential to engage many aspects of relational integration; yet it is important to consider whether the recovery efforts are integrated into the overall theological and communal ethos of the congregation or considered a side ministry for people with "serious problems." A similar challenge emerges for those congregations that offer specialized singles ministries. It may be good to offer those services, but it is important to ask whether singles or people in recovery are integrated into the various aspects of congregational life (including leadership roles) or if they are implicitly stigmatized as different or deficient in some way.

This raises the relational integration observation that it requires high levels of differentiation for a congregation to offer both preventative and healing functions in a particular area. For example, a highly differentiated congregation could offer premarital counseling or other programming aimed at preventing divorce and cultivating healthy marriages, while also offering divorce recovery ministries. This would communicate a dialectical valuing of both marital fidelity and gracious responses to healing after divorce. A similar point could be made about suicide. Religious communities typically take a strong anti-suicide stand about the sanctity of life, but it is a healthy relational integration challenge for those same systems to offer compassionate and healing resources to families who have been impacted by suicide.

Many of these congregational efforts at integration could involve collaboration with psychologists, other social scientists, and psychotherapists. We have found the best relational integration occurs through (a) sustained collaborations over several years and (b) efforts that enhance the integrative capacities of both leaders and lay people. Some congregations will bring in psychologists or psychotherapists as guest speakers to congregants, but we have been most impressed with congregations where leaders also arrange for their own education and development in these areas. This kind of curiosity and growth orientation among leaders sets a positive example. One integrative variation of this is a clinical group practice in Minnesota (Arden Woods Psychological Services) that has partnered for many years with a local church (Salem Covenant) to offer training seminars for pastors and Christian leaders on a Friday morning every other month. These training sessions explore integrative topics, typically presented by one of the clinical staff but in dialogue with these religious community leaders. While attendance is open for each session, this offering has led to a core group of ministers, chaplains, and parish nurses who regularly attend and offer support to one another. This is not only a referral source for the clinical practice but has also built meaningful collaborations between the clinicians and these community leaders.

Finally, we have mentioned the importance of relational supports and consultation groups for clinicians, but we consider them just as important to relational integration for clergy and spiritual leaders. Clergy are at an elevated risk for professional isolation. Systemically, it is crucial to get inputs from outside one's system to maintain one's own leadership of an open, growing system. Some clergy or spiritual leaders find themselves in difficult positions without input from other leaders and cutoff from relationships where they can be candid about struggles in their congregations; they would benefit from the wisdom and support of others. Denominational leaders may not always be safe or adequately neutral to provide this kind of differentiated relationship. Authentic and consistent relationships among clergy or spiritual leaders organized as a learning community and focused on themes of relational integration can offer a holding environment to foster support and growth in practical wisdom.

One of the ongoing challenges for these integrative conversations is to allow differing voices to be heard and sustained in their distinctiveness. To do so is a counter-cultural act in our present "monologic" context. As Walter Brueggemann (2007) observes,

> In Western culture today, we live in a society and in a political economy that moves in every way it can imagine toward monologue. The most visible play in that monologic propensity is the global reach of U.S. imperialism that is increasingly intolerant of local tradition or variation . . . There is no doubt that such a monologic tendency reaches into personal lives that

are dominated by technological conformity and by the pressures of compulsive consumerism. The same propensity reaches into local congregations by a culture of fear that cannot tolerate a thought or a gesture of openness.

(p. 324)

We commend what Brueggemann refers to as "dialogic thickness" for congregations and their leaders as they attend to their relational development in community, with multiple voices from psychological and theological perspectives contributing to a more holistic dialogue and praxis.

Conclusion

In this chapter, we have explored a variety of applications arising from our theoretical model of relational integration—for scholars involved in interdisciplinary dialogue between theology and psychology, for teachers and trainers, for therapists and clinicians, and for those who lead congregations. Our desire is that our own interdisciplinary collaboration around the theory and praxis of relational integration provides new insights and avenues for our readers, both those new to interdisciplinary engagement and those who are already seasoned participants in such conversations. And we hope that our work has an impact on the way interdisciplinary dialogue between psychology and theology is done. Our vision is that psychologists and theologians would contribute to these conversations the best of their work and expertise with humility, curiosity, and a differentiated sense of self.

Bibliography

Bell, C. A., Sandage, S. J., Morgan, T. D., & Hague, D. J. (in press). Relational spirituality, humility, and commitments to social justice and intercultural competence. *Journal of Psychology and Christianity*.

Bordin, E. S. (1979). The generalizability of the psychoanalytic concept of the working alliance. *Psychotherapy: Theory, Research & Practice, 16*(3), 252–260. doi:10.1037/h0085885

Brown, J. K., Dahl, C. M., & Corbin Reuschling, W. (2011). *Becoming whole and holy: An integrative conversation about Christian formation*. Grand Rapids, MI: Brazos.

Brown, J. K., & Sandage, S. J. (2015). Relational integration, part II: Relational integration as developmental and intercultural. *Journal of Psychology & Theology, 43*, 179–191.

Browning, D. S., & Cooper, T. D. (2004). *Religious thought and the modern psychologies* (2nd ed.). Minneapolis, MN: Fortress Press.

Brueggemann, W. (2007). Dialogic thickness in a monologic culture, *Theology Today, 64*, 322–339.

Carter, J. D., & Narramore, B. (1979). *The integration of psychology and theology: An introduction*. Grand Rapids, MI: Zondervan.

Cornish, M. A., Wade, N. G., Tucker, J. R., & Post, B. C. (2014). When religion enters the counseling group: Multiculturalism, group processes, and social justice. *The Counseling Psychologist, 42*(5), 578–600. doi:10.1177/0011000014527001

Cragun, C. L., & Friedlander, M. L. (2012). Experiences of Christian clients in secular psychotherapy: A mixed-methods investigation. *Journal of Counseling Psychology*, *59*(3), 379–391. doi:10.1037/a0028283

Cushman, P. (1995). *Constructing the self, constructing America: A cultural history of psychotherapy*. New York, NY: Da Capo Press.

Cushman, P. (2007). A burning world, an absent God: Midrash, hermeneutics, and relational psychoanalysis. *Contemporary Psychoanalysis*, *43*(1), 47–88. doi:10.1080/00107 530.2007.10745896

Davis, D. E., Rice, K., McElroy, S., DeBlaere, C., Choe, E., Van Tongeren, D. R., & Hook, J. N. (2016). Distinguishing intellectual humility and general humility. *The Journal of Positive Psychology*, *11*, 215–224. doi:10.1080/17439760.2015.1048818

Doran, J. M. (2016). The working alliance: Where have we been, where are we going? *Psychotherapy Research*, *26*, 146–163.

Doran, J. M., Safran, J. D., & Muran, J. C. (2016). The Alliance Negotiation Scale: A psychometric investigation. *Psychological Assessment*, *28*(8), 885–897. doi:10.1037/ pas0000222

Doran, J. M., Safran, J. D., & Muran, J. C. (2017). An investigation of the relationship between the Alliance Negotiation Scale and psychotherapy process and outcome. *Journal of Clinical Psychology*, *73*(4), 449–465. doi:10.1002/jclp.22340

Dueck, A., & Reimer, K. (2009). *A peaceable psychology: Christian therapy in a world of many cultures*. Brazos Press.

Duvall, N. D. (2000, October). *Unconscious theology and spirituality*. Presented at the Institute for Spiritual Formation, Biola University, La Mirada, CA.

Ganje-Fling, M., Veach, P. M., Kuang, H., & Houg, B. (2000). Effect of childhood sexual abuse on client spiritual well-being. *Counseling and Values*, *44*(2), 84–91.

Granqvist, P., & Kirkpatrick, L. A. (2013). Religion, spirituality, and attachment. In K. I. Pargament, J. J. Exline, & J. W. Jones (Eds.), *APA handbook of psychology, religion, and spirituality (Vol. 1): Context, theory, and research* (pp. 139–155). Washington, DC: American Psychological Association.

Greggo, S. P., & Sisemore, T. A. (2012). *Counseling and Christianity: Five approaches*. Downers Grove, IL: InterVarsity Press.

Hall, T. W., & Fujikawa, A. M. (2013). God image and the sacred. In K. I. Pargament, J. J. Exline, & J. W. Jones (Eds.), *APA handbook of psychology, religion, and spirituality (Vol. 1): Context, theory, and research* (pp. 277–292). Washington, DC: American Psychological Association.

Hammer, M. (2011). Additional cross-cultural validity testing of the Intercultural Development Inventory. *International Journal of Intercultural Relations*, *35*, 474–487.

Hodge, D. R. (2001). Spiritual genograms: A generational approach to assessing spirituality. *Families in Society*, *82*, 35–48.

Hodge, D. R. (2005). Spiritual ecograms: A new assessment instrument for identifying clients' strengths in space and across time. *Families in Society*, *86*, 287–296.

Hook, J. N., Davis, D. E., Owen, J., Worthington, E. J., & Utsey, S. O. (2013). Cultural humility: Measuring openness to culturally diverse clients. *Journal of Counseling Psychology*, *60*(3), 353–366. doi:10.1037/a0032595

Hook, J. N., Davis, D., Owen, J., & DeBlaere, C. (2017). *Cultural humility: Engaging diverse identities in therapy*. Washington, DC: American Psychological Association. doi:10.1037/0000037–000

Jankowski, P. J., Sandage, S. J., & Hill, P. C. (2013). Differentiation-based models of forgivingness, mental health, and social justice commitment: Mediator effects of differentiation of self and humility. *Journal of Positive Psychology*, *8*, 412–424.

Johnson, E. L. (Ed.). (2010). *Psychology & Christianity: Five views* (2nd ed.). Downers Grove, IL: InterVarsity Press.

Johnson, J. J. (2009). *What's so wrong with being absolutely right: The dangerous nature of dogmatic belief.* Amherst, NY: Prometheus Books.

Kegan, R., & Lahey, L. L. (2009). *Immunity to change: How to overcome it and unlock the potential in yourself and your organization.* Cambridge, MA: Harvard Business Review Press.

Lewis, T., Amini, F., & Lannon, R. (2000). *A general theory of love.* New York, NY: Vintage.

Maddock, J. W., & Larson, N. R. (2004). The ecological approach to incestuous families. In D. R. Catherall (Ed.), *Handbook of stress, trauma, and the family* (pp. 367–392). New York, NY: Brunner-Routledge.

Majerus, B., & Sandage, S. J. (2010). Differentiation of self and Christian spiritual maturity: Social science and theological integration. *Journal of Psychology and Theology, 38,* 41–51.

Martinez, J. S., Smith, T. B., & Barlow, S. H. (2007). Spiritual interventions in psychotherapy: Evaluations by highly religious clients. *Journal of Clinical Psychology, 63,* 943–960. doi:10.002/jclp.20399

Owen, J., Tao, K. W., Drinane, J. M., Hook, J., Davis, D. E., & Kune, N. F. (2016). Client perceptions of therapists' multicultural orientation: Cultural (missed) opportunities and cultural humility. *Professional Psychology: Research and Practice, 47*(1), 30–37. doi:10.1037/pro0000046

Owens, B. P., Johnson, M. D., & Mitchell, T. R. (2013). Expressed humility in organizations: Implications for performance, teams, and leadership. *Organization Science, 24,* 1517–1538. https://doi.org/10.1287/orsc.1120.0795

Paine, D. R., Jankowski, P. J., & Sandage, S. J. (2016). Humility as a predictor of intercultural competence: Mediator effects for differentiation of self. *The Family Journal, 24,* 15–22.

Powlison, D. (2010). A Biblical counseling view. In E. L. Johnson (Ed.), *Psychology & Christianity: Five views* (2nd ed., pp. 245–273). Downers Grove, IL: InterVarsity Press.

Roberts, R. C., & Watson, P. J. (2010). A Christian psychology view. In E. L. Johnson (Ed.), *Psychology & Christianity: Five views* (2nd ed., pp. 149–178). Downers Grove, IL: InterVarsity Press.

Rose, E. M., Westefeld, J. S., & Ansley, T. N. (2008). Spiritual issues in counseling: Clients' beliefs and preferences. *Psychology of Religion and Spirituality, S*(1), 18–33. doi:10.1037/1941-1022.S.1.18

Safir, S. (2017). *The listening leader: Creating the conditions for equitable school transformation.* San Francisco, CA: Jossey-Bass.

Salimi, B., Sandage, S. J., & Stavros, G. S. (2016). Spiritual transcendence in therapy: A pragmatic, relational, and semiotic approach. *Open Theology, 2,* 581–594.

Sandage, S. J. (2012). The transformation of happiness: A response from counseling psychology. In B. A. Strawn (Ed.), *The Bible and the pursuit of happiness* (pp. 263–286). New York, NY: Oxford University Press.

Sandage, S. J., & Brown, J. K. (2010). Monarchy or democracy in relation integration? A reply to Porter. *Journal of Psychology and Christianity, 29*(1), 20–26.

Sandage, S. J., & Brown, J. K. (2012). Converging horizons for relational integration: Differentiation-based collaboration. *Journal of Psychology and Theology, 40,* 72–76.

Sandage, S. J., Cook, K. V., Hill, P. C., Strawn, B. D., & Reimer, K. S. (2008). Hermeneutics and psychology: A review and dialectical model. *Review of General Psychology, 12,* 344–364.

Sandage, S. J., Jensen, M., & Jass, D. (2008). Relational spirituality and transformation: Risking intimacy and alterity. *Journal of Spiritual Formation and Soul Care, 1,* 182–206.

Sandage, S. J., Paine, D. R., & Devor, N. G. (2014). Psychology and spiritual formation: Emerging prospects for differentiated integration. *Journal of Spiritual Formation and Soul Care, 7,* 229–247.

Sandage, S. J., & Shults, F. L. (2007). Relational spirituality and transformation: A relational integration model. *Journal of Psychology & Christianity, 26,* 261–269.

Schnarch, D. M. (1997). *Passionate marriage: Love, sex, and intimacy in emotionally committed relationships.* New York, NY: W. W. Norton & Co.

Shults, F. L., & Sandage, S. J. (2006). *Transforming spirituality: Integrating theology and psychology.* Grand Rapids, MI: Baker Academic.

Siegel, D. (2010). *Mindsight: The new science of personal transformation.* New York, NY: Bantam Books.

Sorenson, R. L. (2004). *Minding spirituality.* Hillsdale, NJ: The Analytic Press.

Stavros, G., & Sandage, S. J. (Eds.). (2014). *The skillful soul of the psychotherapist: The Link between spirituality and clinical excellence.* Lanham, MD: Rowman & Littlefield.

Tan, S. (1996). Religion in clinical practice: Implicit and explicit integration. In E. P. Shafranske (Ed.), *Religion and the clinical practice of psychology* (pp. 365–387). Washington, DC: American Psychological Association. doi:10.1037/10199–013

Wampold, B. E., & Imel, Z. E. (2015). *The great psychotherapy debate: The evidence for what makes psychotherapy work* (2nd ed.). New York, NY: Routledge.

Wengst, K. (1988). *Humility: Solidarity of the humiliated.* Minneapolis, MN: Fortress Press.

Worthington, E. J., Hook, J. N., Davis, D. E., & McDaniel, M. A. (2011). Religion and spirituality. *Journal of Clinical Psychology, 67*(2), 204–214. doi:10.1002/jclp.20760

Worthington, E. L., Jr., & Sandage, S. J. (2016). *Forgiveness and spirituality: A relational approach.* Washington, DC: American Psychological Association.

INDEX